Mapping the Medieval City

D1453562

RELIGION AND CULTURE IN THE MIDDLE AGES

Mapping the Medieval City

Space, Place and Identity in Chester *c*.1200–1600

Edited by

CATHERINE A. M. CLARKE

UNIVERSITY OF WALES PRESS
CARDIFF
2011

www.uwp.co.uk

British Library Cataloguing-in-Publication Data
A catalogue record for this book is available from the British Library.

ISBN   978-0-7083-2652-7
e-ISBN   978-0-7083-2393-9

Printed by CPI Antony Rowe, Chippenham, Wiltshire

CONTENTS

Series Editors' Preface

Religion and Culture in the Middle Ages aims to explore the interface between medieval religion and culture, with as broad an understanding of those terms as possible. It puts to the forefront studies which engage with works that significantly contributed to the shaping of medieval culture. However, it also gives attention to studies dealing with works that reflect and highlight aspects of medieval culture that have been neglected in the past by scholars of the medieval disciplines. For example, devotional works and the practice they infer illuminate our understanding of the medieval subject and its culture in remarkable ways, while studies of the material space designed and inhabited by medieval subjects yield new evidence on the period and the people who shaped it and lived in it. In the larger field of religion and culture, we also want to explore further the roles played by women as authors, readers and owners of books, thereby defining them more precisely as actors in the cultural field. The series as a whole investigates the European Middle Ages, from *c*.500 to *c*.1500. Our aim is to explore medieval religion and culture with the tools belonging to such disciplines as, among others, art history, philosophy, theology, history, musicology, the history of medicine, and literature. In particular, we would like to promote interdisciplinary studies, as we believe strongly that our modern understanding of the term applies fascinatingly well to a cultural period marked by a less tight confinement and categorization of its disciplines than the modern period. However, our only criterion is academic excellence, with the belief that the use of a large diversity of critical tools and theoretical approaches enables a deeper understanding of medieval culture. We want the series to reflect this diversity, as we believe that, as a collection of outstanding contributions, it offers a more subtle representation of a period that is marked by paradoxes and contradictions and which necessarily reflects diversity and difference, however difficult it may sometimes have proved for medieval culture to accept these notions.

ACKNOWLEDGEMENTS

The essays in this volume were inspired by the Arts and Humanities Research Council-funded interdisciplinary research project 'Mapping Medieval Chester: Place and Identity in an English Borderland City, c.1200–1500'. Directed by Catherine A. M. Clarke, the project also involved Keith Lilley and Helen Fulton as Co-Investigators and Mark Faulkner as Post-Doctoral Researcher, together with Paul Vetch at the Centre for Computing in the Humanities, King's College London, as Technical Director. The digital resources produced by the project can be viewed at www.medievalchester.ac.uk. The essays by Clarke, Lilley, Fulton and Faulkner in this collection were written as part of the AHRC-funded research. The 'Mapping Medieval Chester' project also included a major international conference at Swansea University, 'Mapping the Medieval City' (July 2009). Many of the other essays in this volume were presented as papers at this event, and indeed almost all of the volume contributors were present at the conference, which proved a valuable opportunity to share work in progress and exchange ideas. The volume editor and project team would like to thank the AHRC for the funding which enabled the 'Mapping Medieval Chester' research project, which has expanded to include the collection of essays published here. Thanks also to Gill Alexander of Queen's University, Belfast, for drawing the maps of medieval Chester (Figures 1 and 2) based on the digital atlas produced by the 'Mapping Medieval Chester' project. The editors of the University of Wales Press series 'Religion and Culture in the Middle Ages' have provided insightful and valuable comments on the various drafts of this volume and, finally, the volume editor would like to thank everyone at the University of Wales Press for their expert and cheerful help, especially the commissioning editors Ennis Akpinar and Sarah Lewis, and the press's editor Dafydd Jones.

NOTES ON CONTRIBUTORS

ROBERT W. BARRETT, Jnr, is Associate Professor of English and Medieval Studies at the University of Illinois at Urbana-Champaign. His research crosses the period boundary between the Middle Ages and the Renaissance, focusing on calendrical festivity, early English drama and local identity. In addition to articles on Chester pageants and London Lord Mayor's Shows, his publications include the monograph *Against All England: Regional Identity and Cheshire Writing, 1195–1656* (Notre Dame, 2009). He is currently editing the Chester Whitsun plays for the TEAMS Middle English Texts Series and planning a second monograph on Pentecost in early English literature.

CYNTHIA TURNER CAMP is Assistant Professor of English at the University of Georgia, where her research focuses on English hagiography, especially fifteenth-century Middle English literature and late medieval monasticism. She is currently preparing a monograph on the Middle English and early Tudor lives of Anglo-Saxon saints and an edition of Henry Bradshaw's *Life of St Werburge* and *Life of St Radegund*.

CATHERINE A. M. CLARKE is Senior Lecturer in English and Associate Director of the Centre for Medieval and Early Modern Research at Swansea University. Her research centres on earlier medieval literature and culture, with particular attention to questions of place, power and identity and an emphasis on interdisciplinary approaches. Her publications include the monograph *Literary Landscapes and the Idea of England, 700–1400* (Cambridge, 2006), and she was Principal Investigator on the AHRC-funded 'Mapping Medieval Chester' project.

†JOHN DORAN was Deputy Head of History and Archaeology and Senior Lecturer in Medieval History at the University of Chester. His research focused on the relationship between the popes and the city of Rome from the eleventh to the thirteenth centuries, but he was also interested in the development of Chester and its similar ecclesiastical and civic tensions.

His publications include an edited volume, *Pope Celestine III: Diplomat and Pastor* (Ashgate: Farnham, 2009). John died in October 2012, shortly before the publication of this volume in paperback.

MARK FAULKNER is currently Lecturer in English at University College Cork. His research focuses on medieval literary culture, particularly the composition and reception of English, Latin and French texts in England during the 'long' twelfth century. His publications include 'Ælfric, St Edmund and St Edwold of Cerne', *Medium Aevum*, 77 (2008) and he is currently writing a monograph entitled *Ignota lingua: English literatures 1042–1215*, as well as editing Lucian's *De Laude Cestrie*. He was research assistant on the 'Mapping Medieval Chester' project.

HELEN FULTON is Professor of Medieval Literature at the University of York and was previously Professor of English and Director of the Research Institute for Arts and Humanities at Swansea University. Most of her research is concerned with the interface between medieval literature and politics. She has published widely in the field of medieval Celtic studies with a particular focus on the links between Welsh and English cultural production in medieval Britain. Recent publications include *Welsh Prophecy and English Politics in the Late Middle Ages* (Aberystwyth, 2008) and *Companion to Arthurian Literature* (Oxford, 2009) and she was also Co-Investigator on the AHRC-funded 'Mapping Medieval Chester' project.

JANE LAUGHTON is an independent historical researcher and consultant whose research centres on medieval urban topics. Chester was the subject of her Ph.D. thesis from Cambridge (1994) and has remained a particular focus of interest. She has collaborated with historians and archaeologists to produce multidisciplinary works such as *The Chester Rows Research Project* (1999) and *The City of Chester*: Volume V, Part 1 of *A History of the County of Chester* (2003). Her monograph *Life in a Late Medieval City: Chester 1275–1520* was published in 2008 (Windgather Press, an imprint of Oxbow Books, Oxford).

CHRIS LEWIS worked for the Victoria County History from 1982 to 2009 and was county editor for Cheshire 1995–2002, based at the University of Liverpool. He co-edited the VCH's volumes on the City of Chester (2 volumes, 2003–5) and has published on other aspects of Cheshire history, especially on the central Middle Ages.

KEITH D. LILLEY is Reader in Historical Geography at Queen's University Belfast. Using particularly mapping and cartography as interpretative frames, his research focuses on the materiality and imagining of space, place and landscape during the later Middle Ages. His publications include *Urban Life in the Middle Ages, 1000–1450* (London, 2002), and *City and Cosmos – the Medieval World in Urban Form* (London, 2009), and he was Co-Investigator on the AHRC-funded 'Mapping Medieval Chester' project.

LIZ HERBERT MCAVOY is Senior Lecturer in Medieval Literature and Gender Studies at Swansea University and Director of the Centre for Medieval and Early Modern Research in the School of Arts and Humanities. She has published widely on medieval women, gender issues and anchoritism, including *Authority and the Female Body in the Writings of Julian of Norwich and Margery Kempe* (2004). She has also edited a number of essay collections on aspects of the anchoritic life, including *Rhetoric of the Anchorhold* (2008), *A Companion to Julian of Norwich* (2008) and *Anchoritic Traditions of Medieval Europe* (2010). She has recently completed a second monograph on works written for, about and by medieval anchorites, to be published shortly by The Boydell Press.

LAURA VARNAM is Lecturer in Old and Middle English Literature at University College, Oxford. Her research focuses on the intersection between literature, culture and space, and she co-organised the interdisciplinary conference 'There and Back Again: Re-Fashioning Journey and Place in the Middle Ages' at Balliol College, Oxford in 2008. She is currently writing a monograph entitled *The Howse of God on Erthe: Sacred Space, Community and Material Culture in Late Medieval England*.

ABBREVIATIONS

BL	British Library
EETS	Early English Text Society
CCALS	Cheshire and Chester Archives and Local Studies
DLC	Lucian, *De Laude Cestrie*, ed. and trans. Mark Faulkner (*www.medievalchester.ac.uk*)
DNB	Oxford Dictionary of National Biography
EEA	English Episcopal Acta
MED	Middle English Dictionary
OED	Oxford English Dictionary
Ormerod	Ormerod, G., *The History of the County Palatine and City of Chester*, revised and enlarged edition by Thomas Helsby, 3 vols (London, 1882)
PN Ches.	J. McN. Dodgson (ed.), *The Place-Names of Cheshire*, 5 vols in 7, English Place-Name Society (1970–97)
STC	Short Title Catalogue
TNA: PRO	The National Archives, Public Record Office, Kew
VCH Ches. 3	Harris, B. E (ed.), *A History of the County of Chester*, Victoria History of the Counties of England, 5 vols, vol. 3: *Religious Houses* (London, 1980)
VCH Ches. 5. i	C. P. Lewis and A. T. Thacker (eds), *A History of the County of Chester*, Victoria History of the Counties of England, 5 vols, vol. 5. i: *The City of Chester: General History and Topography* (Woodbridge, 2003)
VCH Ches. 5. ii	C. P. Lewis and A. T. Thacker (eds), *A History of the County of Chester*, Victoria History of the Counties of England, 5 vols, vol. 5. ii *The City of Chester: Culture, Buildings, Institutions* (Woodbridge, 2005)

FIGURES

Shortly before the publication of this volume in paperback, our fellow contributor, John Doran, died at the age of 46. Deputy Head of History and Archaeology and Senior Lecturer in Medieval History at the University of Chester, John was a specialist on medieval Rome and the papacy in the eleventh and twelfth centuries. His essay in this volume, on relations between St Werburgh's and St John's, exemplifies his learning and the new critical insights he brought to medieval scholarship. John's death is a great loss for his colleagues in Chester, for the wider research community, and most of all for his young family. This new edition of *Mapping the Medieval City* is dedicated to his memory.

1

Introduction
Medieval Chester: Views from the Walls

CATHERINE A. M. CLARKE

In September 2008, on a research trip to Chester as part of the AHRC-funded 'Mapping Medieval Chester' project, I picked up the leaflet for a 'Walk around Chester Walls': a 'Unique Circular Walk', which promised to be 'Unmissable! – One of Britain's *Best* Historic Walks'.[1] As I followed the outlined route along the stone walls which encircle the early settlement, the leaflet drew my attention to the wonderful views over the city and its individual buildings, repeatedly emphasizing the multiple strata of history encoded within the urban landscape. Eastgate, for example, was described through a brief account of its various historical incarnations: '[t]he current 18th-century arch replaces a narrow, fortified medieval gateway, which in turn overlay the ruins of the ceremonial entrance to the Roman legionary fortress.' The leaflet's introduction to 'England's Walled City' offered me a concise account of the history of Chester's walls, from Roman fortress and Saxon *burh* through to medieval towers and early modern promenade. For a visitor to Chester, this walk around the walls presents an overview of the city – both literally and metaphorically – which gives an insight into its long, varied and multi-layered history.

As a privileged vantage point over Chester, the view from the walls recurs as a key motif throughout texts associated with the city from the medieval period to the present day. Most recently, the walls have become a 'virtual' point of entry into Chester for remote 'visitors' distant from the city itself. The very popular website 'Chester: a Virtual Stroll around the Walls' (*www.chesterwalls.info*), produced and maintained by local photographer and amateur historian Steve Howe, leads virtual tourists through the landscape and history of the city via a carefully constructed circular route, receiving visits from internet users all over the world. The digital resources produced by the AHRC-funded 'Mapping Medieval Chester' project (*www.medievalchester.ac.uk*) present an interactive digital atlas of the city *c.*1500, allowing users to move around the medieval walls and follow links to related descriptions and accounts in contemporary texts. Whilst working in new, digital media and presenting new possibilities for virtual interaction with the city's material fabric, these online resources continue a long tradition of making the city accessible through the view from its historic walls. Across different texts associated with Chester, with their different cultural contexts, ideological positions and symbolic configurations of the urban space, the elevated perspective from the walls seemingly renders the city uniquely legible and comprehensible, whilst simultaneously revealing the desires and concerns of the author. The diverse views over the city presented in these texts offer a useful starting point for thinking about the different perspectives produced by our own studies, and the different versions of medieval Chester formed by our own critical mappings, whether visual or textual.

The descriptions of Chester's walls by the novelist Henry James are amongst the most well-known accounts of the city. As well as the 1903 novel *The Ambassadors*, which begins with the visit of the American, Lewis Lambert Strether, to Chester, James's collection of travel writing *English Hours* includes a sustained description of the city and its walls. This account is typical of Chester texts in its use of the walls as a device for comprehending the city: as with many writers before him, James's view from this privileged vantage point reveals his own desires and anxieties mapped onto the urban landscape. For James, the walls of Chester represent the fantasy of the authentic ancient city, preserved in all its original integrity. He begins his account of the city by reporting that 'I have been strolling and restrolling along the ancient wall – so perfect in its antiquity – which locks this dense little city in its stony circle,' celebrating the 'brave little walls' as the exemplar of the English practice of 'an ancient property or institution lovingly readopted and consecrated to some modern amenity'.[2] Already here two key themes are clear: the notion of the 'perfection' of the urban enclosure, and the image (later to emerge as ambivalent) of the city 'locked' inside its *enceinte*. James goes on to insist further on the perfect compass of the walls, observing that:

> The wall enfolds the place in a continuous ring, which, passing through innumerable picturesque vicissitudes, often threatens to snap, but never fairly breaks the link; so that, starting at any point, an hour's easy stroll will bring you back to your station.[3]

However, this perfect circumscription of the city is James's rhetorical construction. The walls had already been damaged and compromised in various ways by the mid-nineteenth century, the most major break in the circuit caused by the cutting for the Chester-Holyhead railway in 1846.[4] In fact, James's character Strether in *The Ambassadors* adopts a less idealised and more realistic view of the city's walls when he imagines, '[t]he tortuous wall' as a 'girdle, long since snapped, of the little swollen city, half held in place by careful civic hands'.[5] Strether experiences 'delight' at the views from the walls, but his description of the city resists the indulgence of picturesque fantasy admitted in the *English Hours*.[6] Whilst James's view from the walls reveals Chester as he wishes to see it – the still-perfect embodiment of the ancient European fortress enclosure – he also suggests that the walls represent a 'prime necessity' for the Cestrians themselves in terms of their ability to know and understand their own city.

> For through it, surely, they may know their city more intimately than their unbuckled neighbours – survey it, feel it, rejoice in it as many times a day as they please.[7]

Again here, we have a version of the commonplace that the walls of Chester enable the city to be viewed, known and understood and thus enjoyed. For James too, his walk around the walls allows him to regard the city from above, making sense of the different views which emerge '[e]very few steps'.[8]

> A shaded mall wanders at the foot of the rampart; beside this passes a narrow canal, with locks and barges and burly water-men in smocks and breeches; while the venerable pair of towers, with their old red sandstone sides peeping through the gaps in their green mantles, rest on the soft grass of one of those odd fragments of public garden, a crooked strip of ground turned to social account, which one meets at every turn, apparently, in England . . .[9]

Yet, whilst the walls lift James above the city, allowing him to survey and interpret the urban spaces and activities below, the streets of Chester itself offer a different experience. In his account of the city's famous medieval Rows, James's account becomes more ambivalent, exposing the negative implications of the city 'locked' and 'buckled' within its enclosing fortifications. The streets of Chester do offer picturesque interest and amusement for James, with their 'random corners, projections and recesses, odd domestic interspaces . . . architectural surprises and caprices and fantasies', yet the antique charms of the city are intermeshed with the spectre of 'old-world pains and fears'.[10] The architecture of the Rows suggests an oppressive, constricted way of life within the claustrophobic confines of the walled city. James asserts:

> Fix one of them with your gaze, and it seems fairly to reek with mortality. Every stain and crevice seems to syllable some human record – a record of lives airless and unlighted.[11]

Although James attempts to imagine these quaint buildings as relics of 'Merrie England', his optimism and idealism fail at this point in his tour of the city.

> Human life, surely, packed away behind those impenetrable lattices of lead and bottle-glass, just above which the black outer beam marks the suffocating nearness of the ceiling, can have expanded into scant freedom and bloomed into small sweetness.[12]

Thus, James's fantasy of the authentic ancient city is entangled with anxieties about the confines and pressures of old-world feudal society. The walls of Chester lift James above the crowded, dark and cramped streets of the city, offering him a perspective which transcends the more bewildering and troubling urban spaces within. They offer an elevated view onto Chester's grand historic architecture, expansive surrounding countryside and quaint picturesque scenes: a vantage point which elides the less attractive realities of urban life. However, James's idealised vision of Chester's ancient walls remains implicitly grounded on ambivalence. Whilst the walls fasten the city in an image of perfect, unbroken enclosure and historic survival – a delight for the visitor – they also 'lock' and 'buckle' the citizens into an oppressive, anachronistic old-world geography.

James's paradoxical claim that the elevated, distanced prospect from the walls allows the viewer to 'know [the] city more intimately' resonates across medieval and early modern texts associated with Chester. In many descriptions of Chester, the walls are prominent both as the defining feature of the city, and as the foundation for the structure and perspective of the text itself. The imagined reader, usually constructed as a stranger or visitor to the city, is guided through Chester and its history via a walk around the walls, or through a series of aerial views which replicate its raised vantage points. For example, John Broster's 1821 *A Walk Round the Walls and City of Chester* frames its account of the city through the model of a walking tour, in which the reader is led along a circuit of the walls. Whether *in situ* within Chester itself, or as a remote, 'imaginative' visitor, 'the traveller is in this work conducted regularly from scite to scite'.[13] Typically, the view from the walls in Broster's text opens up an idealised perspective on the city which elides the more uncomfortable, untidy realities of urban life.

> Chester – with respect to its situation – the salubrity of the air – the singular convenience of the rows – the delightful pleasantries of the walls – and the prospects of the adjacent country – merits the notice of the man of taste – claims the attention of the antiquary – and courts the admiration of the stranger.[14]

Broster's vision of the walls as a place of delight and the picturesque reflects their use in this period as a 'popular promenade' around the city.[15] With their wide, open prospects and clean, wholesome air, the walls become metonymic for the 'situation' of Chester as a whole, subtly transforming the city from a site of urban industry, business and crowded communal living into a space of leisure, recreation and pleasure. Such rhetorical devices in Broster's text participate in the reinvention of Chester's walls – and indeed the city as a whole – in the eighteenth and nineteenth centuries, transposing functional civic structures or urban dilapidation and decay into a new imaginative architecture of the picturesque and antiquarian. In Broster's text, Chester (and in particular its walls) emerges as a destination for the tourist, recalling the recent visits to the city of notable, fashionable figures such as John Wesley and Samuel Johnson.[16]

Daniel King's *The Vale-Royall of England, or, The County-Palatine of Chester* (1656) includes a slightly earlier treatise on the city by William Webb, a clerk in the mayor's court, written around 1615. Again, Webb's account of Chester is shaped by the circuit of its walls, and their elevated position informs his imaginative vision of the city. Webb begins with a history of the walls, broadening out to that of the city as a whole (pp. 11–14), before giving an overview of Chester's urban topography.

> The City of *Chester*, is built in form of a quadrant, and is almost a just square, inclosed with a fair stone-wall, high and strong built, with fair Battlements of all the four sides; and with the 4 Gates, opening to the four Winds.[17]

Webb also looks beyond the intramural city, noting that:

> The City extends herself in her Suburbs, with very fair streets, and the same adorned with goodly Buildings, both of Gentlemans houses, and fair Innes for entertainments of all Resorts.[18]

This initial overview of Chester encompasses the complete city in one sustained, sweeping gaze. Webb presents a vision of the city laid out like a map or a bird's eye view: it is visible and available in its entirety to the eye of the spectator. Webb begins his perambulation of Chester just a few lines later, from the Eastgate '[a]t which, we begin the circuit of the Wall'.[19] Yet, already here, the elevated prospect from the walls offers Webb an imaginative vantage point over the city which combines the order and intelligibility of a map with the immediacy and aesthetic pleasure of direct sensory experience.

As it leads the reader around the walls, Webb's text continues to view Chester from above, maintaining the fantasy of the fully-visible and fully-intelligible city. Webb looks out over the River Dee where she 'doth here incline to enlarge herself' but is 'soundly girt in on either side with huge Rocks of hard stone'.[20] Enjoying panoramic prospects over the surrounding landscape, he remarks that:

> [Y]ou may go round about the walls, being a very delectable Walk, feeding the Eye, on the one side, with the sweet Gardens, and fine Buildings of the City; and on the other side, with a Prospect of many miles into the County of *Chester*, into *Wales*, and into the Sea.[21]

Whilst all these views are indeed available in different directions from Chester's walls, Webb here combines them into one (impossible) simultaneous panorama: a fantasy view of Chester experienced both as a combination of 'prospects' and as an aerial view or map. When Webb leads the reader down from the walls into Chester's streets, the text offers a similar conflation of views. He comments that:

> As I led you even now about the walls of the city, which was no very long walk; so now I desire you would be acquainted with the streets and lanes by name; which, methinks it is not any disorder to view them as they lie . . .[22]

This account of the streets 'as they lie' moves the reader through the topography of Chester, constructing a deliberately subjective perspective which aims to replicate a walker's experience of the built environment and the material fabric of the city. Phrases such as '[a]s you descend from the High-cross down the Bridgegate-street . . .' and 'after you have gone certain paces [Cow-Lane] opens into a void place . . .' maintain the imaginative conceit of the reader's simulated walk through the city's spaces.[23] Yet these carefully subjective, focalised views of the city are preceded by an outline of Chester's streets in the form of numbered list and discussion which, again, transcends the perspective of a walker within the city and offers an authoritative, objective, elevated view.[24] The conflation of these different views of the city within Webb's treatise – prospect and aerial plan, focalised experience and objective overview – mirrors the different kinds of mapping current in the seventeenth century and, indeed, included alongside each other in *The Vale-Royall*. Daniel King's volume includes both 'prospect' (panoramic) and 'ground-plott' (aerial, plan) views of Chester, juxtaposed in a single fold-out sheet, offering a dual perspective on the city.[25] For Webb, the overview of Chester from the walls provides the imaginative basis for his textual description, enabling the conflation of multiple perspectives and, most crucially, allowing a vision of the city which is supremely ordered, legible and pleasing.

Taking us much further back into the medieval experience and representation of Chester, the twelfth-century Latin urban encomium *De Laude Cestrie* ('In Praise of Chester') by the monk Lucian also takes the reader on a walk through the city. The text addresses itself to multiple imagined audiences, both within and beyond Chester, commenting that, 'quod habet lector in litera, teneat habitator in oculis et memoria' ('what the reader has in books, the inhabitant may hold in his gaze and memory').[26] Whilst Lucian asserts that the treatise was written 'ad consolationem ciuium' ('for the consolation of [Chester's] citizens'),[27] he repeatedly draws on the idea of the stranger or visitor to the city, using this as a device for presenting the urban landscape in new and fresh ways. He remarks that often 'nec ciuis attendit, peregrinus appendit' ('a stranger ponders what a citizen does not even consider'), and a marginal note at this point in the text reinforces this, with the assertion '[q]uod uni notum, alteri nouum' ('what is known to one, is new to another').[28] This may reflect the twelfth-century tradition of describing cities as if from the experience of a stranger or foreigner, influenced by the accounts of more exotic locations returning via the Crusades and from new trade routes.[29]

Lucian's *De Laude Cestrie* is striking in its use of aerial, elevated views of Chester. Lucian's view of the city repeatedly relies on imagined views from above, which transform urban geography into a series of diagrammatic maps (textual and visual) revealing spiritual truths about divine order and providential plans. For example, Lucian observes that Chester,

[h]abet . . . plateas duas equilineas et excellentes in modum benedicte crucis, per transuersum sibi obuias et se transeuntes, que deinceps fiant quattuor ex duabus, capita sua consummantes in quattuor portis, mistice ostendens atque magnifice, magni Regis inhabitantem graciam se habere, qui legem geminam noui ac ueteris testamenti per misterium sancte crucis impletam ostendit, in quattuor euangelistis.

has two perfectly straight streets intersecting like the blessed cross, which form four roads, culminating at the four gates, mystically revealing that the grace of the Great King dwells in the very city, who, through the four evangelists, showed the twin law of the old and new testaments to be completed through the mystery of the holy cross.[30]

Visualized from above, the streets of the city become an image of the cross and, leading to the four gates, extend into a symbolic representation of the four Gospels which reveal the truth of Christ's incarnation. At other points within the text, Lucian's elevated view of the landscape becomes even more astonishing. Describing the location of four other monasteries around Chester (and the central Benedictine house of St Werburgh's), Lucian again gives a striking representation based on a privileged, aerial perspective.

> Nam a fronte Cumbermare et a tergo Basinwerc et a lateribus, ad euidentissimum modum crucis, competenter et pulcre distinctis spaciis a quattuor monasteriis, uelut preconum laudibus comendatur, ut almum et album sit quicquid medium inuenitur.

> For to the front Combermere, to the back Basingwerk, and to the sides, these monasteries are arranged in the shape of a cross, like the praises of heralds, suggesting that whatever is found in the middle will be bright and nourishing.[31]

In the manuscript, this description is accompanied by a diagrammatic representation of these monasteries set out in the form of a cross (fol. 60v.). As Mark Faulkner has shown, analysis of modern maps and satellite images shows that Lucian's cruciform map of the four monasteries does indeed reflect their position in relation to each other.[32] Yet, of course, this view from above also enables Lucian to develop his account of the city and its surroundings into a sustained religious allegory. He imagines the entire city of Chester as elevated over its surrounding landscape and the wider world, enjoying a privileged view across space and history. He asserts that:

> orientem uersus protendit intuitum, non solum Romanam ante se cathedram et imperium, uerum et orbem prospicit uniuersum, ut tanquam spectaculum proposita sint obtutibus oculorum . . .

> to the east, she enjoys a view not only of the papal seat and Christendom but also sees the whole globe, so that they offer a spectacle to attentive eyes . . .[33]

Topographically, Chester is indeed located on higher ground and is therefore elevated over the (immediate) surrounding landscape of England and Wales. But again here, Lucian extends the city's physically raised position into an allegory for its power, authority and prestige.

This elevated view of Chester and allegorical mapping of space recalls of course the medieval *mappa mundi* tradition, which configures the globe according to ideological and religious imperatives.[34] Just as the *mappa mundi* would have Jerusalem at its centre, so Lucian notes that the marketplace is, fittingly, at the centre of the city.

> Hoc simul intuendum quam congrue in medio urbis, parili positione cunctorum, forum uoluit esse uenalium rerum, ubi, mercium copia complacente precipue uictualium, notus ueniat uel ignotus, precium porrigens, referens alimentum.

Nimirum ad exemplum panis eterni de celo uenientis, qui natus secundum prophetas *in medio orbis et umbilico terre* . . .

It is also worth understanding how fittingly it is that, all things being equal, a marketplace for the selling of things should be placed in the middle of the city, where, with an abundance of merchandise, particularly food available, a native or a foreigner may come to buy provisions. Doubtlessly, as with the eternal bread which came from heaven which, according to the prophets, *was formed in the centre of the earth* . . .[35]

The complex allegory here likens Chester itself to a *mappa mundi*. Through its symbolic association with the 'eternal bread' given to mankind through the incarnation of Christ, Chester's marketplace functions as a type for Jerusalem, at the very centre of the city and Lucian's spiritual vision. Clearly, Lucian's aerial view of the city is informed by these traditions of medieval mapping and allegory. Lucian's text seeks to realise the fantasy of seeing the world from above, of viewing and interpreting space from the perspective of the providential and the divine (a 'God's-eye' view perhaps?). His careful exegesis relies on this imagined aerial vision so that the topography of Chester and its hinterland may assemble itself into this series of diagrams, maps and mnemonics, each of which reveals deep truths about place and identity according to medieval Christian ideology. Lucian's tendency to view Chester from above recalls again the privileged prospect over the city offered by the walls. Whilst his assertion that the city looks out over the whole world ('orbem . . . uniuersum') may be somewhat hyperbolic, the medieval walls of Chester would indeed have allowed Lucian a view over the city and across its surrounding landscape. The accuracy of his topographical descriptions might suggest the use of such a raised vantage point, extended imaginatively in his larger-scale symbolic mappings and diagrams. Lucian's elevated perspective over Chester may be shaped by medieval rhetorical conventions, mapping traditions and the requirements of allegorical writing. Yet, it is also almost certainly informed and inspired by the views available from the city's own walls.

The recurrent motif across these Chester texts of walking through the city or around its historic walls resonates with modern theoretical work on urban space, its uses and representations. Michel de Certeau's influential discussion of the city ('Walking in the City' in *The Practice of Everyday Life*) begins with a description and analysis of the view over New York from the World Trade Center towers, exploring the pleasure and privilege of this unique aerial vantage point before moving down to the realm of experience of the 'ordinary practioners of the city' walking its streets far below.[36] De Certeau explores the 'erotics of knowledge' offered by the elevated view of the urban landscape, discussing 'this pleasure of "seeing the whole", of looking down on, totalizing the most immoderate of human texts', the city itself.[37] This view from above gives the illusion of transcending the subjectivities and narrowly focalised perspectives of those down in the urban environment itself, offering a 'fiction of knowledge' and a fantasy of omniscience or objective apprehension. De Certeau himself links this fantasy back to medieval desires and practices, remarking that,

> The desire to see the city preceded the means of satisfying it. Medieval or Renaissance painters represented the city as seen in a perspective that no eye had yet enjoyed. This fiction already made the medieval spectator into a celestial eye. It created gods.[38]

The descriptions of Chester by James, Broster, Webb and Lucian all, in their different ways, claim this privileged, authoritative perspective on the city, using the elevated view from the walls to re-make the urban space according to imagined desires, ideals and ideologies. In contrast to the spectator viewing the city from above, de Certeau argues that those within the city itself 'make use of spaces which cannot be seen', which 'elude legibility'.[39] Yet it is these walkers within the city who actively produce and give meaning to its spaces. For de Certeau,

> [t]he long poem of walking manipulates spatial organizations, no matter how panoptic they may be: it is neither foreign to them (it can only take place within them) nor in conformity with them (it does not receive its identity from them). It creates shadows and ambiguities within them. It inserts its multitudinous references and citations into them (social models, cultural mores, personal factors). Within them it is itself the effective of successive encounters and occasions that constantly alter it and make it the other's blazon . . .[40]

De Certeau argues that each new movement through the city is shaped by its spatial organizations, whilst also altering and re-making them in turn. Dynamic, contingent and constantly changing, the urban space is differently experienced and produced by each individual walker within it.

More recently, Paul Strohm has developed and refined the theories of de Certeau, as well as other influential writers on space and identity such as Henri Lefebvre and Pierre Bourdieu, with specific reference to the pre-modern city.[41] Whilst Strohm acknowledges that '[e]very urban walker – medieval or modern – makes choices that amount to what Pierre Bourdieu calls "regulated improvisation"', he also asserts that, 'discovering himself or herself within presecured space, the medieval walker renegotiates an itinerary through an especially densely marked terrain'.[42]

In *Three London Itineraries*, a discussion which focuses specifically on texts relating to late medieval London, Strohm argues that,

[t]he peculiarity of medieval space involves the extent to which it is already symbolically organised by the meaning-making activities of the many generations that have traversed it. Which is to say that, as a typical late medieval city, London incorporated a noticeably durable and complicated set of presignifications.[43]

According to Strohm, the medieval walker within the city moves within spaces which are already encoded with meaning and which shape and regulate the individual's experience.

The essays in this volume offer a range of diverse interpretations of medieval Chester, *c.*1200–1500. The contributions include both attempts to recover the experience and understanding of the urban space by individuals and groups within the medieval city and new readings from the vantage point of twenty-first-century disciplinary or theoretical perspectives. As Strohm notes, the spaces of the medieval city are laden with pre-significations. Yet these are not necessarily stable, universal, or agreed upon by all of those whom de Certeau would term 'practioners' of the urban space. Indeed, many recent evaluations of the urban space and its uses have sharpened attention to the dynamics of difference and diversity within the city. Tovi Fenster has shown the ways in which traditional (Lefebvrian) definitions of the city, together with notions of 'use' and 'participation', have tended to rely on discourses of communality and homogeneity, neglecting the ways in which experience of the urban space is shaped by 'patriarchal power relations, which are ethnic, cultural and gender-related'.[44] Just as applicable to investigations of the medieval city as to the city in the modern era of globalization, she emphasises that new critical approaches must 'incorporate issues of difference and cultural, ethnic, racial and gender diversity'.[45] The work of medievalists is already sensitive to many of these issues, particularly in terms of gendered practice and regulation within the city. Diane Watt and Katie Normington, for example, have both reflected on the ways in which women are excluded – or, at least, marginalized – from civic space and how different realms within the city (such as public and private) gather different meanings and possibilities for differently-gendered users.[46]

In medieval and early modern Chester, the meaning and use of urban spaces shifts according to a range of factors and pressures. As the essays in this volume show, the material fabric and topography of Chester itself changes and evolves over the medieval period. The urban environment is also experienced and semanticized differently by different ethnic and cultural communities: citizens, migrants and outsiders; English and Welsh; men and women; those with interests in the city's secular or civic government and those with allegiances to its religious communities (to give just a few examples). Texts and material artefacts produced in medieval Chester represent different responses to the urban space, informed by the requirements of different audiences or users, by different ideological perspectives and by different political agendas. Just as the city is a place of difference and diversity, so the essays in this volume seek to understand medieval Chester in a variety of different ways. Like the textual views over Chester from the city walls, these essays offer vantage points over the city which inevitably reflect our own specific interests in the medieval past, our own sites of imaginative engagement and our own critical, theoretical and ideological priorities. These essays do not necessarily offer a homogenous, uniform perspective on medieval Chester (and do not seek to write a new 'history of medieval Chester', which is already supplied by major works such as the Victoria County History), but instead form a complementary collection of diverse approaches to and interpretations of, the medieval city.

Keith Lilley's essay, 'Urban mappings: visualizing late medieval Chester in cartographic and textual form', explores different kinds of mapping – metaphorical and literal, medieval and modern, textual and visual – and the different ways in which they can extend and challenge our understanding of medieval places and cultures. Lilley describes the process of producing a digital atlas of medieval Chester using GIS (Geographical Information System) software as part of the 'Mapping Medieval Chester' project, reflecting upon the challenges of working with often fragmentary evidence and the many subjective decisions involved. The essay sets this new, digital map of Chester alongside textual mappings of the city by a range of medieval authors, examining the alternative and sometimes apparently contradictory configurations of the urban space offered by different media and cultural perspectives. Lilley rejects any straightforward distinction between 'imagined' and 'real' mappings, arguing that all of these different visualizations of the city – from medieval manuscript to modern digital resource – (re)produce the urban space of Chester according to particular cultural norms, values and desires.

The contribution by C. P. Lewis, 'Framing Medieval Chester: the Landscape of Urban Boundaries', engages with questions central to any process of mapping and understanding the medieval city. How was the space of Chester defined and understood in the Middle Ages and what were the outer limits of the city and its jurisdiction? Lewis gives a detailed analysis of the external boundaries of medieval Chester and its liberties, yet his essay also pays close attention to the multiple borders and edges within the city itself, which he depicts as 'lined and scored with intersecting boundaries of half a dozen kinds, defining parishes and wards, monastic precincts and castle, private and public spaces, layered one upon another' (p. 43). Drawing on a wide range of sources, Lewis vividly reconstructs the ways in which an individual might have navigated the different spaces within the city, whether through experience of its internal material boundaries (such as gateways, the walls of religious precincts, the stairs into the Rows) or through negotiation of less visible jurisdictional boundaries such as parishes and wards.

Although one of the earliest and most extensive examples of urban encomium from medieval England, the *De Laude Cestrie* by the monk Lucian has not received the critical attention it deserves, particularly in terms of what the text can tell us about configurations of place and identity in the twelfth-century city. John Doran and Mark Faulkner offer bold new readings of this neglected text, confirming its complexity and underlining its value for scholars of history, literature and cultural theory alike. John Doran situates *De Laude Cestrie* within its twelfth-century context, tracing responses to local politics within the text and arguing that Lucian aimed to promote cooperation between the monks and clerks of the city in response to unwelcome outside interventions in its religious affairs. Mark Faulkner's essay, 'The Spatial Hermeneutics of Lucian's *De Laude Cestrie*', explores representations of space in the text, focusing on two of Lucian's 'itineraries' through the city. The second of these is reconstructed through analysis of the unusual marginal notes in the manuscript, which seem to record the text's composition and its 'precise temporal and spatial inspiration' (p. 92). Modern theoretical approaches to place and identity are productive here, resonating with Lucian's own opening assertion that space can be decoded and interpreted: 'Tempus et locus et rerum lapsus sensato cuique tribuunt suadibilem, etiam sine literis, lectionem' ('The state of the times, the location of things and the occurrence of events offer persuasive, unwritten instruction to each intelligent being', p. 89).

Liz Herbert McAvoy also considers Lucian in her essay on 'Liminal Spaces and the Anchoritic Life in Medieval Chester', suggesting that he presents the city and its surrounding landscape as an inherently hybrid, unstable, feminine space. Through close literary analysis and interpretation of other documentary evidence, McAvoy shows that the anchoritic life has particular prominence and importance in medieval Chester and its environs. Linking these medieval primary sources with recent theoretical work on gender, space and boundaries, she argues that the 'anchored', fixed, regulated bodies of female English anchorites have special significance in the contested, fluid, and dangerously shifting cultural geography of the Welsh Marches, representing sites of spiritual, ideological – and even national – stability and control. In this provocative and persuasive reading, she challenges us to re-consider works like *De Laude Cestrie* and *Ancrene Wisse* as 'urgent, hyperbolized texts' which respond in their own ways to the hybrid, unstable culture of the Welsh-English borderland.

Laura Varnam and Cynthia Turner Camp both focus on the *Life of St Werburge*, a lengthy late medieval verse hagiography of Chester's patron saint authored by Henry Bradshaw, a monk of St Werburgh's. Drawing on the theoretical work of Mircea Eliade, Varnam explores the triangulations between the sacred, the saint and the city in the poem, with particular attention to the ways in which Bradshaw's text seeks to present the Benedictine community of St Werburgh's as the very centre of late medieval Chester. Her close readings highlight the multivalence of spatial imagery in the *Life*, where 'translacion' functions variously, for example, as a technical term for the relocation of the saint's body in Chester, a way of describing the transformation or re-ordering of space (such as that of a building or the re-arrangement of the diocesan sees), and also a reflection upon Bradshaw's own appropriation of sources and the text's place within literary tradition. Discourses of gender and space also emerge as a key concern in this essay, as Varnam shows the ways in which images of enclosure create parallels between Werburgh's virginity and moral integrity and the walled city itself as embodiments of sanctity. Although written by a Chester monk, the *Life of St Werburge* survives only in the Richard Pynson London edition of 1521. Cynthia Turner Camp confronts the apparent contradiction that 'this decidedly regional saint's life is witnessed solely from the centre', asking how Chester writing might be deployed in and for London. With close attention to the book's paratextual material, including the liminary verses and woodcuts, as well as discussion of the processes and conventions of early print culture, she shows how *Werburge* is positioned for a metropolitan or national audience. Whilst her analysis shows how Werburgh is presented as a universal figure of Christian virtue and sanctity within the text, she also suggests that the *Life* may represent a response by St Werburgh's Abbey to Cardinal Wolsey's proposed Benedictine reforms in 1519–20.

Whilst relations between Chester and Wales and the tensions and cultural exchanges promoted by the city's borderland location, recur as a site of interest in essays throughout this volume, three contributions in particular focus on the interactions between Welsh and English in the city. Helen Fulton's essay 'The Outside Within: Medieval Chester and North Wales as a Social Space' re-examines Chester's frontier situation, challenging notions of a 'hard barrier' between the two cultures (p. 149) and instead exploring the 'overflow' in both directions across this permeable border. She notes however, that Welsh and English understood their 'shared space' differently, and defined themselves in opposition to each other (p. 149). Fulton's essay centres on medieval Welsh poetry relating to Chester, revealing a range of different cultural perspectives on the city from those produced within its official, English culture. Across a range of genres, from religious poetry to satire, these texts suggest the ways in which the Welsh 'transgress[ed] the limits imposed on them by the political border and the city walls' (p. 164). A poem by Tudur Aled, for example, names the religious foundations of Chester – and the abbot of St Werburgh's – in Welsh, an act of linguistic appropriation and challenge directed at some of the city's most powerful institutions. The poems to St John's church and the relics of the 'true cross' held there reflect the Welsh tradition of visiting towns for the purpose of religious worship, subtly incorporating Chester into Welsh religious and cultural space and practice. Fulton's analysis of the Welsh literary material will open new horizons for many students of medieval Chester, and the Appendix to her essay, a catalogue of Welsh strict metre poems with connections to Chester, will facilitate further research and discussion on this important topic.

Looking at the experiences of the Welsh in Chester alongside those of other immigrant communities (Manx and Irish), Jane Laughton's essay uses extensive archival work to ask questions about the interactions between different groups within the city. She 'seeks to determine whether these ethnic immigrants integrated with the long-established English families to form a hybrid community or whether they remained distinctive groupings with their own identities and loyalties' (p. 171). The detailed analysis of medieval documentary evidence here enables Laughton to recover vivid narratives of individuals and their experiences within the city, illuminating issues of habitation, work, kinship and lifestyle for these immigrant groups. The names and stories which emerge through her research are evocative of a diverse, multicultural community in which ethnic groups congregate in particular districts but do not form discrete 'enclaves' (p. 178), and in which individuals from different backgrounds are able to make their own contributions to the life of the city.

Next, Robert W. Barrett's essay reconsiders the question of Welsh-English relations from another literary perspective: that of the Chester

Whitsun plays. Barrett focuses on the Chester *Shepherds' Play*, with its depiction of 'Welsh' shepherds who experience the angelic news of the incarnation from their place in the hills outside the city. Taking its cues from the politically aware critical readings of representations of the Welsh in Shakespeare, Barrett's interpretation of the *Shepherds' Play* is alert to the complex, potentially dangerous political relations and tensions at work here. His analysis centres on the shepherds' feast – a key moment of visual spectacle in the play – offering a challenging new reading which theorizes the cultural or 'biosocial' politics of food and its consumption. The Welsh shepherds' ingestion of English food (butter from Blacon, ale from Halton and Lancashire oatcakes) prompts an investigation of processes of incorporation (literal, physical and cultural) and their limits. Barrett's subtle conclusions resist any easy characterisation of relations between the English and Welsh in medieval Chester, arguing that while 'prejudice against the Welsh was not total during the heyday of the Chester cycle . . ., neither can the shepherds be effortlessly integrated into holistic fantasies of civic and national community' (p. 197).

Finally, my own essay looks beyond the chronological limits of this volume to explore the memory of Anglo-Saxon Mercia in late medieval and early modern Chester, examining sources from Henry Bradshaw's *Life of St Werburge* to early antiquarian writing in the city. The fourteenth-century shrine of St Werburgh in Chester's Benedictine abbey forms the starting point for my discussion. This elaborate stone structure with its Gothic tracery and sculpture in fact elides the absence at its very centre – the missing body of Werburgh herself which, as Bradshaw tells us, 'resolued unto powder' at its translation to Chester. My reading of Chester texts which reconstruct and memorialize the city's Mercian heritage focuses on imaginative responses to absence, loss and desire and the ways in which later literature invents (or in some cases, problematizes) a sense of Anglo-Saxon identity and tradition. Like the carvings of Mercian kings and saints on Werburgh's tomb, these texts seek to supply 'new spiritual and cultural relics' for the city (p. 216), which celebrate Chester's imagined historic identity at the centre of a powerful, autonomous kingdom.

Certain key themes emerge across the essays within this volume, including relations between the Welsh and English, formulations of centre and periphery, nation and region, different kinds of 'mapping' and the visual and textual representation of place, borders and boundaries, uses of the past in the production of identity and the connections between discourses of gender and space. Each essay offers its own perspective on these issues and the volume does not seek to present a homogenous, monolithic interpretation of medieval Chester. Instead, it is designed to generate conversation and debate amongst scholars of different disciplines, working on different locations and periods and to open up directions for future work on space, place and identity in the medieval city.

Notes

[1]   Anthony Bowerman, 'Walk around Chester Walls', with a pictorial map by Chris Bullock (Tattenhall, 1998).
[2]   Henry James, *English Hours* (Oxford, 1981), pp. 35–6.
[3]   Ibid., p. 36.
[4]   A. T. Thacker, 'City Walls and Gates', in *VCH Ches*. 5. i, pp. 213–15, 218. This essay provides an excellent overview of the history of the walls, and the Victoria County History for Cheshire as a whole offers the most authoritative general history of medieval Chester and its hinterland. For further discussion of Chester's medieval walls see C. P. Lewis in this volume, pp. 42–56.
[5]   Henry James, *The Ambassadors*, S. P. Rosenbaum (ed.) (New York, 1994), p. 24.
[6]   In *English Hours*, this element of restraint and temperance comes perhaps from the more cynical 'certain friend' who laments 'the decay of his relish for the picturesque', providing 'a warning against cheap infatuations' (p. 35).
[7]   James, *English Hours*, p. 36.
[8]   Ibid.
[9]   Ibid., p. 38.
[10]   Ibid., pp. 37, 39.
[11]   Ibid.
[12]   Ibid.
[13]   John Broster, *A Walk Round the Walls and City of Chester* (Chester, 1821), p. i.
[14]   Ibid., p. 91.
[15]   Thacker, 'City Walls and Gates', p. 217.
[16]   Ibid.
[17]   William Webb, 'A Description of the City and County Palatine of Chester' in Daniel King, *The Vale-Royall of England, or, The County-Palatine of Chester. Performed by William Smith, and William Webb, Gentlemen* (London, 1656), p. 15 (each inclusion within the volume has its own page numbering). It seems likely that Webb has borrowed this last phrase from Lucian's *De Laude Cestrie*, a text which he cites elsewhere and professes to have found 'comprized in Camden'.
[18]   Ibid., p. 15.
[19]   Ibid., p. 16.
[20]   Ibid., p. 17.
[21]   Ibid.
[22]   Ibid., p. 20.
[23]   Ibid., pp. 24, 22.
[24]   Ibid., pp. 20–1.
[25]   This fold-out occurs after page 36 of Webb's 'Description'.

[26] *DLC*, fol. 88r (text is cited by manuscript folio number). Whilst Lucian addresses these multiple audiences in his work, there is no evidence that the text was widely circulated or known outside Chester.

[27] Ibid., fol. 10r.

[28] Ibid., fols 17r and 5v. Faulkner suggests that, along with the main text of the manuscript, these marginal notes may be in Lucian's hand. See Mark Faulkner's Introduction to *De Laude Cestrie*, *www.medievalchester.ac.uk* (accessed 19 August 2009).

[29] See John M. Ganim, 'The Experience of Modernity in Late Medieval Literature: Urbanism, Experience and Rhetoric in Some Early Descriptions of London', in *The Performance of Middle English Culture*, ed. James J. Paxson et al (Cambridge, 1998), pp. 77–96, esp. p. 87.

[30] *DLC*, fol. 13r.

[31] Ibid., fol. 60v.

[32] See Mark Faulkner, Introduction to *De Laude Cestrie, www.medievalchester. ac.uk* (accessed 19 August 2009).

[33] *DLC*, fol. 12r.

[34] For an overview of the medieval *mappa mundi* tradition, see for example Evelyn Edson, *Mapping Time and Space: How Medieval Mapmakers Viewed their World* (London, 1997).

[35] *DLC*, fol. 13rv.

[36] Michel de Certeau, 'Walking in the City', in *The Practice of Everyday Life* (Berkeley, 1984), pp. 91–110, p. 93.

[37] Ibid., p. 92.

[38] Ibid.

[39] Ibid., p. 93.

[40] Ibid., p. 101.

[41] See the discussion in this volume by Mark Faulkner, pp. 78–98.

[42] Paul Strohm, 'Three London Itineraries', in his *Theory and the Premodern Text* (Minneapolis, 2000), pp. 3–19, p. 4.

[43] Ibid., p. 4.

[44] Tovi Fenster, 'The Right to the Gendered City: Different Formations of Belonging in Everyday Life', *Journal of Gender Studies* 14 (2005), 217–31, p. 217.

[45] Ibid., p. 217.

[46] Diane Watt, 'Faith in the Landscape: Overseas Pilgrimages in *The Book of Margery Kempe*', in Clare A. Lees and Gillian R. Overing (eds), *A Place to Believe In: Locating Medieval Landcsapes* (Philadelphia, 2006), pp. 170–87, esp. p. 175 and Katie Normington, *Gender and Medieval Drama* (Cambridge, 2004), esp. pp. 73–9 (also cited in Watt's discussion).

2

Urban Mappings: Visualizing Late Medieval Chester in Cartographic and Textual Form

KEITH D. LILLEY

'Mapping begets further mappings'[1]

The map is often considered to define a geographer's work, with map-making being seen traditionally as the principal means of pursuing geographical enquiry.[2] But increasingly geographers have become less fixed in their views on cartography, of what a map is and what it is to map, recognizing more the value of metaphorical and less literal, 'maps' and 'mappings'. This shift began to occur in the late 1980s, particularly among cultural and historical geographers interested in maps and landscapes and who were driving geography's so-called 'linguistic turn'.[3] As the subject of language, discourse, metaphor and text all occupied geographers more and more, it gave rise to geographers writing about 'deconstructing the map' and the 'city as text', deploying linguistic and literary terms and approaches in their work.[4] In contrast, cartography of the traditional kind has come to occupy a more marginal place on geography's disciplinary 'map', as cultural and historical geographers' 'mappings' rarely involve producing a piece of cartography and actually making a map.

This chapter aims to swim against the tide in this regard: for writing as a geographer, it reasserts the value of producing traditional cartography, not least in helping us to visualize past landscapes, yet in doing so, I argue, it does not mean that textual and figurative 'mappings' should be ignored, since both they and the normative, 'literal' map offer complementary ways of mapping the medieval city and visualizing its urban spaces and landscapes cartographically.

Paradoxically, just as Anglophone humanities geographers were adopting linguistic and textual approaches in their work, in literature and literary criticism there were those taking an interest in geographical themes, including maps and mapping. The geographer's mantra that 'space matters' has brought cartography into the realm of contemporary and historical English literary studies and arguably brought the two disciplines of geography and literature closer together.[5] This so-called 'spatial turn' takes many different forms, ranging from adopting geographic and cartographic metaphors in studies of textual culture, through to literary and linguistic studies of cartography and visual culture.[6] This is as evident in medieval English literature studies as it is in modern; for example, Nicholas Howe's *Writing the Map of Anglo-Saxon England*, uses 'mapping' in its metaphorical sense to explore Old English texts and their 'imagined geographies', whereas for Kathy Lavezzo, in her book *Angels on the Edge of the World*, the emphasis is placed more on reading, intertextually, both maps (as visual images) *and* texts (as written sources) to show how the English perceived their geographically-marginal place in the medieval world.[7] Combining visual and textual material through the medium of mapping, both literal and metaphoric, provides a rich and lucrative avenue for medieval studies not just in literary history but in historical cartography and geography too.[8]

There are, then, two kinds of mapping that can contribute to our understanding of medieval cultures: 'mapping' in a *metaphorical* sense, and mapping in the more *literal* sense of map-making. Edney warns us not to conflate or confuse the two;[9] but it is through combining both mapping and map-making that we are able to explore how medieval textual, literary 'mappings' of medieval Chester relate to modern cartographic, geographical maps of the city. This was one of the principal aims behind the 'Mapping Medieval Chester' project. The challenge that mapping medieval Chester presents is that it, like many other medieval cities in Europe, was not cartographically represented until the end of the sixteenth century.[10] In fact, Chester's earliest map is William Smith's, in *The Particuler Description of England*, dated 1588, and although by English standards this is an early example, it is not early enough to stand as a 'medieval map' (Figure 1).[11]

However, for exploring textual 'mappings' of the medieval city, Chester does have a rich and relatively early set of texts to draw upon, in particular a description made by Lucian, a monk of St Werburgh's Abbey, whose *De Laude Cestrie* is one of England's most valuable medieval prose descriptions of an urban landscape contemporary with the time of its author.[12] With Lucian's laudatory account of his home city, there is the potential

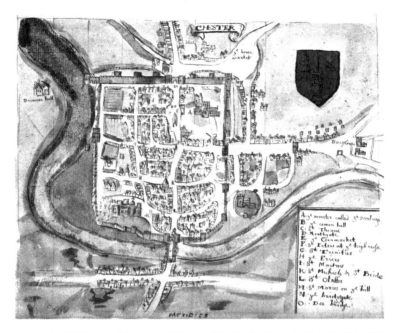

Figure 1. William Smith, map of Chester (1588) (BL Harley MS 1046, fol. 173)
© British Library Board.

to begin to 'map out' his image of Chester and to explore his perceptions
and experiences of its urban spaces.[13] Yet without visual maps of medieval Chester, it is difficult to compare Lucian's textual urban mappings
with contemporary cartographic representations in the way that Lavezzo
has done for textual and visual mappings of medieval England as a whole.
One solution to this is to use modern maps of medieval Chester and reflect
upon how different kinds of 'mappings' – medieval and modern, textual
and visual, metaphoric and literal – relate to one another.

Modern maps of medieval Chester
Modern commentators on medieval Chester have typically adapted
modern street maps to show the city's medieval features such as its street
pattern, walls and gates, monastic houses, parish churches, civic buildings and key landmarks, such as the bridge across the Dee and Chester's
distinctive and particular contribution to medieval architecture, the Rows.
Such maps have long appeared in historical writing on the city, as well
as in archaeological studies, most typically prefacing an article or book
simply as an illustrative device to show the relative positions of the city's

medieval institutions – whether civic, military or religious – and the framework of streets that interconnected them.[14] Maps can of course be used analytically in understanding a city's spatial evolution, while the process of mapping – as an artistic and creative exercise – also opens up our historical and geographical imaginations and can help us to understand places better.[15] In 'Mapping Medieval Chester', the use of maps and mapping sought to achieve both; to move away from simply using maps as a means of illustration. Doing so poses certain methodological problems however, for without medieval maps of the city how is it possible to begin to map its medieval urban landscape? The answer is to use the maps that are available, even though they are post-medieval in date and from them, along with available archaeological and historical evidence, piece together the physical and topographical features that comprised Chester at some period or moment in its distant past.[16] This approach thus makes use of cartographic sources and techniques to create new maps of medieval urban landscapes.[17] In the case of Chester, the existence of early modern and later maps, coupled with an established and well-documented archaeological record, makes this task somewhat easier here than for some other English medieval towns and cities.

A succession of maps and plans of Chester, from Smith's late-sixteenth century manuscript plan through to detailed Ordnance Survey (OS) mapping of the mid- to late-nineteenth century, provides a sequence of cartographic and visual 'snapshots' charting changes in Chester's local urban landscape. Without doubt the most accurately drawn and surveyed of these historic map-sources are the large-scale OS 1:500 scale plans of 1871–3. These show the urban landscape in great detail, including individual buildings and their respective property boundaries (Figure 2). Though these modern OS plans are temporally far removed from the city of the Middle Ages, the urban landscape they show contains an imprint of the medieval townscape. Many of the streets surveyed by the OS in the 1870s, especially those principal thoroughfares located within Chester's city walls, owe their forms and layout to the ninth century, if not earlier.[18] Similarly, plot-boundaries, city walls and gates, ecclesiastical buildings, and other topographical features, all recorded by the Ordnance Surveyors and shown on their detailed plans, are largely inherited from sometime within the Middle Ages, thus making these modern maps an invaluable source from which to begin mapping medieval urban landscapes.

As well as continuity in the urban landscape – from the medieval through to the modern period – there are also townscape discontinuities, or breaks. These too are made evident in Chester's historic maps. Over

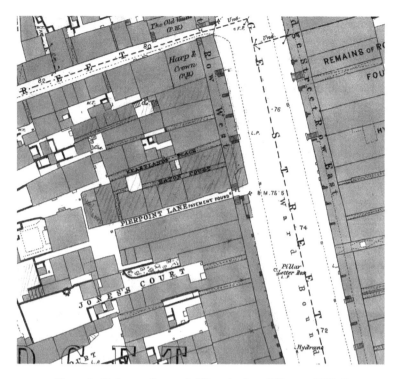

Figure 2. Ordnance Survey 1:500 scale plan of Chester, 1871–3
(detail of Bridge Street).

an intervening period spanning some three hundred years, some areas and features of late medieval Chester had disappeared from the urban landscape. Such losses are evident by comparing, for example, the OS plans with Smith's 1588 plan of the city. A number of other historic town maps and plans, such as the one drawn by Alexander de Lavaux in 1745, chart the process of these intervening erasures from Chester's urban topography and their replacement by successive modern structures and townscapes; yet Chester's medieval skeleton endured and remained visible, at least partially, in these later (re)mappings. Where medieval features were obliterated, notably after the Reformation in the case of monastic houses, local archaeology can often assist us. Over the past half a century archaeologists working in Chester have located lost medieval features and mapped them, revealing the boundaries of former monastic precincts, for example and establishing the ground plans of their associated conventual buildings.[19]

The same has occurred with other medieval features too, including the excavation of some urban properties situated in the commercial heart of Chester, these proving once again the longevity in many cases of the city's street and plot patterns shown by the 1870s OS 1:500 plans.[20] An underlying fossilized medieval urban landscape was inadvertently represented by modern surveyors in their maps of Chester, therefore.

While the city's archaeology, together with a sequence of historic maps and plans of Chester, provides a firm starting point for mapping out the late medieval city's urban topography, attempting to create such a map that is accurate and detailed, both geographically and historically, is by no means without its problems. For example, unlike the historic map-evidence, which covers the whole city and also its suburbs, archaeological and documentary sources are geographically (and temporally) uneven, with evidence good for some parts of Chester but poorer or non-existent in others – Chester is typical in this regard. This presents a methodological challenge for those trying to map the whole city, for clearly it is visually and historically undesirable to have 'blank areas' that are simply showing a current lack of knowledge rather than the lack of any medieval urban occupation. Yet such *terrae incognita* still need to be acknowledged in our urban mappings.

Digital technologies, spatial data and GIS

Visualizing the medieval city cartographically thus requires a process of piecing together a map using various historical, archaeological and geographical sources. Integrating these 'spatial' data to create a modern map of the medieval city can be done by hand, using traditional map-making methods of draughting using tracing overlays and selectively drawing out certain urban features to show in a final finished paper map. With 'Mapping Medieval Chester', however, the process of map-making made use of digital technologies and in particular Geographical Information System (GIS) software, to visualize the medieval urban landscape.

Employing this digital approach offers certain technical and methodological advantages, for using GIS not only makes it possible to include cartographic uncertainty (using later map evidence and a degree of conjecture) but also it can alert future users of maps about which sources were used in the map-making process. This degree of 'cartographic transparency' is easily resolved using GIS but difficult to achieve using paper maps. This is because a GIS is, first and foremost, a database for storing, retrieving and analysing spatial data, which includes maps of course and enables users to keep track of different data and its sources.[21] It also provides a means of converting analogue maps into digital data (through a process of digitization) and allows maps to be quickly and easily generated from this data, either in a digital or a paper format.[22] Tracking data sources is particularly useful in historical mapping where it is necessary to offer transparency in the map-making process, for as we shall see, decisions on what to include and exclude are fundamental to trying to map out medieval urban landscapes, simply because the available evidence is so fragmentary.

The process by which 'digital maps' of medieval Chester were created is methodologically relatively straightforward and easily transferable to other urban contexts. First, by importing digital scans ('rasters') of paper maps, a series of map layers are built up within a GIS, such as Chester's historic town plans discussed earlier. The plans used in creating the Chester GIS include the OS 1:500 plans, as well as Lavaux's 1745 plan, and others from the late 1500s to mid-1800s. In the GIS, each one appears as a separate 'layer'. If required, these historic maps can each be 'geo-rectified', that is, placed in a modern geographical co-ordinate system. Geo-rectifying works much better for more modern maps than it does for early historic maps however, as the latter were usually surveyed and drawn using projection systems that do not translate easily into modern geographical (i.e. latitude and longitude) co-ordinate systems used in GIS software (e.g. ArcGIS). While this again presents a methodological problem, described below, in theory these historic maps should sit one above the other, the layers themselves equivalent to urban topographic 'strata' of particular periods or dates (Figure 3).

Of the historic maps used, the OS 1:500 1870s plans geo-rectified to modern geographical co-ordinates with least difficulty. This was proven by incorporating into the GIS field survey data gathered using a differential Global Positioning System (dGPS).[23] This positional data is imported into the GIS and from it the degrees of 'distortion' in the various historic cartographic layers established and quantified (using tools in the GIS). For Chester, key topographical features and locations were surveyed (in September 2008, by Keith Lilley and Lorraine Barry), establishing their precise geographical positions. What this revealed was the high degree of surveying accuracy achieved by the Ordnance Survey in its 1:500 plans and also to some extent by Alexander de Lavaux in the 1740s. But beyond these particular two map sources, cartographic 'accuracy' – that is, in the modern sense of a consistently scaled and scientifically surveyed map – was lacking, which makes it difficult (and to some extent pointless) to geo-rectify these other maps. Since the OS 1:500 plans are the

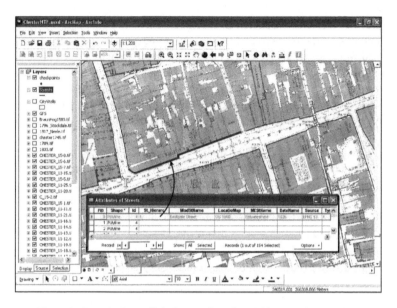

Figure 3. Developing a digital map of medieval Chester using ArcGIS
(Geographical Information System software), showing the digitization of
Eastgate Street in progress and an example of attribute data linked to the
digitized map features.

cartographically most accurate and also (as noted earlier) historically
useful as repositories of relict urban features dating from the Middle Ages,
they were the principal cartographic source used to map out late medieval
Chester, despite their later date.

With the historic map layers imported into the GIS, the second main
stage in the digital mapping process requires selectively digitizing those
urban features of medieval antecedence, which in Chester's case began by
using the OS 1:500 plans. This procedure is carried out 'on screen' using
tools in the GIS software and is a subjective process of deciding which
particular urban features are to be selected and digitized. Decisions are
made based upon the available historical evidence. For example, which of
the streets shown on the OS plans are known (from documentary sources
and archaeology perhaps) to have been in existence before 1500? Did
post-medieval changes take place so affecting their alignment and orientation? The same set of questions also relate to other urban features to be
mapped: to what extent could the alignments of the city's walls, the locations and ground plans of parish churches and the abbey, the plot patterns,

Rows and narrow lanes, all shown by the 1:500 plans, be relied upon, both historically and geographically, to be those present in medieval Chester? Such questioning of the historic map evidence is vital if the finished map is to be believed and trusted. Here, the transparency that GIS offers is useful, for it allows the map's creators (and later its users) to see exactly where the mapped topographical information comes from, for not only are features being digitized in the GIS, each vector – digitized line, polygon or point – can also be described and annotated using 'attribute data' (see Figure 3). With this, each digitized feature (a street or building, for example) is accorded its own unique identification number that links through to an entry in the GIS database. This information can include, for example, from which source the map-feature was digitized, and what the documentary or archaeological evidence is to verify its medieval provenance.

Using Chester's earliest historic maps, together with existing historical and archaeological knowledge of the medieval city, features on the OS 1:500 plans were selectively digitized in stages, starting with street patterns and proceeding through to other constituent urban topographical features, such as the city walls and other structures such as churches, gates and towers on the walls, plot patterns along the medieval streets, the Rows, the bridge over the Dee and the course of the Dee itself. All are shown by the OS 1:500 plans and in the GIS each of these features was digitized as a separate layer, partly because one aim was to be able to re-present them via a web-resource in a way that would allow users to selectively turn each of them either on or off as needed, and partly because making each of the layers – each of the topographic features – independent allows them to be depicted visually differently in the GIS in terms of line weighting, colour, shade and so forth, which helps to communicate more effectively the different cartographic information contained in the GIS (Figure 4).[24]

Since digitizing Chester's medieval urban topography relied primarily upon using the large-scale OS 1:500 plans, this also meant dealing with post-medieval townscape changes, where certain features were either missing completely from the OS plans or substantially altered. To insert these missing or changed features onto the digital map meant sourcing them from elsewhere. Here again GIS offers particular advantages: 'holes' or gaps are made abundantly clear in the GIS if the raster layers (that is historic map scans) are momentarily turned off, particularly in those areas along the western side of the city, just within the circuit of walls, where the majority of the city's religious houses had stood (as well as the castle, which survives today, albeit much altered). To map these 'lost' urban features relies primarily upon scanning archaeological plans.[25] For over

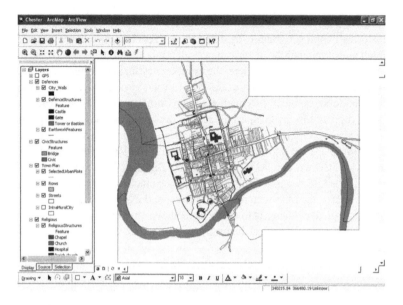

Figure 4. Developing a digital map of medieval Chester using ArcGIS
(Geographical Information System software), the finished resource with layers
(in list on left of screendump) and the map window (right).

thirty years, excavations of Chester's medieval past have compensated for
earlier decades of neglect by former archaeologists who had simply dug
through medieval occupation layers to focus on the city's Roman archaeology. With scanned archaeological plans of excavated and surveyed
medieval features imported into the GIS and geo-rectified to the OS 1:500
layer, it is straightforward to digitize from them selectively the outlines
of former medieval structures, such as the city's lost religious houses and
their precincts, the course of the ditch outside the city walls and the size
and ground plans of churches and chapels, as well as the medieval extent of
the castle and the Rows (as they were before being variously 'restored' or
truncated, in more recent times). There is a dual advantage mapping from
these archaeological plans: first, they are drawn to modern cartographic
standards, so easily geo-rectified and second, they reveal how urban structures and features appeared at the end of the Middle Ages (see Figure 4).

However, this still leaves significant gaps in the digital map; especially
where redevelopment changed an alignment of a street, or removed former
plot boundaries, or obliterated known medieval buildings, including
the city's gates and the structures that had stood in the market place in

front of the abbey gate. In some cases, the locations and shapes of these missing medieval urban features are shown by certain of the city's historic town-plans, but digitizing from these is not straightforward since they geo-rectified comparatively poorly, and generally lacked the level of topographical detail offered by the OS 1:500 plans and the archaeological surveys already used. The need to include these lost, but documented features of late medieval Chester, requires a pragmatic approach of using earlier map-sources selectively as a guide, sometimes by 'locally' geo-rectifying a part of the map to relocate a particular lost feature (which generally worked better than trying to geo-rectify the whole of map), or sometimes simply by redrawing the lost feature (as a vector in the GIS) and then locating it, not necessarily exactly where the historic map showed it to be but where it seemed to belong historically and topographically. In the case of mapping medieval Chester, the latter process was used, for example, to position and delimit the demolished market hall, as well as some of the city's former medieval gates (their positions clearly relating to the alignments of the walls, even if the locally-geo-rectified historic maps had placed them in some other position nearby); while the former method was used to help recreate the earlier alignments of once narrow streets that were widened and 'improved' in the eighteenth and nineteenth centuries, as well as to add in streets that had altogether disappeared, as in the case of Capel Lane near Bridge Gate and part of Castle Street (Figure 5). The sources used to locate these lost features can again be documented through the use of the linked attribute tables and also by using the 'symbology' available in the GIS software. Thus, the more historically and geographically 'secure' mapped features – gained by digitizing from the OS 1:500 and archaeological plans – can be given different visual appearances from those whose location and provenance is less certain.

What results from this digital mapping process then? Rather than a single printed paper map, GIS provides a flexible and interactive map-resource that helps us to visualize Chester's medieval urban landscape. Using GIS allows transparency in the map-making process, and also makes possible both digital and analogue (paper) outputs for further study or dissemination.[26] The resulting maps derived from this process show Chester's late medieval urban landscape and its topography (Figures 6 and 7).[27] These maps are cartographically 'accurate' in the sense that they are drawn to scale, using modern geographical co-ordinate information and accepted cartographic conventions. However, despite this they are nevertheless *subjective* mappings, in that they are a product of particular decisions made by the cartographer as well as decisions made by those

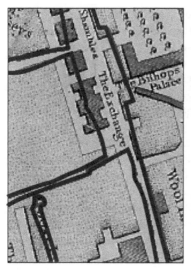

Figure 5. Adding 'lost' urban features into the GIS and indicating localized map distortion: left, the streets as digitized from OS 1:500 plans (dark lines) overlaid onto 1745 Lavaux plan of Chester; right, streets digitized from OS 1:500 plans showing the later alignment of Grosvenor Street cutting across earlier streets and plot-boundaries (shown by 1780s map).

whose sources are drawn upon in the map-making process. Such subjectivity inherent in this sort of historical urban mapping is clear from the account given here, and this should help undermine any claim for a map's (otherwise assumed) 'objectivity' and geographical and historical 'truthfulness' (in this case, as an image of Chester's medieval urban landscape). In this regard, one advantage of creating digital maps in a publically accessible GIS is that it can provide others with opportunities to put forward their own alternative mappings, either by adding new information as it arises in the future or by using existing information but offering different interpretations of it. In this sense, GIS is increasingly being recognized as a more democratic mapping process and tool compared with more traditional print-based cartography.[28]

This exercise in mapping late medieval Chester also helps with reflecting on how urban spaces are experienced and understood through modern techniques of maps and map-making, and how this differs from engaging with the contemporary 'textual' mappings of those who knew the medieval city first-hand. Trying to connect these 'modern' and 'medieval'

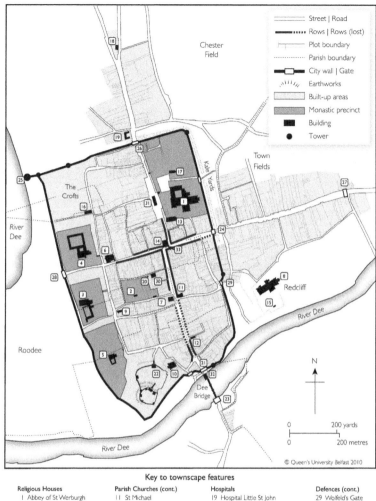

Figure 6. Chester c.1500.

Key to townscape features

Religious Houses
1 Abbey of St Werburgh
2 Carmelite Friary
3 Dominican Friary
4 Franciscan Friary
5 St Mary's Nunnery

Parish Churches
6 Holy Trinity
7 St Bridget
8 St John the Baptist
9 St Martin
10 St Mary (on the Hill)

Parish Churches (cont.)
11 St Michael
12 St Olave
13 St Oswald
14 St Peter

Chapels
15 Hermitage
16 St Chad
17 St Thomas
18 St Thomas the Martyr

Hospitals
19 Hospital Little St John
20 Hospital St Ursula

Defences
21 Bridge Gate
22 Castle
23 Dee bridge-gate
24 East Gate
25 New Tower (Water Tower)
26 North Gate
27 The Bars
28 Water Gate

Defences (cont.)
29 Wolfeld's Gate
   (New Gate)

Civic Buildings
30 Common Hall
31 Market Hall
32 Mills
33 The Pentice

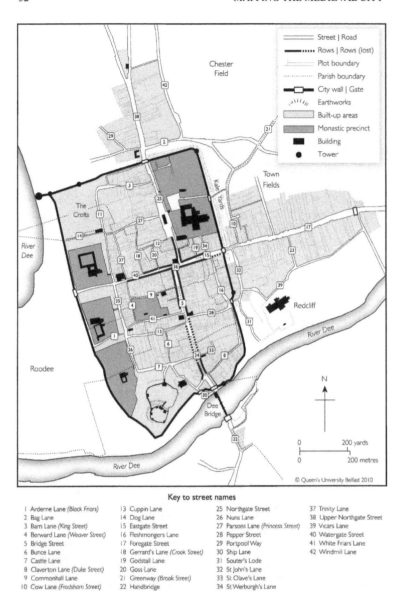

Key to street names

1 Arderne Lane *(Black Friars)*	13 Cuppin Lane
2 Bag Lane	14 Dog Lane
3 Barn Lane *(King Street)*	15 Eastgate Street
4 Berward Lane *(Weaver Street)*	16 Fleshmongers Lane
5 Bridge Street	17 Foregate Street
6 Bunce Lane	18 Gerrard's Lane *(Crook Street)*
7 Castle Lane	19 Godstall Lane
8 Claverton Lane *(Duke Street)*	20 Goss Lane
9 Commonhall Lane	21 Greenway *(Brook Street)*
10 Cow Lane *(Frodsham Street)*	22 Handbridge
11 Crofts Lane *(Linenhall Street)*	23 Love Lane
12 Crook Lane *(Hamilton Place)*	24 Lower Bridge Street

25 Northgate Street	37 Trinity Lane
26 Nuns Lane	38 Upper Northgate Street
27 Parsons Lane *(Princess Street)*	39 Vicars Lane
28 Pepper Street	40 Watergate Street
29 Portpool Way	41 White Friars Lane
30 Ship Lane	42 Windmill Lane
31 Souter's Lode	
32 St John's Lane	
33 St Olave's Lane	
34 St Werburgh's Lane	
35 St Nicholas Lane	
36 The Cross	

Figure 7. Chester streets *c.*1500.

mappings raises some interesting issues: ostensibly they are concerned with the same locality, the city of Chester, yet contrasting them begins to open up how urban spaces are understood, experienced and interpreted as *topoi* – that is, places of particular cultural meaning and value – through textual 'mappings', and how these present a quite different view of the medieval city to that gained from digital 'map-making' with its visually ordered geographical information and orderly urban topographies. Dependent upon the context of those doing the 'mapping' therefore, various cultural meanings are construed through these complementary yet alternative maps and urban 'mappings'.

Alternative maps and mappings

Contrasting the textual mappings of contemporary medieval authors with the digitally-produced maps of Chester raises uncertainties over the location of particular topographical features that are mentioned in the texts but not easily locatable on a map. This is especially obvious in the case of trying to locate 'the cross' which is referred to by various contemporaries in their written accounts of the city. 'The cross' appears, for example, in late medieval Welsh poems describing Chester as a focus of pilgrimage and devotion, including 'Y Grog i bob dyn o gred' ('The Cross, for every man of Christendom') by Guto'r Glyn (fourteenth century), and 'Y Grog odidog y doded dy lun' ('Outstanding Cross, may your image be set') by Llawdden (fifteenth century).[29] A fourteenth-century poem by Gruffudd ap Maredudd imagines the cross in richly symbolic terms which reflect the belief that it incorporated a fragment of the 'true cross' discovered by St Helen.

> Doeth Gaerlleon, deg anrhegion digynrhygedd
> (Didrai foliant, Duw da farant dioferedd!),
> Didrist Grist Groes, organ hoedloes aur gynhadledd,
> Delw fireinryw, er pryny byw o'r pren a'r bedd.
>
> (I will gild my praise of the Cross of Christ
> At the chancel-boundary of shining, most famed Chester;
> St Helena obtained it, a spiritual treasure,
> On the third day by custom (a golden search) of summer.)[30]

The question of this cross's location is an important one for understanding alternative perceptions of medieval Chester from the Welsh (as opposed to English) perspective, but how sure can we be of its location? Is this 'cross' interred in an ecclesiastical building ('at the chancel boundary') in the city, and thus mapable and locatable? Moreover, can we be sure that it is always the same cross being referred to in these contemporary Welsh and English texts, since other crosses also feature in Chester's local urban landscape? These include topographic locations where a cross is (or once was) sited for all to see, including, importantly from a Welsh perspective, on the western approach to the city, as a recent observer has noted:

> The modern traveller from the west will most likely enter the city on the A483, which crosses the river Dee via the Grosvenor Bridge, breaching the ancient city walls just above their south-west corner. To the left the river flows west and then north, leaving a bulge of dry land between its waters and the city wall. This area is known as the Roodee, a name which derives from *rod* [long o], meaning 'cross', and *eg* [long e], 'marsh', 'meadow' or 'island', and which is first attested in a thirteenth-century charter of St Werburgh's abbey. Nowadays the Roodee is covered by Chester Racecourse, but formerly a cross did indeed stand upon it. Its red sandstone pedestal is still visible today, standing rather forlornly just inside the race track on the eastern side, facing the city centre.[31]

This particular cross is marked on some historic maps such as the OS 1:500 plans and marked an intersection between two medieval parishes, perhaps predating them in origin, with the cross being used as a parochial marker.[32] But it not the only mapable cross in Chester. The more obvious cross lay at the city's centre, in the street outside St Peter's church. This is where the 'high cross' of Chester stood, and it is clearly shown on Smith's plan of 1588, as well as others of around that time (see Figure 1). It was typical of the period to have a 'high cross' in the centre of a city and not neces- sarily a market cross (the main market place in Chester was to the north, outside the abbey gates).[33] It gave rise in Chester's case to the local street name 'The Cross' which appears on the OS 1:500 plans. The Cross was also the intersection of the city's four main axial streets which cut Chester into four quarters. This too was understood by (English) contemporaries. For example, in his description of the city, Lucian uses it as a metaphor for Christ and for the crucifixion:

> Habet eciam plateas duas equilineas et excellentes in modum benedicte crucis, per transuersum sibi obuias et se transeuntes, que deinceps fiant quattuor ex duabus, capita sua consummantes in quattuor portis, mistice ostendens atque magnifice, magni Regis inhabitantem graciam se habere, qui legem geminam noui ac ueteris testamenti per misterium sancte crucis impletam ostendit, in quattuor euangelistis.
>
> (Chester also has two perfectly straight streets intersecting like the blessed cross, which form four roads, culminating at the four gates, mystically revealling the marvellously innate grace of the Great King, who, through the four evangelists, showed the twin law of the old and new testaments to be completed through the mystery of the holy cross.)[34]

Locating 'the cross' in Lucian's mind meant 'mapping' Christ's body onto and through Chester's urban topography. This 'cross' is not just an intersection of streets – a crossing place – but a manifestation of Christ's enduring temporal and spatial presence in Lucian's (urban) world, the city thus 'crossing itself' as a sign of Christ's body. Through its cross-shaped form of streets, Lucian extends 'the cross' beyond one topographical location (The Cross), so that it encompasses the whole city and its people. By so doing, Lucian is using the city's topography to connect Chester with Christ and to the wider world.[35] So while it is possible to see Lucian's cross as spatially locatable, as a place on the map centred on The Cross, topographically locating it as such potentially diminishes its significance in Lucian's figurative and allegorical 'mapping' of city's *topoi*. Such alternative mappings are not easily accommodated in our digital maps of the medieval urban landscape, as GIS-based map-making requires a fixed feature or location.

As a case in point therefore, trying to locate Chester's medieval crosses (by connecting textual 'mappings' with mapped urban topography) raises some interesting methodological questions. First, with Chester's 'cross', mapping out topographies from textual mappings makes it clear that there are (seemingly) many alternative crosses; some of which can be geographically located while others cannot. Second, even where it is possible to locate and map a cross, the very process of attempting to place it on a modern map perhaps means we lose something of its particular cultural meaning and significance. These 'alternate mappings' raise yet further, more theoretically orientated questions on how urban spaces are produced through linking textual and cartographic mappings.

The digital map of Chester created using the cartographic and archaeological evidence shows clearly enough the perimeter of the city's medieval defences (Figure 4). They form a rectangular shape and to a large part are still evident in the modern urban landscape. As an enduring physical feature they proved beneficial as a means of geo-rectifying the historic map-layers in the GIS, for they are repeatedly shown by Chester's cartographers (Figure 2). Cartographically, therefore, they loom large in map-makers' imaginations (Figures 6 and 7). The city's defences also feature prominently in written accounts of medieval Chester and are referred to by both Lucian and Bradshaw. Lucian aligns the four main gates with the four points of the compass, presenting symmetries and symbolic associations which recall the medieval *mappa mundi* tradition.[36] Thus Lucian remarks that:

Que, a uentis quattuor, portas quattuor habens: a oriente prospectat Indiam; ab occidentem Hiberniam; ab aquiline maiorem Normanniam; a meridie eam quam diuina seueritas, ob ciuiles et naturals dicordias, Britannis reliquit angularem angustiam.

(Chester has four gates corresponding to the four winds: from the East it looks out towards India; from the West towards Ireland; from the North to greater Normandy; from the South to the place where God's severity left the Welsh a narrow corner to punish their innate rebelliousness.)[37]

Here, Lucian is presenting a stylised vision of 'the city' as a defended and defensible place which enables an allegorical and moral reading. It invokes an imagery and iconography of the heavenly and earthly Jerusalem, as depicted in many contemporary medieval illuminated manuscripts and chronicle accounts, for example. The defended city of Chester, as defined by its walls, thus links it symbolically and topographically with the holiest of all cities, Jerusalem, the spiritual and geographical centre of the Christian world. Chester's walls offer it and its people spiritual as well as material protection against outside forces, such as the Welsh (Lucian's reference to the Welsh reflects the Gildasian tradition of their apostasy and punishment by God),[38] while also connecting the city to the four corners of the world, even though its location (on the western edge of England) placed it geographically on the periphery, on the margins.

Lucian's account of the city's defences seems to define Chester therefore, both in terms of its role as a defended and defensible city and in terms of its relationship as a city linked to a broader (Christian) geography and (Biblical) history. Similarly, Chester's walls and gates are also a recurrent focus in later medieval descriptions too, such as Henry Bradshaw's *Life of St Werburge*.[39] Here the circuit of walls stands metonymically for the integrity and limits of urban community, and an assault on the material fabric of the walls represents and attack on the city and its values. In one account of such an attack on the city by 'innumerable barbarike nacions', Bradshaw notes:[40]

> They set theyr ordinaunce against the towne
> Vpon euery side / timorous for to se,
> Namely at the northgate they were redy-bowne
> By might, police to haue entred the cite.
> The citizens dredyng to be in captiuite,
> Made intercession vnto this holy abbasse
> For theyr deliueraunce in such extreme case (II: 765–71)[41]

This assault focused on the city's north gate and the 'holy abbasse', Werburgh does indeed intervene at this desperate moment: her shrine is set up on the north gate and, despite being struck by a stone thrown by one of the attackers, 'in his rancour',[42] the saint saves the city from attack. Like Lucian, Bradshaw sees the city's defences and the city as one – Chester is not only defended by its walls but defined by them.

Of course, the walls only encompassed part of the built up area of medieval Chester as a whole. As is common with many medieval towns and cities, Chester had extensive extramural suburbs (especially beyond East Gate) that were as integral to the urban landscape as the intramural part of the city and just as large in its areal extent. The digital mapping of Chester's late medieval topography begins to present a rather different view of the defended city and its walls to those 'mapped out' by both Lucian and Bradshaw (Figure 6).[43] The urban area within the walls was in part taken up by some large open spaces, especially along the western side of the city where religious houses of the mendicants occupied extensive blocks of land, probably because even by the thirteenth century these were areas that were not proving popular with townspeople.[44] It seems that the walls of Chester were extended westwards in the later twelfth century under the Earls of Chester, beyond the smaller circuit of the earlier Anglo-Saxon defences (mostly built upon an earlier Roman alignment). This extension of the walled circuit enlarged Chester's intra-urban area considerably and was perhaps 'intended as an experiment in town-planning' on the part of the Earls, to help develop their city and attract newcomers.[45] If so, it was an unsuccessful experiment, for as the topographical map of Chester *c*.1500 shows, the area within and alongside these western defences remained poorly built-up throughout the Middle Ages (see Figure 7). Instead, it was the built-up area that lay *outside* East Gate that thrived, on the route leading towards London; that is, a suburb beyond the walls.

Reading Lucian's and Bradshaw's texts as urban mappings, these extramural suburbs of Chester effectively lie 'off the map' since they are outside the city's walls. Their textual exclusion and marginalizing of the city's suburbs, in effect, half of the medieval urban landscape, reveals interesting insights into how Lucian and Bradshaw saw Chester – principally as a walled city – with its defences principally (re)producing its *urban* space. Their particular 'mappings' of Chester see it as a defended city, defined and bounded by its protective walls, whether or not the area of the walled city actually physically corresponded to where its population lived. Chester's identity as a city was thus more easily defined by its walls than by its overall physical (sub-)urban extent, as mapped through its urban topography. Does this then indicate that these alternate 'urban mappings' are in fact contradictory – one medieval and 'imagined' and the other modern and 'real'? I would suggest not.

Final thoughts

The textual mappings and the digital map of Chester are simply different means of (re)producing urban space(s) – the idealized forms of Chester's walled circuit described by Lucian and Bradshaw are just as 'real' as those mapped out using our GPS survey equipment and historic town-plans. The modern maps too, and the spaces they seek to show, are themselves also a product of our historical and geographical imaginations and a reflection of the norms and values that we bring to bear through map-making processes. The modern maps are thus no more or less 'truthful' than the textual 'mappings' of Lucian and Bradshaw.[46]

Thus, the urban mappings engaged with here are not polar opposites but rather complementary approaches that help us understand how medieval urban space(s) worked. The textual 'mappings' of Chester by Lucian and Bradshaw present a hierarchical urban topography as defined by the city's defences, where the walled circuit differentiated inside from outside, order from disorder; drawing a line between what was 'urban' and what was not. The GIS map-making exercise and its cartography presents instead a rather more 'flattened' image of medieval Chester, in which the city's urban topography is made as much as possible to look the same, right across the map, and give no more weight to one place in it than somewhere else. Placing the two alternate mappings side by side, as it were, accentuates these interpretative differences, helping us to reflect on how we today understand medieval urban spaces through our (digital) mappings of them, while suggesting to us too something of how urban spaces were also seen and understood at the time, by those Cestrians who knew the city through negotiating its streets and living within the material and spiritual protection offered by its circuit of walls.

Notes

[1]   Denis E. Cosgrove, 'Introduction: mapping meaning', in D. E. Cosgrove (ed.) *Mappings* (London, 1999), pp. 1–23, p. 13.

[2]   On the place of cartography in geography's disciplinary history see, for example, David Livingstone, *The Geographical Tradition: Episodes in the History of a Contested Enterprise* (Oxford, 1993); Felix Driver, *Geography Militant: Cultures of Exploration and Empire* (Oxford, 2001) and John Pickles, *A History of Spaces: Cartographic Reason, Mapping, and the Geo-coded World* (London, 2003).

[3]   For example, Denis E. Cosgrove and Stephen Daniels (eds), *The Iconography of Landscape: Essays on the Symbolic Representation, Design and Use of*

Past Environments (Cambridge, 1988); Trevor Barnes and James Duncan (eds), *Writing Worlds: Discourse, Text and Metaphor in the Representation of Landscape* (London, 1992) and James Duncan and David Ley (eds), *Place / Culture / Representation* (London, 1993).

4   J. B. Harley, 'Deconstructing the map', *Cartographica*, 26 (1989), 1–20 and James Duncan, *City as Text: The Politics of Landscape Interpretation in the Kandyan Kingdom* (Cambridge, 1990).

5   For example, Pamela Gilbert, *Mapping the Victorian Social Body* (New York, 2004).

6   On the 'spatial turn' see Barney Warf and Santa Arias (eds), *The Spatial Turn. Interdisciplinary Perspectives* (Oxford, 2009).

7   Nicholas Howe, *Writing the Map of Anglo-Saxon England. Essays in Cultural Geography* (London, 2008) and Kathy Lavezzo, *Angels on the Edge of the World: Geography, Literature, and English Community, 1000–1534* (London, 2006).

8   It is an approach that is also now being advocated by historians of medieval cartography; to re-contextualize maps from the Middle Ages, seeing them in their various manuscript settings rather than detaching them – sometimes literally – from those (con)texts where maps were historically placed. For example, see Evelyn Edson, *Mapping Time and Space: How Medieval Map-makers Viewed their World* (London, 1999).

9   Matthew H. Edney, *The Origins and Development of J. B. Harley's Cartographic Theories*, *Cartographica*, 40 (2005), 1–143, p. 9.

10   On medieval maps of European towns and cities see, Paul Harvey, 'Local and regional cartography in medieval Europe', in J. B. Harley and David Woodward (eds), *History of Cartography: Cartography in Prehistoric, Ancient, and Medieval Europe and the Mediterranean*, vol. 1 (Chicago, 1987), pp. 464–501. For a list of printed maps and plans for Chester see Cheshire and Chester Archives and Local Studies, *Printed Maps in the Cheshire Record Office* (Chester, 2001).

11   William Smith, *The Particuler Description of England. With the portratures of certaine of the cheiffest citties & townes*. BL Harley MS 1046, fol. 173. Visual depictions of English medieval cities are particularly scarce, though examples do exist, for example Bristol (*c.*1480), in Ricart's *Kalendar*, and arguably too the images of cities in Dublin Trinity College Library MS 505: see *The Maire of Bristowe is Kalendar by Robert Ricart, Town Clerk of Bristol 18 Edward IV*, Lucy Toulmin Smith (ed.) (London, 1872); Elizabeth Ralph, 'Bristol, *circa* 1480', in Richard A. Skelton and Paul D. A. Harvey (eds) *Local Maps and Plans from Medieval England* (Oxford, 1986), pp. 309–16 (the original manuscript map is at Bristol Record Office: BRO 04720, fol.5b) and John Scattergood, *Manuscripts and Ghosts. Essays on the transmission of medieval and early Renaissance literature* (Dublin, 2006), pp. 228–51.

12   See Catherine A. M. Clarke, *Literary Landscapes and the Idea of England, 700–1400* (Cambridge, 2006) and *DLC*.

13   See Keith D. Lilley, *City and Cosmos. The Medieval World in Urban Form* (London, 2009) and Robert W. Barrett, *Against all England: Regional Identity and Cheshire Writing, 1195–1656* (Notre Dame, 2009).

14   A case in point is Jane Laughton, *Life in a Late Medieval City. Chester 1275–1520*

(Oxford, 2008), where the street map appears opposite the title page. Another
similar example appears in *The Rows of Chester. The Chester Rows Research
Project*, A. Brown (ed.) English Heritage Archaeological Report 16 (London,
1999), p. 5.

[15] See Keith D. Lilley, 'Landscape mapping and symbolic form: drawing as a creative medium in cultural geography', in Ian Cook, David Crouch, Simon Naylor,
and James Ryan (eds) *Cultural Turns/Geographical Turns* (London, 2000), pp.
231–245.

[16] On the principles of this approach see Keith D. Lilley, 'Mapping the medieval
city: plan analysis and urban history', *Urban History*, 27 (2000), 5030.

[17] For example, Keith D. Lilley, Christopher D. Lloyd and Steven Trick, *Mapping
Medieval Townscapes: a digital atlas of the new towns of Edward I*, University
of York (2005), accessible via *http://ads.ahds.ac.uk/catalogue/specColl/atlas_
ahrb_2005* (accessed 30 September 2009).

[18] See N. J. Alldridge, 'Aspects of the topography of early medieval Chester',
Journal of the Chester Archaeological Society, 64 (1981–3), 5–31.

[19] Simon M. Ward, *Excavations at Chester. The Lesser Medieval Religious Houses,
Sites Investigated 1964–1983* (Chester, 1990).

[20] Keith Matthews, *Excavations at Chester. The Evolution of the Heart of the City,
Investigations at 3–15 Eastgate Street 1990/1* (Chester, 1995).

[21] On GIS generally see Paul A. Longley, Michael F. Goodchild, David J. Maguire
and David W. Rhind (eds), *Geographical Information Systems. Principles,
Techniques, Management and Application* (second edn, abridged) (Hoboken NJ,
2005).

[22] See Ian N. Gregory and Paul S. Ell, *Historical GIS. Technologies, Methodologies
and Scholarship* (Cambridge, 2007).

[23] Using dGPS in such urban surveys is described in detail elsewhere: see Keith D.
Lilley, Christopher D. Lloyd, Steven Trick and Conor Graham, 'Analysing and
mapping medieval urban forms using GPS and GIS', *Urban Morphology*, 9, 1–9.

[24] For the 'Mapping Medieval Chester' web-resource see *www.medievalchester.
ac.uk* (accessed 30 September 2009).

[25] In the case of Chester these plans were kindly made available by the city archae-
ologist, Simon Ward.

[26] The project's various map outputs are available at *www.medievalchester.ac.uk*
(accessed 30 September 2009) including (1) themed maps of Chester *c.*1500 (2)
an interactive (and linked) digital map and (3) downloadable GIS spatial data.

[27] For the maps see *www.medievalchester.ac.uk/mappings/static.html* (accessed 30
September 2009).

[28] See Pickles, *History of Spaces*.

[29] See I. Williams and J. Ll. Williams (eds), *Gwaith Guto 'r Glyn* (Cardiff, 1939), p.
283 and Iestyn Daniel (ed.), *Gwaith Llwadden* (Aberystwyth, 2006), p. 78. My
thanks to Helen Fulton for these references and the following discussion of them.
See *www.medievalchester.ac.uk* (accessed 30 September 2009).

[30] Text and translation from Barry J. Lewis, *Welsh Poetry and English Pilgrimage:
Gruffudd ap Maredudd and the Rood of Chester* (Aberystwyth, 2005), pp. 30, 37.

[31] Lewis, *Welsh Poetry and English Pilgrimage*, p. 1.

32   *PN Ches.* V (I:i), p. 63.
33   Ibid., V (I:i), p. 12.
34   *DLC*, fol. 13r.
35   See Lilley, *City and Cosmos*, pp. 23–5.
36   Indeed, it is possible to read *De Laude Cestrie* as a verbal *mappa mundi*. It presents a view of the entire world, with Chester positioned ambivalently as both periphery and centre and the fact that it is accompanied in the manuscript by Easter Tables recalls the context and transmission of many medieval visual maps. See for example Evelyn Edson, 'World maps and Easter Tables: medieval maps in context', *Imago Mundi*, 48 (1996), 25–42.
37   *DLC*, fols 12rv.
38   See Gildas, *The Ruin of Britain*, Michael Winterbottom (ed. and trans.) (London, 1978).
39   Henry Bradshaw, *Life of St Werburge*, ed. Carl Horstmann, EETS OS 88 (London, 1887). For this discussion of Bradshaw, I am indebted to Catherine Clarke: see her account and discussion of Bradshaw's *Life of St Werburge* at *www.medieval-chester.ac.uk* (accessed 30 September 2009).
40   Alan T. Thacker suggests that this episode is to be associated with 'Edward the Confessor and Harold Godwinson's conflict with Gruffudd ap Llywelyn, king of Gwynedd, in the 1050s and early 1060s'. See A. T. Thacker, 'Early Medieval Chester 400–1230', in *VCH Ches.* 5. i, pp. 16–33, p. 24.
41   For discussion and a selective edition of Bradshaw's *Life of St Werburge* see *www.medievalchester.ac.uk* (accessed 30 September 2009).
42   H. Bradshaw, *Life of St Werburge*, l. 783.
43   As an illustration of this partiality in the textual 'mappings' of Chester, see the plot of text citations accessible at *http://mapserver.cch.kcl.ac.uk/medchest/high-bandwidth.php* (accessed 30 September 2009).
44   See Ward, *Excavations at Chester*, pp.1–2.
45   Alldridge, 'Aspects of the topography of early medieval Chester', p. 30.
46   This particular theoretical position on maps and mapmaking derives largely from a critical cartographical history developed in the 1980s through the work of J. B. Harley, an historical geographer who realised that all maps, whatever form they take, are culturally constructed. He took his inspiration in particular from textual criticism, and literary history, and applied this critical thinking to cartography. See J. B. Harley, *The New Nature of Maps. Essays in the History of Cartography*, Paul Laxton (ed.) (Baltimore, 2001).

3

Framing Medieval Chester: the Landscape of Urban Boundaries

C. P. LEWIS

Boundaries – paradoxically because of their defining peripherality – were central to the lived experience of late medieval Chester, for citizens and outsiders alike. In obvious ways, physical boundaries such as walls and ditches constrained and directed routes through and out of the city, and marked off areas of the town which had different characteristics. Jurisdictional boundaries, too, whether manifested physically or not, affected lives: dictating whether and where a person might trade or practise a craft, where a family worshipped, who had authority over misdemeanours and much besides. The external boundary of the liberties of the city was especially important because it defined what Chester was and in particular where the special freedoms of citizens ended. In other words, boundaries must be part of any attempt to map the city.

Late medieval Chester was a small place.[1] From the northern outskirts where the roads from Wirral converged on the abbey's chapel of St Thomas it was just a mile through the walled town and over Dee bridge to Handbridge in the south. East–west from the Bars to Watergate was barely three quarters of a mile. Nowhere, except the leper hospital of St Giles on the eastern boundary, was more than ten minutes walk from the Cross at the heart of the city. Moreover Chester was compact. Houses, shops, churches, workshops and markets were concentrated on the four main thoroughfares, with open areas in the backlands behind the streets, large monastic and friary precincts and gardens on all sides and the extensive meadows of the Roodee and the Earl's Eye close at hand. The open aspect of the country outside the town walls underlined how small and dense was the urban core. There were no stands of woodland nearby and vantage points on the northern and eastern walls looked out across the city's unhedged fields and Hoole heath, while from Watergate the prospect to the west was of the tides and shifting sands of the wide, long estuary of the Dee.

This rather small place was nonetheless lined and scored with inter-secting boundaries of half a dozen kinds, defining parishes and wards, monastic precincts and castle, private and public spaces, layered one upon another. Most obvious now of the physical boundaries – because of their survival almost complete – are the city walls,[2] emblematic in the Middle Ages of high urban status. City walls were prominent both in the visualiza-tion of towns and in the expression of urban identity, from as early as the twelfth century in the case of London.[3] At Chester, the fortifications may have represented the city even in the tenth century, when a coin of Edward the Elder (899–924) depicted a tower.[4]

Travellers approaching Chester from Wirral (downhill towards North-gate), or along the level Roman road towards Eastgate would have seen the city first as high walls and gates. The approach from Wales through Handbridge offered a different aspect, looking up from Dee bridge to the town spreading up the steep slope of Bridge Street. In 1200, the only church towers breaking the skyline were at the abbey and St John's, but from 1300 onwards, others rose at the friaries and the larger parish churches, so that by 1500 there were nine or ten.[5]

The city walls, completed as a circuit perhaps in the 1160s, were a complex structure.[6] Anyone with an eye for variations in stonework must have been aware of their ancient character and multiple origins, to say nothing of more recent repairs and piecemeal alterations. Long stretches on the north and east retained the chamfered plinths and massive squared blocks set in courses that betray Roman origin. In 1264, a town ditch was dug around those two sides, and remained an open feature well after 1500, by when the circuit included eight or nine watchtowers, the four main gates (at least two of which had separate passages for carts and pedes-trians) and at least six smaller posterns (for foot passengers only), much of it being embattled. The walls did not define Chester in any formal sense, but what they enclosed must have seemed the essence of the city to all but the extramural community at St John's church.

The city walls loomed large in other ways. Responsibility for repair had passed probably in the twelfth century from the men of Cheshire as a whole to the city in particular. The citizens *owned* this emblematic boundary. After 1200, successive kings periodically granted murages, a local tax for repairs, collected over a specified number of years; in the fifteenth century the city took full control and exacted murage whenever it liked. The four main gates were in the hands of hereditary serjeants, who saw to their locking overnight and took tolls on goods brought into the city by 'strangers' and 'foreigners'. For outsiders, too, the city walls were highly significant.

Other high walls formed boundaries between different sorts of space *within* Chester, notably around the precincts of the religious houses. The two largest precincts were at the abbey, occupying much of the north-east quarter of the walled town and at the collegiate church of St John, in the eastern suburb. In 1200, their precincts were probably bounded at least in part by ditches, earth banks, and fences; rebuilding in stone came later, and over the whole period 1200–1500 the precincts were progressively shut off from the city. At the abbey, there was a wall of some kind by the later thirteenth century along the southern side of the precinct, behind Eastgate Street, but the surviving great gate and high walls to the west were only built in the early fourteenth century and a licence to enclose and crenellate the abbey was obtained only in 1377.[7]

Both of the major precincts were complex areas with intricate internal plans, littered with buildings of varied functions, materials and architectural styles. A seventeenth-century plan of St John's, reflecting the layout before the Dissolution, shows a large rectangular area, walled on three sides and with gardens sloping down to the Dee on the fourth. In the centre was the impressive collegiate church. There was a main precinct gate and a secondary gate in the north wall. Along the eastern wall were the chapel of St Anne and the petty canons' houses; along the west other domestic buildings, including the dean's and bishop's houses. Freestanding structures around the precinct included two further chapels and a cross; other houses leaned up against the walls of the church itself.[8] The abbey precinct was similarly crowded with buildings of all kinds.[9] The nunnery and the three orders of friars which settled in Chester from the 1230s (Dominicans, Franciscans and Carmelites) also had walled precincts.[10] The friaries colonized the western side of town, closed off certain streets, took over at least one existing chapel (the Dominicans' St Nicholas), and erected high walls which made their precincts places apart despite the friars' close interactions – both friendly and hostile – with the citizens.

All the precincts were as busy and crowded with buildings as the main streets of Chester, but busy and crowded in different ways: passing through the precinct gates took a person into a world which looked different (dressed stone rather than timber framing and plaster), sounded different (the din of manufacture and commerce muffled by the high walls), and was differently peopled (by gender and age) and differently controlled (a single authority – abbot, dean or prior – in place of the complex social hierarchy of the town). The castle, bounded by walls and ditches, was another place apart, less a single bounded enclave than a set of spaces nested within one another. The outer ditch and gatehouse gave on to the large open expanse of the outer bailey, behind which were another deep ditch and gatehouse, leading into the taller walled circuit of the inner bailey, lined by the individual towers of the oldest part.[11]

All medieval English towns of any size had walled precincts and many had castles; Chester alone – almost uniquely in Europe – had the Rows, where boundaries of another kind were a marked feature of the urban experience.[12] The Rows – stretching along much of Eastgate, Bridge and Watergate Streets by 1350 – consisted of an elevated public space, the Row walkway, which threaded through private space in three dimensions. In the fully evolved form of the Rows, the walkway typically passed over private undercrofts used for storage, alongside a chain of tiny booth-like shops and under the more private rooms of the houses, which were jettied out over the walkway on timber posts. The roofs of the porches built out into the street to protect the undercroft doors from the weather provided sloping spaces (called stallboards) where traders set out their goods. The Rows became public space in the Middle Ages through use and custom rather than prescription, but the porches and the stairs up from street level were built on the public road and as a result the corporation took rent for them and probably had some powers of regulation over the stairs. The Row walkways and stallboards must have been at least as uneven and irregular in the Middle Ages as they are now, conveying the sense of being in a very particular sort of bounded space, and adding an extra dimension to the materiality of physical boundaries in the city.

Crossing the physical boundaries between different sorts of space in Chester typically involved passing through the narrow dark space of a substantial stone gatehouse under the eye of a porter or a toll collector, or ascending a flight of stairs from the open street into the gloom of the Rows. But jurisdictional boundaries mattered just as much as stone or timber walls. The city included nine parishes and four (later nine) wards; the abbey precinct was exempt from the city authorities; the castle was not in any sense jurisdictionally part of Chester and there was a further anomaly called Gloverstone in front of the castle gates.

Jurisdictional boundaries intercut with one another in complicated ways. Four of the parishes (St Martin, St Michael, St Olave and St Peter) lay entirely within the walls.[13] Holy Trinity also covered a manor outside

Chester (Blacon), and St Bridget's included the Earl's Eye. St John's was mostly extramural with barely a foothold inside the walls; St Mary's included rural townships north and south of the city; St Oswald's (the abbey's parish) was even further flung. Parish boundaries mattered for all kinds of reason, payment of tithes and administration of the sacraments being only the most obvious. Their layout within the walled city was intricate, having evolved through the subdivision of the two earliest, St Oswald's and St Mary's. These two retained a monopoly on burials within the city almost throughout the Middle Ages, which was both lucrative and symbolically charged. In broad terms parish boundaries were arranged to allow each householder to attend the church nearest his front door, a rule of thumb that applied in many other towns. Thus the boundary between St Peter's parish and St Bridget's and St Michael's was drawn almost exactly half-way down Bridge Street. But there were many exceptions, like the inclusion in St Michael's of some houses on the 'wrong' side of Lower Bridge Street. This is not the place to expound, let alone try to explain, all the peculiarities of parochial topography. In the Middle Ages no one found it necessary to write them down or draw them on a plan or (probably) mark their boundaries on the sides of houses: they were so central to the way that Cestrians mapped the city in their heads that they were remembered.

Wards, the civic divisions, were recorded and probably developed much later than parishes, and were based on much simpler principles. At first there were four wards (or quarters) coinciding with the four main streets; from the 1460s onwards they were subdivided so that by 1507–8 there were nine wards, each covering a section of one of the main streets, and by 1533 fifteen. The city administered its property and ran local government ward by ward, so that for example, in 1487 brewers were summoned by the constables of their wards to have their measures checked and stamped.[14] The inhabitants had constant reminders of which ward was theirs.

Arguably the most important boundary for Cestrians, however, was what bounded and defined Chester as a whole: the liberties, located beyond the fields and meadows at some distance from the town. The liberties were the area within which freemen Cestrians exercised their rights. Full formal independence from the county came with Henry VII's charter of 1506, which made Chester a county in its own right,[15] but the citizens' freedoms were repeatedly confirmed in writing long before there was any need for a definitive description of the liberties as a territory. Around 1200, Earl Ranulph III confirmed the citizens' rights 'in the city of Chester' without specifying what he meant by 'the city', and in the 1230s, Earl John granted them liberties as citizens, again without geographical definition. The earliest reference to territory was in Edward I's charter of 1300, which was concerned with powers and privileges 'within the liberty of the city', implying that the liberty was a known quantity but not giving its extent.[16]

The liberties excluded three enclaves situated within the urban core. The castle, seat of the Anglo-Norman and royal earls, was reckoned part of the county. Gloverstone, a small area in front of the outer gatehouse, was also county rather than city, the eponymous 'glover stone' marking the boundary of the two jurisdictions until Gloverstone was obliterated during the early nineteenth-century rebuilding of the castle.[17] The abbot of Chester claimed exemption from the city's courts not only for the abbey precinct but also for his tenants throughout Chester. Over the course of the fifteenth century, the city authorities wore away at the exemption until it was definitively restricted to the precinct in 1509.[18]

The boundary of the liberties was first written down in the time of the Black Prince, Edward III's son and earl of Chester. In 1351, his administration began *quo warranto* proceedings for the earldom, inquiring 'by what warrant' (Latin *quo warranto*) communities and individuals claimed their franchises and exemptions and expecting to be paid handsomely to confirm them. By May 1351, the citizens of Chester had offered £300 to have their charters ratified and the bounds of their franchise fixed; the Prince's central administration then instructed his senior officers locally (the justice and chamberlain of Chester) to view the bounds in person.[19] They had perambulated the boundaries by May 1353, when the chamberlain was ordered to return a copy of the written bounds.[20] The Prince's charter was issued in March the following year, so that the bounds are generally dated to 1354,[21] but it is clear from the charter that they had not been unknown or in dispute, simply that they had never been written down:

> in the aforesaid charters [of 1300 and 1327] ... some lands, meres, limits, or boundaries to which the precincts of the said city ought to extend and within which the liberties of the same city ought to be exercised are not specified.[22]

The 1354 bounds described a circuit of 11½ miles, starting in the south-eastern corner at Heronbridge on the banks of the Dee and going anticlockwise. The few fixed points included a marl pit and two further bridges, but most of the circuit followed linear features rather than jumping from point to point. Apart from where the boundary crossed the Dee estuary, there was only one stretch of about 100 yards where the feature being followed was neither named nor implied. The stability of the boundary over subsequent centuries, and later documentary evidence which starts with a new perambulation by mayor Henry Gee (1539–40) allow the bounds of 1354 to be plotted with a high degree of confidence.

Much of the boundary followed watercourses, variously designated stream (*rivulus*), sike (*sichetus*), 'the water of Bache pool' (*aqua de le Bachpol*) – the abbot's millpond – and a creek or inlet of the estuary called Landpool (*le Londpul*) or Blackpool (*le Blakepul*). On the west, the boundary crossed the head of the estuary, and in the east followed the river bank (*ripa aque de Dee*). Elsewhere it ran along ditches (singular, *fossatus*) and roads or tracks (all called *via*). About half the circuit followed streams, sikes and pools; 20 per cent ditches, and 10 per cent each roads, river bank, and estuary. Use of the river bank rather than the centre of the river is an unusual feature discussed below. The northern and southern boundaries were markedly differently. North of the Dee, over 80 per cent of the boundary followed watercourses and less than 10 per cent ditches; south of the river only 28 per cent followed watercourses and 55 per cent ditches. The northern boundary was thus essentially 'natural', the southern very largely man-made, a distinction which points to historical differences also examined below.

The boundary of the liberties was certainly old in 1354, but it was not immemorial, and it may be significant that the written perambulation made no claim for its antiquity, since some of the other liberties confirmed by the Black Prince's charter *were* claimed as ancient. The liberties as a territory had undoubtedly evolved from the earlier hundred of Chester, documented only by Domesday Book in 1086, but the boundaries of the two do not correspond in detail, and the points of difference are worth spelling out.[23] Chester hundred evidently disappeared at some point in the twelfth century, in part because the powers exercised by its hundred court overlapped with – and could be conveniently subsumed into – those of the borough court. Probably, it went during a larger reorganization of the Cheshire hundreds.[24]

The Domesday hundred – actually a half-hundred rated at 50 hides – consisted of the city and a ring of eight manors 'outside the city', located variously at Newton, *Redeclive*, Handbridge, and *Lee* (Overleigh and Netherleigh). The city accounted for most of the assessment (46½ hides), and the insignificance of the rural penumbra is underlined by the fewness of its ploughteams (not quite 6½, all told) and population (25 households). Handbridge, Netherleigh, and Overleigh comprised the bulk of what was later the liberties south of the river and need no further discussion here. *Redeclive*, named from the 'red cliff' of sandstone along the north bank of the Dee around St John's church, comprised two small manors held by the bishop (who owned St John's) and a secular landowner. It probably occupied the fields east of St John's, between Foregate Street and the river and perhaps land north of Foregate Street; Love Lane was perhaps its western boundary. To the east, the block of urban properties south of Foregate Street backed on to a curving rear lane, in the eighteenth century called the Headlands from a field of the same name to the south. 'Headlands' as a field name is associated with open fields and may derive from a time when all the land between the river and Foregate Street was ploughed and part of *Redeclive*.

In the north the liberties were smaller than the hundred, since they excluded the township of Newton, whose name and location close to Chester suggest that it originated literally as a new *tūn* (perhaps in both senses, settlement and township) within the larger territory of Chester. In the early 1090s, one of Earl Hugh's barons, William fitz Nigel, gave it to the earl's new Benedictine abbey in Chester and it must have been early and continuous possession by the abbey which kept it out of the liberties, in contrast with the way in which his manor of St Thomas's to the south – acquired piecemeal and considerably later – stayed within the liberties.[25]

On the south side of Chester, the liberties of 1354 were larger than the hundred of 1086, taking in parts of Lache on the west and Claverton on the east. In 1086, Lache was a small manor belonging to the minster church of St Werburgh, administratively in Atiscross hundred.[26] Its division into two parts is explicit in the 1354 bounds, which ran 'as far as the vill of Lache and thus through the middle of that vill (*per medium ville istius*) to Landpool in Saltney', *villa* here probably signifying a township rather than a settlement. The division into two is apparent in later evidence. Lache Hall, a minor gentry house until the mid-eighteenth century and a farmhouse in the nineteenth,[27] stood within the liberties, near the boundary, but its medieval predecessor may well have occupied the moated site a short distance to the south-east and outside the liberties.[28] As late as the seventeenth century, a reference to 'Lache within the liberties of the city of Chester' indicates that part of Lache was known to lie on one side of the boundary while the rest had ceased to be a separate township and had been merged with its neighbour as the township of Marlston cum Lache. Further work is needed to establish the historical circumstances in which the boundary of Chester hereabouts was pushed southwards to take in part of Lache.

Claverton in 1086 was a somewhat larger manor than Lache, also in Atiscross hundred and distinct from the small holdings in Handbridge, Netherleigh, and Overleigh immediately to its north; on the other hand it had burgesses in Handbridge as well as Chester and in 1086 had the same owner as one of the Handbridge manors. Claverton lost status in the thirteenth century and there came to be a single manor of Handbridge owned by the nuns of Chester which included land in Claverton and whose open fields were divided between a nearer town field within the liberties and a further town field in Claverton township.[29] Parochially, Claverton and Handbridge belonged to same Chester parish, St Mary's.

Although the 1354 bounds did not say so, it seems clear that they divided Claverton in two, not least because this stretch of the boundary was man-made, following Green ditch alias Mere ditch (*Grenediche similiter vocatum le Merediche*). Mere ditch means simply 'boundary ditch', while its alternative name suggests that it was not filled with water. Those were not its only names. In the second half of the thirteenth century, it had been called the Great ditch (*le Gretedich*) and although that name was not recorded after 1281, the much later name of Grey ditch (first recorded in Henry Gee's perambulation of 1539–40 as *the Myre Dyche otherwise called the Gray Dyche*) sounds more like a corruption of 'great' than of 'green'.[30] Its naming as the great ditch suggests that it enjoyed a certain standing in the collective mind of Cestrians, as well as hinting at the effort needed to dig it. The circumstances in which the great green boundary ditch was dug through the middle of Claverton might be elucidated by further documentary and topographical research, one pointer being that in 1086 Claverton and Lache were both part of Atiscross hundred; their dismemberment and division between the liberties and Broxton hundred may prove to have had some connection with the disappearance of Atiscross hundred, probably when the Welsh overran its more westerly parts in the twelfth century.

The territory of Chester also expanded to the east after 1086. In Domesday Book the single manor of Boughton belonged to the canons of St Werburgh's,[31] but afterwards there were three distinct territories bearing its name. The township outside the liberties, eventually called Great Boughton but throughout the Middle Ages just Boughton,[32] remained in the hands of the canons' successors at Chester abbey and was part of the abbey's parish of St Oswald.[33] Inside the liberties, the street running west from the boundary towards Eastgate has always been called Boughton and was historically in St John's parish. On the boundary between Great Boughton and Boughton, the precincts of the leper hospital of St Giles became an extra-parochial place called Spital Boughton. The 1354 bounds zig-zagged along ditches and roads around the east side of the hospital, their longest stretch following a ditch called Bishopditch (*Bispediche*) which turned through three right angles; the ditch must have been so named because it marked the eastern limits of the territory attached to the bishop's church of St John.

At the western end of Boughton, the street ran into Foregate Street at a point marked by a toll gate across the road, first recorded in 1241 and in the Middle Ages variously called the Bars, Foregate, or the gatehouse in Foregate Street. It consisted of a substantial wall across the width of the road, pierced by an elliptical arch. A postern was added in 1609 and the structure was demolished in 1767, but the name of the Bars was retained for what is now a busy point on Chester's inner ring-road.[34] The Bars almost certainly marks the early limits of Chester on this side, before the annexation of part of Boughton. Some kind of toll barrier here, on the most important trade route into Chester, is likely from an early date. The topo-graphy north and south of the Bars has been so altered in modern times – by the canal in the 1770s and City Road and Grosvenor Park in the 1860s[35] – that is it impossible to be sure where the rest of the original boundary ran.

The annexation of part of Boughton into the liberties can be explored a little further by considering St Giles's hospital. Leper hospitals were normally sited in suburbs and near busy roads, as here at the convergence of the main roads from Northwich and Whitchurch, but there does not seem to be any particular association with boundaries.[36] Because the 1354 bounds followed its precinct ditches, St Giles's must have existed before that boundary was adopted. The date of the hospital, however, is elusive. Recent research on the origin of leper hospitals has argued that they began as informal groups of lepers gathered in places favourable for collecting alms from passers-by, and were gradually formalized into permanent establishments through acts of patronage and episcopal sanction. Their 'founders' – meaning the agents of formalization rather than the original settlers – typically 'provided a site for the hospital, designated a form of alms to be carried out there and gathered an endowment to provide those alms'.[37] Those insights allow a clearer perspective of the claims which the hospital at Chester made about its foundation and early history, much later, in answer to the *quo warranto* proceedings of 1499. The brethren claimed, first, that they were freed from the jurisdiction of the justice [of Cheshire] and the sheriff [of Chester?] by a certain Earl Hugh of Chester under a charter granted to 'the infirm brethren living at St Giles's outside Chester' ('infirmis fratribus apud sanctum Egidium deforis Cestriam existentibus'). Evidently, in 1499 the brethren showed a charter bearing that phrase, which is indeed plausible wording for a document issued by Hugh II, earl 1153–81.[38] The earl's grant was to a group of lepers *already* settled at St Giles's (obviously the chapel must have existed too), and St Giles's was described as *outside* Chester, but whether that meant merely 'outside the town' – which it certainly was – or more precisely 'outside the liberties' has to be left open. The brethren's second claim was that Earl Ranulph had granted them a long list of tolls on goods at Chester market and the right to fish with one boat in the Dee; both of those charters were also exhibited in 1499 though, like Earl Hugh's, they do not survive except in the portions copied into the *quo warranto* roll.[39] 'Earl Ranulph' has been taken to be Hugh II's son, Ranulph III (1181–1232),[40] partly because he is known to have given the leper hospital small sums annually from an estate in Lincolnshire which he acquired in 1198 and from the shrieval revenues of Chester on the anniversary of his father's death[41] and partly because he certainly took the other hospital in Chester, St John the Baptist, outside the Northgate, under his protection in a charter which can be dated between 1190 and 1194.[42] But both those facts could be read as reasons to think that he was *not* the major benefactor of St Giles's hospital whose charters the brethren showed in 1499. In fact, there is no reason why the earl who endowed the leper hospital should not be Ranulph II (1129–53). A grant of market tolls and fishing rights fits into the pattern of his activities since he established a market in Northgate Street and gave boats on the Dee to several religious houses, including Chester nunnery.[43] If St Giles's hospital was fully established before 1153, the extension of Chester's boundaries into Boughton could have taken place as early as the later twelfth century.

Mapping Chester's boundaries in the late Middle Ages requires one imaginative leap well beyond the liberties in order to take in the admiralty powers which the mayor of Chester claimed over the whole of the Dee estuary, from Heronbridge (significantly the starting point of the 1354 bounds) down to Arnold's Eye, a reef at the north-westernmost tip of Wirral.[44] Admiralty jurisdiction – over shipping, fisheries and other matters – was confirmed by the Black Prince in the 1354 charter, and claimed as ancient custom.[45] This, incidentally, provides a context for the location of the 1354 bounds on the right bank of the Dee downstream from Heronbridge (rather than mid-stream), placing the whole width of the river unambiguously under Chester's authority.

The mayor had a rival in the Dee, who emerges in the early fourteenth century when Robert of Eaton, ancestor of the Grosvenors of Eaton, claimed to be serjeant of the Dee with powers over fishing, wrecks, ferries, and tolls – exactly the powers that the mayor exercised as admiral. The claim was presumably made in respect of his lordship of the manor of Eaton, which lay a little way upstream but not contiguous with the liberties. The principal difference from the mayor's claim is that the Grosvenors asserted their rights downstream from Eaton, not from Heronbridge. More work is needed on this topic, but certain facts about the manor of Eaton are relevant. Eaton belonged to Earl Hugh of Chester in Domesday Book and to the earls of Mercia before 1066. It was not a large place, assessed at only 1½ hides and with only two ploughs and four peasant families in 1086.[46] The Domesday manor cannot have been any more extensive than the later township of Eaton, since Claverton and Eccleston immediately downstream, and Poulton immediately upstream, were all recorded separately in Domesday Book.[47] Yet Eaton was worth the prodigious amount of £10, more than those other three places combined even though they had much larger arable resources, nine ploughs between them to Eaton's two. The difference was made by Eaton's rights in the Dee, since the other manorial resource recorded there was a render of 1,000 salmon owed by six fishermen. That was easily the biggest salmon render recorded anywhere in 1086 – a corresponding render from the Severn by the burgesses of Gloucester numbered just sixteen and other salmon renders in Devon and Herefordshire were of thirty (twice) and only six fish.[48] A working hypothesis is that the Eaton salmon render and the rights in the estuary which it reflected, was a perquisite of the pre-Conquest and Norman earls which had been attached before 1066 to their principal rural manor near Chester, but which had either originated in association with the earls' interests in Chester or had become associated with the city at some later date, allowing the earls' successors at both places – the mayor in the city and the lords of Eaton – to stake a claim.

The expansions of the territory of Chester discussed here, taking in parts of Lache, Claverton and Boughton, were all made at the expense of the county, and can be linked to the growth of civic institutions and increasing independence from the earls of Chester, processes which began in the later twelfth century but proceeded much more rapidly in the first half of the thirteenth and were crystallized especially by the Crown's acquisition of the earldom in 1237.[49] The existence well before 1250 of mature, independent civic administration helped to ensure that the enlarged boundaries of the liberties were stable even before they were first written down; once fixed even more firmly by writing in 1354, they were unaltered for centuries afterwards. Much had changed in Chester's boundaries in the central Middle Ages, 900–1200. What Chester was, as a territory and a type of place, had evolved from Æthelflæd's refortification of 907, to the two boroughs (earl's and bishop's) documented in Domesday Book, to the unitary city evident by 1200. Other things became fixed in the half century 1200–50: the city walls were already complete and the parishes fully functioning, but the castle was now enlarged to its full extent, the friars arrived and established their precincts and the Rows began to reach their full development. This means that for most of the period treated in other contributions to this volume, the bounded space of Chester as a whole as well as its main internal divisions (both physical and administrative) were stable and relatively unchanging. That, surely, has much relevance for the multiple ways in which Cestrians and outsiders of the late Middle Ages responded to the city and mapped its features in their minds, their writings and their daily lives.

Notes

[1]   This article makes extensive use of the factual material presented in *VCH Ches.* 5. i and ii. The maps included in the present volume (Figures 6 and 7) provide some visual context for this essay; in addition, a range of further maps of medieval Chester (including representations of the city's parishes, as well as key civic and ecclesiastical features) is available at *www.medievalchester.ac.uk* (accessed 30 September 2009).

[2]   *VCH Ches.* 5. ii, pp. 213–18.

[3]   Derek Keene, 'Text, visualisation and politics: London, 1150–1250', *Transactions of the Royal Historical Society*, 6th series 18 (2008), 69–99 at 77–80.

[4]   *VCH Ches.* 5. ii, p. 215, citing C. E. Blunt et al., *Coinage in Tenth-Century England* (Oxford, 1989), pp. 35–8, plate 4.

[5]   *VCH Ches.* 5. ii, pp. 130–1, 135, 144–5, 155–6, 185–90, 242 and 244.

[6]   Ibid., pp. 218–25; for illustrations of the medieval gates see also *VCH Ches.* 5. i, plates 19, 21–2.

[7]   *VCH Ches.* 5. ii, p. 194.

[8]   Ibid., pp. 131–2.

[9]   Ibid., pp. 191–5.

[10]   *VCH Ches.* 5. i, pp. 82–3; *VCH Ches.* 5. ii, pp. 240–5.

[11]   *VCH Ches.* 5. ii, pp. 207–9.

[12]   Ibid., pp. 225–35; Andrew Brown, ed., *The Rows of Chester. The Chester Rows Research Project*, English Heritage Archaeological Report 16 (London, 1999).

[13]   Paragraph based on *VCH Ches.* 5. ii, pp. 12–15; N. J. Alldridge, 'Aspects of the topography of early medieval Chester', *Journal of the Chester Archaeological Society*, 64 (1981), 5–31.

[14]   *VCH Ches.* 5. i, p. 62; *VCH Ches.* 5. ii, p. 15.

[15]   *VCH Ches.* 5. i, p. 62.

[16]   Ibid., p. 9, citing charters printed in R. H. Morris, *Chester in the Plantagenet and Tudor Reigns* (Chester, 1893), pp. 482–3, 485–7, 490–3.

[17]   *VCH Ches.* 5. i, pp. 51, 103, 212; *VCH Ches.* 5. ii, p. 211; Morris, *Chester*, pp. 107–11.

[18]   *VCH Ches.* 5. ii, pp. 25, 27.

[19]   *Register of Edward, the Black Prince, preserved in the Public Record Office*, 4 vols (London, 1930–3), III, pp. 20–1.

[20] Ibid., p. 104.

[21] The local copy of the charter is Cheshire Record Office, ZCH 18, printed and translated in Morris, *Chester*, pp. 496–9.

[22] Ibid., pp. 496–7.

[23] Great Domesday Book is cited hereafter as GDB, followed by folio number, a or b (for recto or verso), and 1 or 2 (for the column), from *Domesday Book, seu Liber Censualis Willelmi Primi*, 2 vols (London, 1783), I; followed in parentheses by the abbreviated county name and the entry number in *Domesday Book*, John Morris et al (eds), 34 vols (Chichester, 1974–86).

[24] Summarized in F. R. Thorn, 'Hundreds and wapentakes', in *The Cheshire Domesday [Introduction and Translation]* (London, 1991), pp. 26–37 at 36.

[25] *VCH Ches*. 5. ii, pp. 322–3, 328.

[26] GDB 263b1 (Ches. A/22).

[27] Ormerod, II, p. 823.

[28] There was a single manor of Marlston cum Lache, so we should not think that the moated site can represent Marlston manor, as *PN Ches*. IV, p. 164.

[29] *VCH Ches*. 5. ii, pp. 324, 329; for the town fields, P. J. W. Higson, 'Pointers towards the structure of agriculture in Handbridge and Claverton prior to parliamentary enclosure', *Transactions of the Historic Society of Lancashire and Cheshire*, 142 (1993), 56–71.

[30] *PN Ches*. V (1), p. 53, where the idea that Old ditch was yet another name for this stretch is simply mistaken: the perambulation followed Green ditch or Mere ditch to the Bromfield–Chester road and [then] to Old ditch ('usque quondam viam que ducit de Bromfeld versus Cestriam usque Oldediche'), then followed that ditch (i.e. Old ditch) northwards to another road ('et sic sequendo fossatum illud versus partem borialem usque ad quondam viam').

[31] GDB 263a2 (Ches. A/5).

[32] *PN Ches*. IV, pp. 123–4.

[33] Ormerod, II, pp. 771–2.

[34] *VCH Ches*. 5. ii, p. 225; *PN Ches*. V (1:i), p. 79.

[35] *VCH Ches*. 5. i, p. 235; *VCH Ches*. 5. ii, pp. 87, 302.

[36] Sheila Sweetinburgh, *The Role of the Hospital in Medieval England: Gift-Giving and the Spiritual Economy* (Dublin, 2004), p. 28. More work is needed on this topic.

[37] Sethina Watson, 'The origins of the English hospital', *Transactions of the Royal Historical Society*, 6th series 16 (2006), 75–94, esp. 78–9, quotation at 85.

[38] *The Charters of the Anglo-Norman Earls of Chester, c. 1071–1236*, ed. Geoffrey Barraclough, Record Society for the Publication of Original Documents relating to Lancashire and Cheshire 126 (1988), no. 198. It must date from after his majority in 1163, and not from 1174–7 when he was temporarily deprived of the earldom.

[39] Ibid., no. 222.

[40] Ann J. Kettle, 'The hospital of St Giles, Chester', *VCH Ches*. 3, pp. 178–80, p. 178.

[41] *Charters of Anglo-Norman Earls*, nos. 236–7.

[42] Ibid., no. 221.

43   *VCH Ches*. 5. ii, pp. 95, 111.
44   For the location, *PN Ches*. IV, pp. 299–300.
45   *VCH Ches*. 5. i, p. 55; *VCH Ches*. 5. ii, p. 84.
46   GDB 263b2 (Ches. 1/13).
47   GDB 265a1, 267a1, 268b2 (Ches. 6/1; 17/1; FD5/2).
48   GDB 109a1, 109a2, 165b2, 179b2 (Devon 17/32; 17/48; Glos. 10/14; Herefs.
      1/7).
49   On all this see *VCH Ches*. 5. i, pp. 25–8, 38–43.

4

St Werburgh's, St John's and the
Liber Luciani De Laude Cestrie

Two religious communities dominated Chester throughout the Middle Ages. Both were ancient, both perhaps royal, foundations.[1] Both had undergone radical changes at various times, had enjoyed royal and noble patronage and nurtured myths designed to enhance their status within the city and the region.[2] Each was in competition with the other in the eleventh and twelfth centuries. It is thus surprising to find Lucian, monk of St Werburgh's and author of the *Liber Luciani De Laude Cestrie*, identifying his patron as one of the canons of St John's and extolling the virtues of his house.[3] Indeed, Lucian had himself been schooled at St John's, although he claimed not to have been a native of the city.[4] However, as is often the case with Lucian, things may not have been quite as they seemed. In reality, Lucian's work included almost nothing which could be interpreted as referring directly to St John's church or its canons. The perceived shortcomings of the text have been lamented by many scholars.[5] Yet within Lucian's complicated and often confusing narrative, there are indications that contemporary events in Chester lay behind the subject matter chosen for the text and that, far from being simply allegorical and abstruse, it was interpreting a wider debate within the Church in a local context.

It is impossible to establish the origins of either St Werburgh's or St John's.[6] The latter was probably the more ancient foundation, its otherwise inconvenient extramural site near to the Roman amphitheatre indicating that it may have been constructed above the grave of an early Christian martyr.[7] The *Annales Cestrienses*, compiled by the monks of St Werburgh's in the thirteenth century, recount that St John's was founded by King

Æthelræd of Mercia in 689.[8] Although the canons were unable to identify the founder of their church in 1318,[9] their forebears in the twelfth century were conscious of the royal connections of the church, both ancient and more recent. John of Worcester reported that in 973 Edgar had gone to pray at St John's having been rowed up the Dee from his palace, perhaps at Farndon, by eight kings as a sign of their submission.[10] St Werburgh's was also an ancient foundation. The later tradition kept in the abbey was that Æthelflæd, the 'lady of the Mercians', had caused the body of St Werburgh to be brought to Chester and housed in a new minster built on the site of an ancient church.[11] Thacker has pointed out the plausibility of this tradition and the likelihood that the earlier church was an Anglo-Saxon foundation.[12]

Henry Bradshaw, who based his *Life of St Werburge* on local sources, supplied the idea of the dedication of this earlier church to SS Peter and Paul. He recounted the translation of the body of St Werburgh to Chester in 875 and the building of a minster on the site of the earlier church by Æthelflæd, while a new church of SS Peter and Paul was built in the centre of the city.[13] However, Bradshaw went on to cite an inscription in St John's church which suggested that the founder of the new minster was Edmund, the third son of Edward the Elder.[14] The obvious interpretation of such an inscription would be that St John's had been founded or endowed by Edmund, but this would not have suited the monk's purpose. Just as his report of the progress of Edgar had the king visiting St Werburgh's shrine after he left St John's, so here he took the idea of a royal foundation and applied it to his own church.[15] Moreover, the index to the 1887 edition of the *Life of St Werburge* by Horstmann cited this passage as the foundation and building of Chester cathedral, a title not enjoyed by the abbey church until 1541 and only briefly by St John's.[16] Such misinterpretation of sources and invention of evidence was not confined to the sixteenth century, however. It seems to be a fair reflection of the rivalry which existed between the two churches in the eleventh century and beyond.[17] That rivalry was exacerbated by the contemporary competition between the earls of Chester and the bishops of Lichfield.

On the eve of the Norman Conquest, Chester had two prestigious minster churches. Each had recently been given rich gifts by Earl Leofric of Mercia and Lewis has suggested persuasively that Chester was being drawn into a regional network intended to provide stability to the local church by linking it to the family interests of the earls of Mercia.[18] After the Conquest, Chester appears to have remained attractive to the bishops of Lichfield, to the extent that the synod of London presided over by

Archbishop Lanfranc in 1075 gave permission to the Norman bishop, Peter (1072/3–c.1085), to translate his see from Lichfield to Chester.[19] It is very likely that St John's had long been associated with the bishop of Lichfield.[20] It was situated outside the Newgate in the east of the city in an area which was already an 'episcopal burh'.[21] The Domesday survey documented the bishop's extensive property rights in Chester, where his ownership of fifty-six houses compared favourably to his sixteen in Shrewsbury and fourteen in Stafford.[22] The survey also recorded the customary dues assigned to the bishop in the city, such as the fine for those who worked or traded on Sundays and holy days, suggesting a close connection between the bishop and the city even before the translation of the see.[23] Such a connection can also be traced in the common interest of both St John's and the bishop in properties beyond the city.[24] More importantly, perhaps, the removal to Chester was prompted by the poverty of the cathedral chapter in Lichfield.[25]

The foundation of a cathedral at Chester would no doubt have added to the prestige of the city. It is striking then, that Lucian made no mention of a cathedral there. Peter is reported to have instituted canons in St John's and this may have represented the establishment of a cathedral chapter.[26] The rebuilding of the church may have been started under Bishop Peter, although recent research suggests that the present church was not begun before 1100.[27] Indeed, the letter of Lanfranc cajoling Peter for his mistreatment of the monks of St Mary's, Coventry and their property, suggests that the bishop himself quickly turned his attention to a richer rival.[28] Yet Peter is reported to have been buried at Chester and the petition to William I requesting the appointment of Robert came from the clergy and people of Chester.[29] All that can be said with certainty is that Peter's successor, Robert de Limesey (1085–1117), while involved in a diplomatic mission to Rome, secured the approval of Pope Paschal II for the translation of his episcopal see from Chester to Coventry. The pope addressed Robert as bishop of Coventry and confirmed the move because the 'town' of Chester was a humble and impoverished place unworthy of the dignity of an episcopal throne.[30]

The idea that St John's may have appeared to be as grand a church as St Werburgh's in the later eleventh century has been undermined recently; in reality, it was very much the poor relation.[31] The Domesday survey recorded that St John's had a *matricularius* and seven canons, living in eight houses quit of customary dues, while St Werburgh's had a *custos* and twelve canons occupying thirteen houses in the city. The wealth of the latter was considerably greater than the former.[32] Indeed, it may have been the wealth of Coventry which enabled Robert and his successors to rebuild St John's in a grand style, but it was no longer a cathedral.[33] And although the bishops of Coventry and Lichfield were often referred to as bishops of Chester in the twelfth century and kept a house for their own use at St John's, there is only one recorded visit to the city by any of the bishops from 1072 to 1208, that of Hugh de Nonant in 1192.[34] Keeping Chester in the episcopal title, however, did not mean that St John's was a cathedral.[35] Indeed, the strange legend of King Harold living on at Chester for many years after the Conquest as a hermit of St John's seems to have been exploited by the canons in the later twelfth century precisely in order to bolster the flagging reputation of their church.[36]

The relationship between the canons of St John's and the bishops of Coventry and Lichfield does not appear to have been close after the translation of the see away from Chester. While evidence is lacking for the twelfth century, the thirteenth-century bishops granted benefices in St John's to members of their *familiae*, with little evidence that those so rewarded were resident in Chester.[37] It appears likely that an archdeacon of Chester was resident in the twelfth century, but while appointed by the bishop it seems that he could not be removed by a successor.[38] The long dispute between the chapters of Coventry and Lichfield over the right to elect the bishop provides occasional hints that the canons of St John's attempted to assert their own influence, but to little avail.[39] The setting up of a new chapter at Lichfield by Bishop Roger de Clinton (1130–48), based on that at Rouen and his extensive rebuilding of the cathedral at Lichfield, all while St John's remained unfinished, confirm that Chester was less important than the other diocesan centres.[40]

Archbishop Theobald summoned the monks of Coventry to Leicester in order to elect Roger's successor. That the election of Walter Durdent (1149–59) led to an immediate appeal to the holy see from the clergy of Lichfield and Chester suggests that Roger had indeed enhanced the position of Lichfield but also that the canons of St John's were discomfited by this development.[41] Bishop Walter and Lawrence, the prior of Coventry, argued their case before Pope Eugenius III, who reportedly enforced an agreement which ensured that while the properties of the monks of Coventry were protected from the bishop, the episcopal throne would always remain in Coventry, whose prior would have first voice in the episcopal election.[42] While this report is from the thirteenth century, it reflects the contents of the papal bulls purportedly granted by Innocent II and Lucius II, reinforcing the bishop's rights, and the subsequent bull of Eugenius III, which restored the rights of the monks.[43] Incidentally,

Eugenius III's bull outlined the peripheral nature of the bishop's authority in Chester, stating that he owned,

> in suburbio Cestr(ie), ecclesiam sancti Iohannis cum pertinentiis suis et vicum qui vocata Forieta; infra muros Cestr(ie) quatuor mansura.

> (in the suburb of Chester, the church of St John with its appurtenances and the street called Foregate; within the walls of Chester, four houses.)[44]

The involvement of the popes merely confirmed that this was a quarrel between the canons of Lichfield and the monks of Coventry; the canons of St John's had little to gain from the outcome. Furthermore, the setback for the bishop was likely to provoke a hungrier assessment of assets which he might exploit elsewhere in his diocese. This impression was strengthened by Bishop Walter assigning the prebend of William de Vilers, archdeacon of Chester from before 1140 until 1152, to one of his household clerks, Walter, precentor of Lichfield. To make matters worse, this Walter was one of the bishop's relatives and was also surnamed Durdent.[45] The statute of residence issued by Archbishop Baldwin of Canterbury at Lichfield between 1195 and 1198 confirmed that 'the archdeacon', probably of Chester, had a stall in the cathedral chapter and was henceforth required to reside in Lichfield for three months each year.[46] Yet this presence gave little influence to the clergy of Chester, since the election of the bishop was normally accomplished without reference to the chapter at Lichfield.[47] Just as St John's was not a cathedral in the twelfth century, there is little reason to maintain that its canons were supporters of their bishop or his rights. Indeed, Lucian's text suggests that they were just as likely as the monks of St Werburgh's to view him as an outsider and a predator.

St Werburgh's was the most prominent church in Chester in 1070. As the city went from being a backwater on the edge of the kingdom of Mercia to the capital city of a tight-knit marcher earldom and the residence of a powerful and ambitious Norman earl, the minster became his property.[48] St Werburgh's benefited particularly from the protection of Earl Hugh (1071–1101), who was able to prevent the loss of estates to Norman incomers, nearly all of whom were his men.[49] Furthermore, its status as the most important of the city churches was reinforced by the adoption of the minster for the earl's new monastery of Benedictine monks.[50] Chester was a particularly homogeneous earldom and the earl's foundation was richly endowed by his vassals and by his and their successors.[51] Recent archaeological research at St Werburgh's suggests, moreover, that rebuilding work may have been well underway at the time of the visit of Anselm of Bec in 1092 for the institution of the new foundation.[52] Indeed, the generous

re-endowment of the new abbey, the reinforcement of its rights and privileges, the doubling of its estates, the rebuilding on a monumental scale and
the collaboration of the most prestigious prelate of the Norman world must
surely have added to the self-confidence of the new house.[53] The establishment of the abbey was intended by the earl as a direct response to the
presence in Chester of the Norman bishop, and it may well have been this
that sealed the fate of the 'cathedral' at St John's.[54]

While St Werburgh's abbey enjoyed the protection of the earls of
Chester, the monks had little to fear from the bishops of Coventry and
Lichfield. Surviving *acta* relating to the abbey are few and mostly drawn
from the monks' 'cartulary', in reality a series of abbreviated abstracts (or
poor copies of them).[55] Most of the *acta* are general or specific confirmations of properties and rights.[56] A mandate of Pope Alexander III survives,
ordering the bishop to put a stop to the archdeacon of Coventry making
illegal exactions from clergy and laity, while a similar mandate concerning
the archdeacon of Chester found its way into the decretal collection of
Gregory IX.[57] The tradition of St Werburgh's was that some of the earls
had been persecutors of the monks, such as Earl Richard (1101–20), who
died in the White Ship disaster, his fate, according to Henry Bradshaw,
for indulging his wife's prejudices against the monks and intending to
introduce a new order to the house.[58] In 1131, Earl Ranulf II (1129–53)
founded Basingwerk Abbey (Flintshire) using some of the original endow-
ments of St Werburgh's, although there is no hint of this in the abbey's
chronicle and Lucian himself mentioned Basingwerk with approval.[59]
There may have been a lingering memory in St Werburgh's of the perils of
the twelfth century. Bishop Richard Peche (1160–82) granted the abbot of
St Werburgh's the right to publish sentences, after three warnings, against
those who withheld rents and debts to the detriment of the abbey; the
abbot's sentences would be confirmed by the bishop.[60]

The death of Earl Hugh II (1153–81) invited outside interference
in Chester. His son and heir, Ranulf III (1181–1232) had been born in
1170 and his wardship was held by Henry II until 1187. On the death of
Abbot Robert II (1174–84) on 31 August 1184, the abbey was seized by
the king, who passed it on to Hugh de Nonant, bishop-elect of Lichfield,
who was to achieve notoriety for his treatment of the monks of Coventry
and Canterbury.[61] In the same year, according to the abbey's chronicle,
Henry II and Baldwin, archbishop of Canterbury, appointed Robert de
Hastings (1184–94) as abbot.[62] The wording of the chronicle suggests
the displeasure of the monks and may contain a hint that there was a
rival candidate from within St Werburgh's: 'Sed et Henricus II. Rex et

Baldwinus archiepiscopus posuerunt unum abbatem ad Cestriam nomine Robertus de Hastinges' ('But King Henry II and Archbishop Baldwin placed *one* abbot at Chester, namely Robert de Hastings').[63]

In 1194, the chronicle recorded that:

> Confirmatus est abbas Galfridus in abbatia de Cestra disceptans et litigans coram archiepiscopo Huberto Cantuariensi contra Robertum de Hastinges quondam abbatem Cestrie tandem patrocinante Sancta Werburga et glorioso Comite Cestrensi Rannulpho Galfridus optinuit dignitatem suam reddendo annuatim supradicto Roberto de Hastinges xx marcas duobus terminis et sic pacificati sunt.

> (Abbot Geoffrey was confirmed in the abbey of Chester after much dispute and litigation with Robert de Hastings, the former abbot of Chester, before Hubert, archbishop of Canterbury; at last, through the assistance of St Werburgh and of the glorious Earl Ranulf of Chester, Geoffrey obtained his dignity by returning to the said Robert of Hastings twenty marks annually in two payments, and thus peace was restored between them.)[64]

Robert resigned his office in 1194, but the date of his death is unknown, and while no date is recorded for the election of Geoffrey (1194–*c.*1208), his assumption of the abbacy in 1194 was recorded as a vindication of a long-held right.[65] It is noteworthy that Ranulf made a substantial gift to the church of Coventry on 30 July 1192, at the behest of Bishop Hugh; this charter, which was placed on the altar along with a gold ring by the earl, was later clarified, no doubt because at the time it was issued Hugh had dispossessed the monks and instituted secular canons.[66] Ranulf had also been at Lichfield on 6 April 1192 and witnessed the grant by John, Count of Mortain, of the church of Bakewell to the cathedral at Lichfield.[67] It was assumed that Ranulf had accompanied Richard I on the Third Crusade and had returned to Chester no longer a minor determined to put the affairs of his family monastery in order.[68] However, Ranulf did not take part in the Third Crusade and it may be that the death of Archbishop Baldwin at Acre in November 1190 deprived Robert de Hastings of his protector.[69] The series of papal confirmations acquired by the monks in the pontificate of Clement III (1187–91) may have represented an earlier attempt to secure the removal of Robert de Hastings by securing the right of free election.[70]

The northern chronicler, William of Newburgh, reported the actions of Hugh de Nonant in Coventry and related them to the wider attack on Benedictine monks in the 1180s.[71] He noted that Baldwin, although himself a Cistercian, had sought to replace monks with secular canons in the great cathedrals.[72] Hugh, 'homo callidus, audax, inverecundus, et ad ausus improbos literature eloquentiaque instructus . . .' ('a cunning, bold and shameless man, learned in dishonest letters and eloquence'), was himself far more evil than Baldwin and conspired to destroy the famous and peaceful old monastery at Coventry, which had been worthy to share the episcopal title with Chester, to exclude the monks and to use their properties in order to provide prebends for his clergy.[73] Thus, he spread discord among the prior and the monks in order to provoke disquiet and scandals, enabling him at last to expel them with armed force as incorrigible disturbers of ecclesiastical peace.[74] The expulsion seems to have been the culmination of a visitation by the bishop which led to a disturbance in the cathedral, during which Hugh claimed that the monks had assaulted him and shed his blood.[75] Hugh, like Bishop Peter a century before, was also reported to have destroyed some of the documents of the monks.[76] Hugh then sought confirmation of his decision from the pope which, the monks having been unable to present themselves at Rome within six months, was duly received.[77] As William was writing, the monks of Coventry were dispersed and penniless. The forlorn figure of Moses 'qui *fuit* prior Coventr' ('who *was* prior of Coventry') sued for *novel disseisin* in the royal court in the autumn of 1194.[78] The ultimate success of the monks in January 1197 could not have been predicted and would have been unknown to Lucian if he were writing before 1195. As a monk himself, he would surely have shared the horror and disgust evident in Richard of Devizes' account of the treatment of the monks by their bishop; and Hugh de Nonant was not only their bishop, but Lucian's bishop.[79] And he had been instrumental in imposing Robert of Hastings as abbot of St Werburgh's, hated by his fellow monks of Christ Church for his treachery in supporting Baldwin.[80]

Hugh de Nonant was not only the persecutor of the Coventry monks, but the most outspoken opponent of monastic cathedral chapters and the mainstay of support for Archbishop Baldwin in his attempt to establish a secular chapter at Hackington, a suburb of Canterbury.[81] The case elicited an exaggerated response from monastic chroniclers, who claimed that there was a conspiracy to have monks removed from all of the cathedrals in England, that the bishops had taken personal oaths to this effect and that the king was behind the initiative.[82] All of these assertions had some truth to them and it is likely that Lucian was also caught up in this atmosphere. Indeed, it would be rather strange if he had been immune from the publicity surrounding the case, which saw all the major ecclesiastical figures and religious houses of Europe taking sides.[83] The monks of Canterbury had clearly recognized Hugh de Nonant as their chief antagonist, and when Baldwin had besieged them within their monastery, provoking a debate among the bishops, they remembered that Hugh had said to the king in London that "'... infra duos menses in nulla sede episcopali in regno vestro erit aliquis monachus, quia justum non est", et adjecit, "Monachi ad diabolos.'" ("'... within two months there will be no monk in any episcopal see in your kingdom, for it is not right", adding "Monks to the devils"'.)[84] When a committee was appointed to reach a compromise on the matter, Hugh of Chester and Reginald Fitz Jocelin of Bath were left out as known supporters of one side or the other.[85] Hugh also attempted to prevent the involvement of William Longchamp, bishop of Ely, in the case as a papal legate;[86] he later appended his seal to the decision of King Richard in favour of Archbishop Baldwin[87] and witnessed Richard's confirmation of the establishment of the new college at Lambeth.[88] After the death of Baldwin, Richard's brother John sent Hugh de Nonant, among other bishops, to prevent the election of the bishop of Ely by the monks.[89]

Seen in the context of the anxiety provoked in Chester by the minority of Ranulf III and the appointment of a fearsome opponent of Benedictine monks as bishop of Lichfield, the observations of Lucian on monks and secular clerks begin to make sense. Had he felt that his own community was in competition with St John's he had ample scope to reflect the views of Richard of Devizes, who freely displayed his contempt for secular canons, or 'clericorum irregulariter regularium' ('irregular clerks regular').[90] That he did not do this was not because he had any great regard for St John's and its community, since he praised clerks in general terms without reference to his neighbours. Rather, Lucian was attempting to encourage cooperation between clerks and monks in Chester to ensure that the city was protected from predatory outside influences.

One indication of the context in which Lucian wrote is the reference to schism in the Church.

Nunc autem frequenter ob gladium scismatis diuisa patitur et discessa gemitum cordis; contemptum et comtumaciam sustinens a filiis suis; qui transeuntes ad alienos scalam reputant scolam sceleris; et raciones laicorum quasi ritus gentium imitantes edificant gimnasium in ierosolimis; casam episcopalem relinquentes ob curiam principis; et felicitatem suae promotionis aucupantes ex palatio regis.

(Now, however, divided and forsaken on account of the sword of schism, she suffers anguish of heart, enduring the contempt and contumacy of her sons who, passing over to strangers, consider the ladder as a school of wickedness, and, mimicking the arguments of laymen as if they were the rites of the pagans [cf. 2 Paralipomenon 28:3], they build the gymnasium [cf. Tertullian] in Jerusalem, abandoning the bishop's house for the prince's court, and seeking the good fortune of their promotion from the king's palace.)[91]

The reference to schism could be a reflection of the preoccupation in the twelfth-century Church with repeated disputed elections to the papacy, the most recent of which had lasted for twenty years from 1159.[92] However, given that the schism of double election had affected St Werburgh's so recently and had been healed only after protracted litigation, Lucian was probably referring to the experience of his own house.

Lucian's description of schism used the language of the hunt which he also used in his denunciation of grasping bishops and he seems to have suggested that the bishops of his day had forsaken their clerical calling and become laymen in alliance with the king.

Si enim monachi monasterium non exierent, milui monasterium arpagarent. [. . .] Quibus fuit olim studium nimis benigne prospicere. quieti monacorum. Et solebant alta compassione ne illorum ocium sanctum tumultus premeret prouidere. [. . .] Set nunc mundus monachis molestus est quia gregorius rebus humanis exemptus est.

(For if monks do not leave the monastery the hawks will spear it with their talons. [. . .] Once it was their [the bishops'] purpose to be provide with great kindness for the peace of the monks. And they used with the greatest compassion to make provision lest tumult should destroy their peace. [. . .] But now the world has become troublesome for monks because Gregory [i.e. Pope Gregory the Great] has been released from human affairs.)[93]

Lucian seems to have included some veiled criticism of the bishops with whom his monastery had personal dealings. In his discussion of the role of the bishop he noted that the bishop should be a man who 'dicit patri et matri nescio uos, et fratribus suis, ignoro illos' ('says to his father and mother, "I do not know you", and about his brothers, "I do not recognize them"').[94] The bishops of Lichfield certainly used the resources of their churches to endow their friends and families.[95]

The atmosphere of hostility towards Benedictine monks, especially from the bishops appointed in the 1180s, was intensified by the satirical writings of a group of secular clerks.[96] While the attacks on the monks of Canterbury and Coventry can be seen in the context of bishops trained in the schools and in the developing discipline of canon law rejecting the monastic cathedral chapter as an anomaly, it is probable that Lucian saw them as an attack on monks generally.[97] The chancellor of Richard I, William Longchamp, bishop of Ely, had enacted draconian legislation restricting the activities of Benedictine monks at a council held at Westminster in 1190.[98] Lucian may thus have been noting that the monks were not out of their cloisters for pleasure. Indeed, elsewhere in the treatise, he praised the seclusion of monks and asked 'si monacus es quid facis

in urbibus?' ('if you are a monk, what are you doing in cities?').[99] Lucian
probably thought of St Werburgh's as set apart from the city. When the
monastery was founded, the monastic buildings were deliberately built on
the north side of the abbey church in order to provide a secluded precinct
for the monks in the north-eastern corner of the city.[100]

In the preamble to his treatise, Lucian recorded how he took refuge in
St John's church during a busy day of litigation at the earl's court.[101] It was
here that he met his patron, but it is notable that he praised him without
making further specific reference to St John's. Indeed, Lucian's treatise
divided Chester by its gates, so he had ample opportunity to praise St
John's if he had so desired. His lengthy discussion of 'the gate of St John'
dealt mainly with St John the Baptist and his relationship with Christ and
St Peter.[102] His observation that St John ruled over the east of the city may
be a passing reference to the episcopal properties outside the walls, but
there is little that would single out the community of canons for praise.[103]
That is not to say, however, that the treatise is entirely of a moral and allegorical tone. There appears to be an oblique and ironic reference to Hugh
de Nonant when Lucian praised Chester through its clergy: 'hodie cernitur
clara, quia literatum habet episcopum, liberalem archdiaconum, lucidum
clerum' ('for today it [the threefold nature of Chester] is clearly discerned,
for she has a learned bishop, a liberal archdeacon and an enlightened
clergy').[104] Lucian was surely referring to Hugh when he added to the
above passage:

> Si . . . posse fieri, ut sortiatur ipsa ciuitas episcopum, non ut nunc, set illiter-
> atum, hebetem, et bavosum; archdiaconum auarum, odilibilem, et obscurum;
> clerum non lucidum quidem set liuore mutuo et libidinum fece, inferni clibano
> deputandum . . .
>
> (But if . . . it should be that the city could come out with a bishop not as now, but
> unlettered, dull and drivelling; an avaricious, hateful and benighted archdeacon;
> a clergy not shining but indeed bruised together and soiled with desire, fit to be
> consigned to the oven of the underworld . . .)[105]

Lucian was at least afraid of what might befall Chester in the future
and it is significant that his response to the threat was to write a treatise in
praise of his city. Praising the city for Lucian involved praising the secular
clergy of the city. However, whereas Hugh de Nonant was reported to
have told secular clerks that they were like gods, sons of the Most High,
in contrast to the vileness of monks,[106] Lucian was in no doubt that the
monk's contemplation was more important than the active life of the
clerk.[107] Lucian's intention, however, was not to prove the superiority of

the monk or, indeed, of St Werburgh's over St John's, although the assumption can clearly be detected in the work. His main purpose was to ensure the collaboration of monks and clerks in the interests of the city itself, as he showed in his second definition of the city, where he averred that had it not been for the religion of the monks the city would have perished.[108]

Lucian likened the secular clerk to the priests of the Old Testament, chosen by lot from among the men of the tribe of Levi for a very public office.[109] The monk, on the other hand, pursued a life of self-denial voluntarily chosen. He illustrated the voluntary nature of the monastic life by citing the Nazirites of the Old Testament. This was an unusual parallel to adopt, but the voluntary nature of the Nazirite's vocation seems to be what appealed to Lucian. The Nazirite was required to abstain from the consumption of wine or grape products, to grow his hair and to avoid contact with dead bodies.[110] The prohibitions against wine and defilement by corpses were precisely those which were to be observed by the priests performing temple service.[111] For Lucian, however, the importance of the Nazirites was as an Old Testament symbol of the monk, a parallel to the clerk, who was represented by the prophets. All would be well if monks and clerks would work together:

> Et si coniuncti per spiritum idem sapiunt et idem uolunt, hostibus terrori sunt et magnum angelis dei gaudium faciunt. Qui et tempora sua inuicem adiuti, dulcius poterunt et cum maiori tranquillitate transigere; et quicquid a patre petierint facilius impetrare.

> (And if joined by the spirit they know and want the same things, they are a terror to their enemies and they bring great joy to the angels of God. And if in their time they help each other, they are able to complete their tasks more sweetly and with greater tranquillity; and whatever they ask of the father, they will more easily gain.)[112]

The insistence of Lucian on the need for unity and cooperation among the monks and clerks of Chester appears at first sight to jar with the preoccupations of the twelfth century, characterized by pejorative accounts of rival religious bodies in the search for patronage.[113] Yet this is an insistent message, and one which is put repeatedly in the context of ecclesiastical authority. Thus, Lucian noted that:

> Habet autem episcopus in genere clericum et monacum tanquam duos filios ... Clericus maior episcopi filius est et natu prior; monacus autem minor ... Ille debet iubente episcopo docere populum; iste feruente studio deo conciliare seculum.

> (The bishop has two sons in kind, the clerk and the monk ... The clerk is the eldest son of the bishop, being born earlier, the monk meanwhile is the younger

... The clerk is to teach the people at the bishop's command; the monk with fervent study is to reconcile the world to God.)[114]

Lucian also noted that monks and clerks should cooperate under the bishop for the good of the people.[115]

The *Liber Luciani De Laude Cestrie* provides the reason for this rather unusual stance. Lucian referred to the bishops of his day and their lack of care for monks. He also provided a contrast to this in his depiction of the ideal bishop, a discussion of what a bishop ought to be and how he should relate to the monks under his care.[116] It may be argued that such an account had little relevance to Chester, which was not an episcopal city and which rarely felt the presence of its bishop. If Lucian had the monks of Coventry or Canterbury in mind as he wrote, he would nevertheless have had reason to fear the influence of the bishop of Lichfield and the archbishop of Canterbury in Chester. Both prelates used the resources of St Werburgh's in the 1190s to provide rewards for members of their households.[117] Baldwin stayed at Chester, where his protégé had been intruded as abbot, from 24 to 27 June 1187 and from 14 to 18 April 1188; in his capacity as papal legate, he confirmed the possessions of the monastery and 'conducted much business'.[118]

For Lucian, the ideal bishop was the vicar of Christ on earth, one who made Christ present especially in the exercise of mercy:

> Sedet episcopus, immo sedet xpc, eructans dulcedinem, effundens gratiam, erogans pietatem; nichil affectans ante tronum suum nisi gaudium creature, salutem animarum.

> (The bishop sits, but rather Christ sits; pouring forth sweetness, spreading grace, bestowing piety, caring for nothing before his throne except the joy of the creature and the salvation of souls.)[119]

The bishop was called to quell storms, as Christ did when he called the apostles from their boats to serve on land.[120] The key for the bishop's ability to promote peace was the health of the monasteries in his care. He should ensure that there is peace:

> ... saltim in monasteriis ad audientiam uerbi dei, uelut silentium in celo sic pax et ueneratio deferri possit. Habet quippe aepiscopus ecclesiam tanquam domum, set monasterium tanquam talami sinum ...in locis religiosis, et monasteriis seruorum dei, habere satagit ubi caput reclinet.

> (... at least in monasteries, so that the words of God can be heard, just as though silence in heaven can bring peace and reverence to the earth. For indeed the bishop has the church as a house, but the monastery as his intimate chamber ...in religious places, and especially within the monasteries of the servants of God, the bishop has a fitting place to rest his head.)[121]

Lucian was preoccupied with the burgeoning legal culture in the Church. He saw the bishop as a judge and a lawgiver, whose presence was necessary because of the troubled times in which he lived, and who:

> ... habens in caliginosis clarissimam scripture lucernam, et in nocte temporis, solem iusticie xpm tenens; denique secundum illam uocem gaudentis atque gratulantis, ista est ierusalem in medio gentium posui eam et in circuitu eius terras; satis mirabiliter inter insanos tuta, dormiens inter belligerantes, et faciens paradisum domino super terram.

> (... uses the gospel to dispel the dark of the night, holding Christ, the sun of justice, and then, according to that rejoicing and congratulatory voice, 'This is Jerusalem. I have set her down in the midst of the nations and the countries round about her' (Ezekiel 5:5); miraculously enough she is safe among the madmen, sleeping among the war makers and creating a paradise for the Lord upon the earth.)[122]

For good measure, Lucian recorded the prerogatives of the Roman pontiff, perhaps emphasizing the papal protection recently accorded to St Werburgh's, but also no doubt reflecting the faith of the monks of England that the papacy would ultimately protect their order, a hope which was to be vindicated with the election of Innocent III in 1198.[123] It is surely significant that in his treatise Lucian reserved the term *cathedra* to St Peter and the pope.[124]

Lucian's purpose in writing his treatise in praise of Chester was to ensure cooperation between the monks and clerks of the city. He wrote after a period of schism within his own monastery, itself the result of the minority of Earl Ranulf, which placed Chester at the mercy of outsiders. The insularity and peculiarity of the earldom were to continue, ensuring that Magna Carta was issued separately in the earldom and that no members were returned to Parliament before the sixteenth century.[125] What Lucian's treatise demonstrates is that local sensibilities were more important in twelfth-century Chester than regional or national concerns. The involvement of Henry II in the affairs of the city was unwelcome and left the abbey of St Werburgh's prey to the king's agents, among them Hugh de Nonant and Archbishop Baldwin. By 1195, the immediate problem of the disputed election within the monastery had been solved, at considerable cost to the monks, while the menace of Hugh de Nonant was still present, exemplified by the sufferings of the expelled monks of Coventry. In this context, local rivalries could only be harmful to Chester. Whether Lucian admired the office of the clerk as much as he claimed may be doubted, but in the interests of the city it was necessary to foster cooperation between monks and clerks. His treatise was an attempt to shore up the confidence of the city in the face of its recent losses, and thus competition among religious houses was not likely to be helpful. In the late-twelfth and thirteenth centuries the canons of St John's and the monks of St Werburgh's did indeed cooperate as Lucian had suggested, protecting their ancient burial rights in the city in the face of newcomers, be they nuns, friars or hospitals.[126] Their common interests were more important than the differences between them, as Lucian had said at the beginning of his treatise:

> Ubicumque enim duo simul bene uidentur, consensus amborum quasi tercius in numero reputatur. Nam et robur et decor et honestas ibidem pensantur (robur contra inimicos, decor ad parilitatem, honestas ad uolitum); haec secundum scripturas et secundum mores.

> (For wherever two seem to be well together, the consensus of both is held to be worth that of three. For there is held to be both strength and worthiness and honesty (strength against enemies, worthiness to be considered equal, honesty as to the will); and these things are so according to the scriptures and according to custom.)[127]

Notes

[1] For a general account of the history of the city in the earlier Middle Ages, see *VCH Ches*. 5. i, pp. 16–33.

[2] For a general overview of St Werburgh's, see A. Kettle, 'The Abbey of Chester', in *VCH Ches*. 3, pp. 132–46; for St John's, see A. T. Thacker, 'The Collegiate Church of St John', in *VCH Ches*. 5. ii, pp. 125–33.

[3] Oxford, Bodleian Libary, MS Bodley 672, fols 5r–6v; partial edition by M. V. Taylor, *Extracts from the MS Liber Luciani de laude Cestrie*, Record Society for the publication of original documents relating to Lancashire and Cheshire 64 (1912), 1–78, pp. 38–9; I am grateful to Dr Mark Faulkner for providing me with his transcript of Lucian's text. For the alternative suggestion that Lucian may in fact have been a monk of Combermere, see Faulkner in this volume, pp. 78–98.

[4] MS Bodley 672, fol. 5v: 'quia puer ibi dudum literas didiceram' ('for as a boy long ago I was educated there'); Taylor, *Liber Luciani*, p. 38.

[5] J. Doran, 'Authority and care. The significance of Rome in twelfth-century Chester', in *Roma Felix – Formation and Reflections of Medieval Rome*, ed. É. Ó Carragáin and C. Neuman de Vegvar (Aldershot, 2008), pp. 307–32, pp. 308–10.

[6] A. T. Thacker, 'Chester and Gloucester: Early Ecclesiastical Organization in Two Mercian Burhs', *Northern History*, 18 (1982), 199–211, pp. 200–4.

[7] Ibid., p. 201.

[8] *Annales Cestrienses; or chronicle of the Abbey of S. Werburg, at Chester*, R. Copley Christie (ed.) Record Society for the publication of original documents relating to Lancashire and Cheshire 14 (1886), p. 10.

[9] D. Jones, *The Church in Chester 1300–1540*, Remains Historical and Literary

Connected with the Palatine Counties of Lancaster and Chester, Chetham Society, Third Series VII (Manchester, 1957), p. 6.

[10] R. R. Darlington and P. McGurk (eds), *The Chronicle of John of Worcester*, J. Bray and P. McGurk (trans.), 3 vols (Oxford, 1995–98), vol. ii, pp. 424–5; Thacker, 'Chester and Gloucester', p. 201.

[11] Ibid., p. 203; id., 'Werburh', DNB, 58, pp. 164–5; *Polychronicon Ranulphi Higden monachi Cestrensis*, ed. C. Babbington and J. R. Lumby, Rolls Series 41, 9 vols (1879–86), vol. vi, pp. 126–8, 176–8, 366; Henry Bradshaw, *The Life of Saint Werburge of Chester*, C. Horstmann (ed.), EETS OS 88 (London, 1887), pp. 139–53; a thorough review of the traditions is provided in *The Chartulary or Register of the Abbey of St Werburgh Chester*, in Remains Historical and Literary Connected with the Palatine Counties of Lancaster and Chester, J. Tait (ed.), Chetham Society New Series 79 (Part 1) and 82 (Part 2) (Manchester, 1920, 1923), Part 1, pp. vii–xxii.

[12] Thacker, 'Chester and Gloucester', p. 201

[13] Bradshaw, *The Life of Saint Werburge*, pp. 149–52.

[14] Ibid., p. 151.

[15] Ibid., pp. 171–2.

[16] Ibid., p. 207; in reality, of course, Bradshaw did not write of a 'cathedral' at all.

[17] I am grateful to Dr C. P. Lewis for making available to me a revised chapter on 'The Greater Churches', based on his unpublished thesis, 'English and Norman government and lordship in the Welsh borders 1039–87' (DPhil thesis, Oxford University, 1985).

[18] *The Chronicle of John of Worcester*, vol. ii, pp. 582–3; *Annales Cestrienses*, p. 14; Lewis, 'The Greater Churches', pp. 8–9.

[19] *The Letters of Lanfranc Archbishop of Canterbury*, H. Clover and M. Gibson (eds) (Oxford, 1979), p. 76.

[20] Thacker, 'Chester and Gloucester', p. 202; Lewis, 'The Greater Churches', p. 9.

[21] Ibid., p. 9.

[22] *The Domesday Survey of Cheshire*, J. Tait (ed.), Remains Historical and Literary Connected with the Palatine Counties of Lancaster and Chester, Chetham Society New Series 75 (Manchester, 1916), pp. 27, 79.

[23] Ibid., p. 87.

[24] Thacker, 'Chester and Gloucester', p. 202.

[25] M. J. Franklin, 'The bishops of Coventry and Lichfield, c.1072–1208', in G. Demidowicz (ed.), *Coventry's First Cathedral. The Cathedral and Priory of St Mary. Papers from the 1993 anniversary symposium* (Stamford, 1994), pp. 118–38, pp. 118–19.

[26] William of Malmesbury, *De gestis pontificum Anglorum*, N. E. S. A. Hamilton (ed.), Rolls Series 52 (London, 1870), p. 309; *Coventry and Lichfield 1072–1159*, M. J. Franklin (ed.), English Episcopal Acta 14 (Oxford, 1997), pp. xxx–xxxi.

[27] R. Gem, 'Romanesque architecture in Chester c.1075 to 1117', in A. Thacker (ed.), *Medieval Archaeology, Art and Architecture at Chester*, The British Archaeological Association Conference Transactions 22 (Leeds, 2000), pp. 31–44, p. 41.

[28] *The Letters of Lanfranc*, Clover and Gibson (eds), pp. 110–12.

[29] Franklin, EEA 14, pp. xxxii and 124 (i.e. Appendix VII: Fasti 1072–1159,

compiled by C. N. L. Brooke, pp. 123–31); see also pp. 31–2 for the 'smoak penney', which provides evidence that St John's was indeed a cathedral for a short time.

30 *Patrologia latina*, clxiii, 95–6: 'quia et Lichefeldensis locus et Cestrensis villa, ubi praedecessoribus tuis vel tibi hactenus sedes fuerunt, pro exiguitate ac paupertate sui episcopalis dignitatis solium non merentur' ('since both the district of Lichfield and the town of Chester, where your predecessors and yourself have held your sees until now, do not merit the dignity of the episcopal throne because of their paltriness and poverty'); see also Franklin, EEA 14, pp. xxxv and 5; cf. Franklin, 'The bishops of Coventry and Lichfield', p. 119.

31 R. Gem, 'Romanesque architecture in Chester', pp. 38–41; V. Jansen, 'Attested but opaque: the early Gothic east end of St Werburgh's', in A. Thacker (ed.), *Medieval Archaeology, Art and Architecture at Chester*, pp. 57–65; R. V. H. Burne, *The Monks of Chester. The History of St Werburgh's Abbey* (London, 1962), pp. 24–5.

32 Thacker, 'Chester and Gloucester', pp. 201 and 204; *The Domesday Survey of Cheshire*, Tait (ed.), pp. 92–3 (St John's), pp. 93–100 (St Werburgh's), pp. 117–19 and 127–9 (lands claimed by St Werburgh's).

33 Lewis, 'The Greater Churches', pp. 9–10, for an assessment of the policy of the bishops in the century after the Conquest.

34 Ormerod, I, pp. 93–5, for the episcopal title; itineraries for the bishops are given in the following: Franklin, EEA 14, pp. 132–4 (and 102 for the episcopal title); *Coventry and Lichfield 1160–1182*, M. J. Franklin (ed.), English Episcopal Acta 16 (Oxford, 1998), p. 120; *Coventry and Lichfield 1183–1208*, M. J. Franklin (ed.), English Episcopal Acta 17 (Oxford, 1998), pp. 132–6, p. 134 (and pp. 29–30 for Hugh's visit, which was perhaps in order to celebrate the feast of St John the Baptist); for the bishop's house at St John's, *VCH Ches*. 5. ii, p. 132.

35 Burne, *The Monks of Chester*, p. 111; Ormerod, I, p. 232, citing a visit of Richard II to 'Chester cathedral', but based on unreliable evidence.

36 A. Thacker, 'The cult of King Harold at Chester', in T. Scott and P. Starkey (eds), *The Middle Ages in the North West* (Oxford, 1995), pp. 155–76, pp. 162–5; S. Matthews, 'The content and construction of the *Vita Haroldi*', in G. R. Owen-Crocker (ed.), *King Harold II and the Bayeux Tapestry* G. R. Owen-Crocker (Woodbridge, 2005), pp. 65–73, p. 73.

37 Franklin, EEA 14, p. liii.

38 Ibid., pp. lii and 128.

39 Id., 'The bishops of Coventry and Lichfield', pp. 128–9.

40 Id., EEA 14, pp. xlii–iv, 90.

41 Id., 'The bishops of Coventry and Lichfield', p. 128.

42 Ibid., p. 129.

43 Id., EEA 14, pp. 89–97; *Patrologia Latina*, clxxx, 1512–14 (Eugenius III).

44 Franklin, EEA 14, p. 96. The Domesday survey also listed fifty-six houses belonging to the bishop, without mentioning that fifty-two of them must have been around St John's: *The Domesday Survey of Cheshire*, J. Tait (ed.), p. 78.

45 Franklin, EEA 14, pp. xliv–v, 64–5 no. 66.

46 *Canterbury 1193–1205*, C. R. Cheney and E. John (eds), English Episcopal Acta 3 (Oxford, 1986), pp. 185–6 no. 528; Franklin, EEA 17, pp. 138–9.

47 Id., 'The bishops of Coventry and Lichfield', p. 127.
48 Lewis, 'The Greater Churches', pp. 14, 27–8; *VCH Ches.* 5. i, pp. 25–7.
49 Lewis, 'The Greater Churches', pp. 14–16.
50 Ibid., p. 16; Kettle, 'Chester Abbey', *VCH Ches.* 3, pp. 132–3.
51 Tait, *Chartulary*, Part I, 'Charters of the Earls', pp. 13–82, esp. pp. 15–22; Burne, *The Monks of Chester*, pp. 5–18, 196–201 and Lewis, 'The Greater Churches', pp. 28–9.
52 Gem, 'Romanesque architecture in Chester', p. 41.
53 MS Bodley 672, fols 8v–9r; C. P. Lewis, 'Avranches, Hugh d', first earl of Chester (*d.* 1101), magnate and founder of Chester Abbey', DNB, vol. 3, pp. 1–3.
54 Id., 'The Greater Churches', p. 31.
55 Tait, *Chartulary*, Part I, pp. xxviii–xxxv; Franklin, EEA 14, pp. 102–5.
56 Ibid., pp. 12 no. 13, 13 no. 14 and 48 no. 49 and Franklin, EEA 16, pp. 14–15 no. 14, pp. 15–16 no. 15, 16 no. 16, 18 no. 19 and 18 no. 20.
57 *Canterbury 1162–1190*, C. R. Cheney and B. E. A. Jones (eds), English Episcopal Acta 2 (Oxford, 1986), pp. 93–5 no. 115; *Liber Extra (= Decretales Gregorii IX): Corpus Iuris Canonici*, E. Friedberg (ed.), ii (Leipzig, 1881), I.23.6; P. Jaffé, *Regesta Pontificum Romanorum ad annum 1198*, S. Loewenfeld, F. Kaltenbrunner, and P. W. Ewald (eds), 2 vols (Leipzig, 1885–8), no. 13857.
58 Bradshaw, *The Life of Saint Werburge*, pp. 182–5.
59 Tait, *Chartulary*, Part I, pp. xxvii, 30; *Annales Cestrienses*, p. 22; MS Bodley 672, fol. 61r; Taylor, *Liber Luciani*, pp. 58–9; G. White, 'Ranulf (II) [Ranulf de Gernon], fourth earl of Chester (*d.*1153), magnate', DNB, vol. 46, pp. 53–6, p. 56.
60 Franklin, EEA 16, pp. 17–18 no. 18.
61 *Annales Cestrienses*, p. 30; *The Great Roll of the Pipe for the Thirty-First Year of King Henry II A.D. 1184–1185* (London, 1913), p. 142; *Cheshire in the Pipe Rolls, 1158–1301*, R. Stewart-Brown (ed.), Record Society for the publication of original documents relating to Lancashire and Cheshire 92 (London, 1938), p. 15; Burne, *The Monks of Chester*, pp. 12–13; for Hugh de Nonant, see M. J. Franklin, 'Nonant, Hugh de', DNB, vol. 40, pp. 991–3; idem, EEA 17, pp. xxvi–xlvii; D. E. Desborough, 'Politics and Prelacy in the Late Twelfth Century: The Career of Hugh de Nonant, Bishop of Coventry, 1188–98', *Bulletin of the Institute of Historical Research*, 64 (1991), 1–14.
62 *Annales Cestrienses*, p. 34.
63 Ibid., p. 34; cf. Kettle, 'Chester Abbey', *VCH Ches.* 3, p. 135; Doran, 'Authority and Care', pp. 325–9.
64 *Annales Cestrienses*, p. 44.
65 *Heads of Religious Houses in England and Wales 940–1216*, D. Knowles, C. N. L. Brooke and V. C. M. London (eds) (Cambridge, 1972), p. 39.
66 *The Charters of the Anglo-Norman Earls of Chester, c.1071–1237*, G. Barraclough (ed.), Record Society for the publication of original documents relating to Lancashire and Cheshire 126 (Gloucester, 1988), pp. 219–20 no. 219; clarification in *The Great Register of Lichfield Cathedral, known as* Magnum Registrum Album, H. E. Savage (ed.), Collections for a History of Staffordshire edited by the William Salt Archaeological Society (Kendal, 1924), p. 241 no. 500.
67 Magnum Registrum Album, Savage (ed.), p. 60 no. 131.

68 Burne, *The Monks of Chester*, pp. 13 and 16–17.

69 J. W. Alexander, *Ranulf of Chester. A relic of the Conquest* (Athens, Georgia, 1983), p. 4; R. Eales, 'Ranulf (III) [Ranulf de Blundeville], sixth earl of Cheser', DNB, vol. 46, pp. 56–9, p. 57.

70 Tait, *Chartulary*, Part I, pp. 109–12, 115–16; Doran, 'Authority and Care', pp. 328–30.

71 William of Newburgh, in *Chronicles of the reigns of Stephen, Henry II, and Richard I*, R. Howlett (ed.), 4 vols, Rolls Series 82 (1884–9), vol. i, pp. 393–6; for the Coventry case, see Knowles, *The Monastic Order in England. A history of its development from the times of St Dunstan to the Fourth Lateran Council 940–1216*, second edn (Cambridge, 1963), pp. 322–4.

72 William of Newburgh, vol. i, 393–4.

73 Ibid., vol. i, pp. 394–6.

74 Ibid., vol. i, pp. 394–5.

75 Gervase, *The historical works of Gervase of Canterbury*, ed. W. Stubbs, 2 vols, Rolls Series, 73 (1879–80), i, pp. 461 and 469–70; and Franklin, EEA 17, pp. xxxii.

76 Gervase, vol. i, p. 461; Franklin, EEA 14, pp. xxxi and 97; *The Letters of Lanfranc*, Clover and Gibson (eds), pp. 110–13.

77 William of Newburgh, vol. i, p. 395.

78 Franklin, 'The bishops of Coventry and Lichfield', pp. 136–7.

79 *The Chronicle of Richard of Devizes of the Time of King Richard the First*, J. T. Appleby (ed.) (London, 1963), pp. 69–73 and see pp. 86–7.

80 Gervase, vol. i, pp. 335–6.

81 Knowles, *The Monastic Order*, pp. 318–22; C. Holdsworth, 'Baldwin [Baldwin of Forde] (*c.*1125–1190), Archbishop of Canterbury', DNB, vol. 3, pp. 442–5, pp. 444–5 for the Hackington dispute.

82 Knowles, *The Monastic Order*, p. 320, citing Gervase, vol. ii, p. 402; Gervase, vol. i, pp. 540–1; and William of Newburgh, vol. ii, p. 392.

83 Knowles, *The Monastic Order*, p. 322.

84 *Epistolae Cantuarienses*, in *Chronicles and Memorials of the Reign of Richard I*, ed. William Stubbs, Rolls Series 38, 2 vols (London, 1864–65), vol. ii (1865), p. 318; Gervase, vol. i, p. 470.

85 *Epistolae Cantuarienses*, p. 317; Gervase, vol. i, p. 470 has Richard I expressing this opinion.

86 *Epistolae Cantuarienses*, p. 318.

87 Ibid., p. 323.

88 Ibid., p. 324.

89 Ibid., p. 346.

90 *The Chronicle of Richard of Devizes*, Appleby (ed.), pp. 70–1.

91 MS Bodley 672, fols 119v–120r; the ladder refers to the twelve steps recommended by St Benedict in chapter 7 of his rule: *The Rule of St Benedict*, J. McCann (trans.) (London, 1952), p. 38; for Tertullian's question, 'What has Athens to do with Jerusalem?', see *Ante Nicene Fathers* 3, A.C. Coxe (ed.) (New York, 1918), p. 246.

92 I. S. Robinson, *The Papacy 1073–1198* (Cambridge, 1990), pp. 472–94.

[93]   MS Bodley 672, fol. 116r.

[94]   MS Bodley 672, fol. 128v.

[95]   Franklin, EEA 14, pp. lii–liv; idem, EEA 16, pp. xxxv–xl; idem, EEA 17, pp. liii–lx.

[96]   Knowles, *The Monastic Order*, pp. 313–16.

[97]   Ibid., p. 318; Franklin, 'The bishops of Coventry and Lichfield', p. 135.

[98]   'Jocelini Cronica', in T. Arnold (ed.), *Memorials of St Edmund's Abbey*, Rolls Series 96, 3 vols (London, 1890–6), vol. i, p. 259; Knowles, *The Monastic Order*, pp. 323–4.

[99]   MS Bodley 672, fol. 131v.

[100] Burne, *The Monks of Chester*, p. 5.

[101] MS Bodley 672, fol. 5v; Taylor, *Liber Luciani*, p. 38.

[102] MS Bodley 672, fols 17–23.

[103] Ibid., fol. 22v: 'iure sibi sibi assumpsit orientalia ciuitatis'.

[104] MS Bodley 672, fol. 8v; Taylor, *Liber Luciani*, p. 41.

[105] MS Bodley 672, fol. 8v.

[106] *The Chronicle of Richard of Devizes*, Appleby (ed.), 72: 'Ego dico, dii estis et filii Excelsi omnes'; Hugh was also reported as saying: '"Ego," ait, "clericos meos deos nomino, monacos demonia"' ('I call my clerks gods, and the monks devils').

[107] MS Bodley 672, fols 5v–6r: 'Ibi sapiuit in gutture mentis, quantum a se different salum maris et sinus matris: in uno turbamur, in altero consolamur' ('There he savours in the taste of the mind how different from each other are the salt of the sea and the bosom of the mother: in the one we are much troubled, in the other consoled.')

[108] Ibid., fols 8v–9r: '. . . religione monacorum . . . et precipue si religio non fuisset, ciuitas interisset . . .'

[109] Ibid., fols 117r–121v specifically, but generally there are references throughout fols 116r–138v.

[110] Num 6:1–21, cf. Judges 13:4–5, 7, 13–4 and 16:17 (Samson); 1 Sam 1:1 (Samuel); Acts 18:18 (St Paul's vow at Cenchrae); A. L. Barbieri, 'Nazirites', *New Catholic Encyclopedia*, 10, 287–8. A recent discussion of Nazirites and their significance is provided by E. Diamond, 'An Israelite self-offering in the priestly code: a new perspective on the Nazirite', *The Jewish Quarterly Review*, New Series 88 (1997), pp. 1–18.

[111] Ibid., p. 3.

[112] MS Bodley 672, fols 123r–123v.

[113] *Libellus de Diversisi Ordinibus et Professionibus qui sunt in Aecclesia*, G. Constable and B. Smith (eds) (Oxford, 1972), pp. xviii–xxiii.

[114] MS Bodley 672, fols 129v–130r.

[115] Ibid., fols 131r–131v.

[116] Ibid., fols 127–131v.

[117] Franklin, 'Nonant', p. 993; J. Tait (ed.), *Chartulary*, Part I, pp. 125–6.

[118] Cheney and Jones, EEA 2, p. 221 no. 260; *Annales Cestrienses*, p. 36.

[119] MS Bodley 672, fols. 127r–127v.

[120] Ibid., fol. 128r.

[121] Ibid.

[122] Ibid., fols 129r–129v.

[123] Ibid., fol. 129v; Knowles, *The Monastic Order*, pp. 325–7.

[124] Ibid., fols 23r (St Peter), 26r (St Peter), 28r (Rome), 33r (Rome, in marginal note), 33v (Peter, in marginal note).

[125] Eales, 'Ranulf III', DNB, vol. 46, p. 57.

[126] Tait, 'Chartulary', Part II, pp. 299–302 nos 522–6.

[127] MS Bodley 672, fol. 4v.

5

The Spatial Hermeneutics of Lucian's
De Laude Cestrie

MARK FAULKNER

Sed nec in arctois sedem tibi legeris urbibus, Wigornia, Cestria, Herefordia, propter Walenses uite prodigos.

(Neither should you choose a seat in the Marches, Worcester, Chester, or Hereford, because of the Welsh, who are prodigal with the lives of others.)[1]

W riting in the early 1190s, Richard of Devizes imagines a French Jew telling a young compatriot about the English cities he should avoid. He groups Worcester, Chester and Hereford together as northern (*in arctois*), perhaps Marcher, locations, which collectively suffer regular Welsh violence. Richard's satirical description imputes innate, indescriminate hostility to the Welsh and implies that Chester and the two other cities are frontier towns on England's wild west.

We find a much more ambivalent image of Wales in Lucian's *De Laude Cestrie*, a text probably datable to the 1190s and thus the contemporary of Devizes' *Cronicon*. Here Wales is 'eam quam diuina seueritas, ob ciuiles et naturales discordias, Britannis reliquit angularem angustiam' ('the narrow corner which God's severity left the Welsh to punish their innate rebelliousness'),[2] but also a valued trading partner which is particularly generous in supplying Chester with meat.[3] The Welsh are frequent visitors to Chester[4] and the proximity of the city to Wales has made its citizens 'per longam transfusionem morum, maxima parte consimiles' ('through a long exchange of customs, for the most part similar') to those across the border.[5] So unconcerned does Lucian seem about the Welsh, that his text has been seen to usher in 'a period of newly established peace'.[6]

Yet it would be a mistake to accept Lucian's endorsement of Welsh merchants and to ignore his fears about the country's 'innate rebelliousness' and the gradual effect of Welsh culture on Chester. Lucian's vision of urban space is conditioned by a range of generic influences from classical rhetoric, to biblical hermeneutics, to Neo-Platonist philosophy, to Pauline ecclesiology. While recent scholarship has made particular progress exploring Lucian's application of biblical hermeneutics to Chester's urban environment and the inevitable elisions and distortions this entails, other influences on Lucian's text have received less attention, a neglect which risks distorting Lucian's complex, ambivalent attitude to Chester space. We can see these complexities in Lucian's attitude to the Welsh. Traditional historiography told Lucian that a history of repression is often the consequence of moral turpitude; the conventions of urban encomium dictated Chester must be depicted as both amply provisioned and hospitable; and the nascent twelfth-century interest in realistic description justified Lucian recording his anthropological observation of how readily people adopt the customs of their neighbours. Such generic influences moreover constitute just one aspect of the 'production of space' in *De Laude Cestrie*.

This essay attempts to come to a nuanced understanding of how Lucian saw urban space, by triangulating three types of evidence: first, what we know about Chester's urban environment in the late twelfth century; second, how Lucian chooses to depict urban space; and third, how Lucian himself interacted with urban space. The intellectual roots of this approach lie in Henry Lefebvre's triad of spatial pratice / representations of space / representational spaces (equating to how space is perceived / conceived / lived)[7] and in Paul Strohm's essay 'Three London Itineraries', with its emphasis on understanding:

> the city's own previous investment in its symbolization; (2) various discursive conventions, appropriate to the genre of writing; and (3) a number of characteristally 'literary' ways of deploying material.[8]

The first half of this essay accordingly explores the generic affiliations of *De Laude Cestrie*, locating its origins in the classical tradition of epideictic rhetoric, the hermeneutic transformations of biblical exegesis and the philosophy of Neo-Platonism and suggesting that these influences explain Lucian's habitual representation of space. The essay then turns to two occasions when Lucian describes himself walking through the city and beyond to look at his own *representational space*. The first of these itineraries took Lucian from St Werburgh's Abbey to the Parish Church of St Michael to the Cathedral of St John, where an unnamed canon explained the etymology of the city's Latin name, *Cestria*, and provided the inspiration for writing *De Laude Cestrie*, while the unpleasant prospect of a visit to the Earl's Castle darkened his mind. The second, apparently a record of the composition of a section of the text in 1195, must be reconstructed from a series of ambiguous marginal notes in the only surviving manuscript of *De Laude Cestrie*. Analysing each itinerary in turn, this essay contrasts Lucian's lived experience of the city with the spatial developed in his text. Seen through this lens, Lucian's ambivalence to the Welsh can be seen to reflect different strands of his livelihood – the literate man aware of the traditional historiography that attributes military failure to moral laxity, the preacher advocating the Pauline doctrine that all men are equal in Christ and the grateful Cestrian who likes a bit of Welsh beef – and as neither a xenophobic dismissal of the Marches nor an endorsement of 'a period of newly established peace'.

Lucian's Mental Maps: Generic Influences on De Laude Cestrie

The primary generic influence on Lucian's *De Laude Cestrie* was classical rhetorical tradition. The opening rubric in Lucian's autograph manuscript calls the text the *Liber Luciani De Laude Cestrie*. Lucian's chosen title reflects his debt to the medieval discourses of *laus* and *uituperio*, long taught in the schools as the twin purposes of epideictic (demonstrative) rhetoric.[9] Cities were one of the recommended themes for this discourse. Quintillian for example, advised:

> Laudantur autem urbes similiter atque homines. Nam pro parente est conditor, et multum auctoritatis adfert vetustas, ut iis qui terra dicuntur orti, et virtutes ac vitia circa res gestas eadem quae in singulis: illa propria quae ex loci positione ac munitione sunt. Cives illis ut hominibus liberi sunt decori.

> (Cities are praised on similiar lines to men. The founder stands for the father, age gives authority (as people are said to be autochthonous), and the virtues and vices seen in actions are the same as with individuals, the only special features being those which come from the site and the fortifications. Citizens are a credit to cities as children are to parents.)[10]

Priscian's *Praeexercitamina*, a translation from Hermogenes' Greek *Progymnasmata*, gives similar principles:

> Quin etiam urbium laudes ex huiscemodi locis non difficulter acquires. Dices enim et de genere, quod indigene, et de victu, quod a deis nutriti, et de eruditione quod a deis eruditi sunt. Tractes vero, quomodo de homine, qualis sit statura, quibus professionibus est vsa, quid gesserit.

(Moreover, you will be able to undertake the praise of cities without difficulty by using these principles: for you will speak concerning its origins, which are innate, concerning their livelihood, which is nourished the gods, and concerning their learning, which is taught by the gods. Just as in the case of a man, you will treat its manners, institutions and its pursuits.)[11]

Similar instructions to praise the origins of a city, its site and fortifications and the virtues of the citizens feature in many rhetorical handbooks[12] and it is extremely likely that Lucian studied the *laudes urbium* while he was at school at St John's Cathedral in Chester, where he tells us he was first educated.[13] Each student may once have composed his own *De Laude Cestrie*.

The influence of these rhetorical handbooks on Lucian's *De Laude Cestrie* is readily apparent. The text begins with a lengthy discussion of the etymology of Chester's Latin name, *Cestria* (fols 7v–12r), interpreted as 'cis tria', loosely 'threefold', and explained with three threefold etymologies, before describing the city's site, gates, river, streets and marketplace (fols 12r–13v). Lucian then turns to Chester's gates again, correlating each with a church: St John's with the East Gate, St Peter's with the West Gate, St Werburgh's with the North Gate and St Michael's with the South Gate (fols 16v–88r). He discusses Chester's three churches dedicated to the Virgin Mary (fols 88r–112r), then returns to 'pauca que restant' ('a few little things that remain'), describing the suburbs, the possible etymology of Chester from the Old English word *ceaster*, 'fortified settlement', and the customs of the inhabitants (fols 112r–14r). It is clear that all the themes suggested in the handbooks – the city's origins, its site and fortification and the virtues of its citizens – are present.

In this, *De Laude Cestrie* is comparable to other contemporary city descriptions, such as the description of London which William Fitz Stephen prefixed to his *Life* of Thomas Becket.[14] Fitz Stephen outlines London's praiseworthiness at the very beginning of his text:

Felix est aeris salubritate, Christiana religione, firmitate munitionum, natura sitis, honore civium, pudicitia matronali; ludis etiam quam jocunda, et nobilium est fœcunda virorum.

(It is blest in the wholesomeness of its air, in its reverence for the Christian faith, in the strength of its bulwarks, the nature of its situation, the honour of its citizens and the chastity of its matrons. It is likewise most merry in its sports and fruitful of noble men (ll. 23–6).)[15]

Both texts include some detailed descriptions of the inhabitants drawn from life.[16] The resemblance between Fitz Stephen's *Descriptio* and Lucian's

De Laude Cestrie remains superficial however. Fitz Stephen's text emphasizes the customs of London's citizens; Lucian's Chester's churches.
Lucian's approach to the city is also markedly different. Fitz Stephen sees
London through the lens of the Latin classics and, by figuring the city
through these texts, asserts London's status as both New Troy and New
Rome.[17] Lucian, by contrast, sees Chester as a microcosm of the Christian
universe past, present and future: God's fingerprints are everywhere.

Lucian's interpretation of the *laudes urbium* model is indebted to
twelfth-century theology, but perfectly compatible with the prescriptions
of the rhetorical handbooks which, as we saw, attributed a city's advantages to the gods. The twelfth-century Neo-Platonists saw the world
as a universe, a single whole unified by God's harmony of purpose.
Contemplating this universe gave both delight and the prospect of a closer
understanding of God.[18] As Arnold of Bonneval wrote in his commentary
on Genesis:

> Et [Deus] quasi magni corporis membra, rerum naturas, distinguens propria loca
> et nomina, congruas mensuras et officia assignauit . . . Complectitur omnia, intra
> solidans, extra protegens, supra fovens, infra sustinens, arte investigabili ligans
> diversa, temperatura mirabili astringens in pacem et in unam jungens contraria,
> premens levia ne effluant, sustinens ponderosa ne ruant.

> (God distributed all things of nature like the members of a great body, assigning
> to all their proper places and names, their fitting measures and offices . . . He
> encloses all things, strengthening them from within, protecting them from
> without, nurturing them from above, supporting them from below, binding
> contraries with perceptible art, joining opposites into one and with marvellous
> moderating power enjoining peace upon them, holding down lightweight things
> lest they fly off, holding up ponderous things lest they crash downwards.)[19]

Such considerations applied not only to the natural world, but also to
man-made objects. When Master Gilbert asked himself 'Can one consider
things manufactured by man – footgear, cheese, and like products – as
works of God?', he answered by averring that these were all works of God
made through the intermediary service of man, just as 'we customarily say
that some rich man has built many buildings which in fact a carpenter has
built'.[20]

Lucian's *De Laude Cestrie* is perhaps the fullest application of this
Neo-Platonic theology to survive from the Middle Ages. It colours almost
everything Lucian writes about Chester, as he repeatedly quotes Eliphaz's
advice to Job that 'nothing is done without voice cause' (Job 5:6). A simple
example is his commentary on the location of the marketplace in the centre
of Chester at the crossroads of the city's two main Roman roads:

Hoc simul intuendum quam congrue in medio urbis, parili positione cunctorum, forum uoluit esse uenalium rerum, ubi, mercium copia complacente precipue uictualium, notus ueniat uel ignotus, precium porrigens, referens alimentum. Nimirum ad exemplum panis eterni de celo uenientis, qui natus secundum prophetas *in medio orbis et umbilico terre*, omnibus mundi nationibus pari propinquitate uoluit apparere. Illud precipue prudens aliquis gaudenter attendat, quod Deus omnipotens paterna bonitate prospexit, et ad salutem ciuium, altius et eminentius ordinauit. Nam siquis stans in fori medio, uultum uertat ad ortum solis, secundum ecclesiarum positiones, inueniet Iohannem Domini precursorem ab oriente, Petrum apostolum ab occidente, Werburgam uirginem ab aquilone, archangelum Michaelem a meridie. Nichil illa scriptura uerius: *super muros tuos Ierusalem constitui custodes* (Isa. 62:6). Nichil hac euidentia dulcius cui tales Deus contulit seruatores; sollempne munus, suaue misterium. Confortat animos et pascit intuitum

(It is also worth understanding how fittingly it is that, all things being equal, a marketplace for the selling of things should be placed in the middle of the city, where, with an abundance of merchandise, particularly food available, a native or a foreigner may come to buy provisions. Doubtlessly, as with the eternal bread which came from heaven, which, according to the prophets, *was formed in the centre of the earth*, God wanted to supply all nations of the world equally. Let everyone wise observe this joyfully because almighty God provided for us with paternal goodness, and arranged fully and nobly for the prosperity of the citizens. For anyone standing in the middle of the marketplace may turn his face to the east and examine the position of the churches, noting John, precursor of the Lord, to the east, Peter the apostle to the west, Werburgh the virgin to the north, and Michael the Archangel to the south. There is nothing truer than this verse: *Upon thy walls, O Jersualem, I have appointed watchmen* (Isa. 62:6). Nothing is sweeter than this evidence that God gave us such guardians: it is a sacred offering and a charming mystery. It comforts men's spirits and encourages contemplation.)[21]

Here biblical hermeneutics are skilfully deployed to justify the Neo-Platonic confidence that God is visible in the *universitas*. Lucian compares the marketplace to Christ, 'the eternal bread which came from heaven', who was born in Jerusalem, a city often described as being in the centre of the world (e.g. Ezek. 5:5 and Ps. 73:12). The centrality of the marketplace and of Jerusalem serve to demonstrate the universal availability of the Christian gospel, a tenet of Pauline ecclesiology which is fundamental to Lucian's description of Chester as a city open to all.[22] The analogy between Chester and Jerusalem is then developed as Lucian imagines someone standing in the middle of the marketplace, noticing the surrounding churches and recalling Isaiah's words. Lucian states that the homology should be both comforting and thought-provoking, traditional

outcomes of monastic contemplative practice, but like Isaiah's words, it
is also a hortatory warning: Chester, like Jerusalem, must remain a pious
Christian city.

Lucian's recent critics would not be slow to point out the distortions and
ironies latent in this passage. In reality, the crossroads and the marketplace
were not in the 'very centre of the city' and St Peter's was not to the west.
The layout of the streets was Roman and thus antedated the arrival of the
'eternal bread from heaven'. It is likely the right to sell and even buy in
the marketplace were restricted. Nonetheless, Lucian seems to be aware of
these problems and anticipates (or answers) such criticism in his gnomic
marginal comment 'caritati sic est, cauillationi aliquid deest', which probably means, loosely, 'this comes from love, not quibbling'.

However, to show that Lucian's representation of urban space is not
mimetic but involves the distortion of the topography of the city only gets
us so far. As geographers have recently begun to acknowledge, no mapping
can reproduce reality in its full complexity and each mapping is controlled
by the set of conventions and preconceptions which underlie it.[23] The
form of *De Laude Cestrie* was profoundly influence by classical rhetorical
handbooks, biblical hermeneutics, Neo-Platonic philosophy and monastic
models of psychology and inevitably bears their stamp. While much of *De
Laude Cestrie* accordingly focuses on teasing out spiritual lessons from
Chester's urban environment, the city also emerges as a lived-in space,
particularly in the two itineraries which this essay examines. While these
itineraries are no more or less literary constructs than other parts of the
text, they do enable us to see Lucian's spatial hermeneutic more clearly.

Itinerary I: The Individual and His City

Lucian describes the Sunday he decided to write the *De Laude Cestrie* in
vivid detail:

> Non excidit memorie, nec periit recordationi quod michi ante menses aliquot,
> ex duricia diuitum tribulanti, tripliciter in ciuitate trisillaba contulisti. Nam pro
> responso monasterii missus et curiam comitis aditurus, post missas in basi-
> lica Archangeli Michaelis explicitas, temporalis negocii certitudinem nactus,
> eciam uenerandi precursoris ecclesiam credidi uisitandam, quo potens meritis,
> exaudicione piissimus, Eterni Regis clementiam uotis omnium impetraret. Ede
> sacra egressus, cum in atrio paululum subsisterem et ex loci facie, quia puer
> ibi dudum literas didiceram, res humanas uersari et reuersari sciens, presentia
> preteritis compararem; tu cum de proximo transires et literate lucis dulcedinem
> dissimulationis tenebris tegere non ualeres, clericum probans et clarius agens,

salutacione oblata, alacriter accessisti, hilariter astitisti, amabiliter deduxisti. De sinu pectoris tui uenit quod honestatem refunderet, quod humilitatem saperet, quod gratiam redoleret. Fecunde unum debriat quod alteri de facili profluebat, quia plerumque quod nec ciuis attendit, peregrinus appendit. Quod unus uelut parum optulit, alter plurimum reputauit, quia nichil adeo demulcet animum, ut caste impensum caritatis obsequium.

Fateor eo die differenter ac uarie temporis tractus effluxit: castellum tedio, set ecclesia solatio fuit; in definicione negocii distulit me turgiditas et superbia secularium, set refouit honestas et amor domesticorum; et quicquid lesit aula principis, leniuit uberius atrium Precursoris. Ibi sapuit in gutture mentis quantum a se differant salum maris et sinus matris; in uno turbamur, in altero consolamur. Tempestas docet quid tranquillitas donet; quicquid inuexit asperum fremitus pelagi, mitigauit et fouit misericordia proximi.

(I have not forgotten that, some months ago, with the exacting rigour of your rich mind, you explained to me the three syllables of the city in three ways. Having been sent with the monastery's answer and about to visit the earl's residence, after hearing masses in the church of the Archangel Michael, and having obtained confidence to conduct my earthly business, I thought it also worth visiting the church of our venerable predecessor, where that virtuous and most piously devoted man can obtain the mercy of the eternal king for everyone who requests it. After I had left the holy church, when I briefly came to a stop in the precinct, because of its appearance, familiar since as a boy I had once learnt my letters there, I then compared present circumstances with those past, knowing human affairs to be fickle; you came over from nearby, and did not labour to conceal the sweetness of literary illumination with the darknesses of dissimulation, but, proving yourself to be a man of learning, by making things clearer, and having been greeted, you approached me eagerly, gladly stood by me, and amiably instructed me. From your breast came something which smacked of integrity, savoured of humility, and bore the odour of goodwill. What readily flows forth from one, completely intoxicates another, because often a stranger ponders what a citizen does not even consider. One person has often valued highly what another has offered as if it were little, because nothing soothes the spirit as much as an unexpectedly generous offering of affection made with integrity.

I must admit that time passed that day in a variety of ways: the castle was a nuisance, but the church was a consolation; the pride and pomposity of the age confounded me in the settlement of my business, but the integrity and affection of the community revived me; and whatever wounds the Earl's palace inflicted, the precinct of the Forerunner of God fully soothed. There the throat of my mind tasted how much the salt sea and maternal love can differ; we are buffetted by one, consoled by the other. A storm teaches what calm weather can grant; whatever the harsh roaring of the ocean inflicted, the mercy of my kin softened and soothed.)[24]

Lucian here describes walking from St Werburgh's Abbey to Chester Castle, and, nervous about his forthcoming business, dallying by attending Mass at St Michael's and visiting St John's. This was a roundabout route, which moved from within the city walls to without the walls, and from the ecclesiastical precincts of Chester's two main religious foundations, St John's and St Werburgh's, to an independent parish church to the secular space of the castle. Lucian gives us most information about his visits to St Michael's and St John's, and it is on these two churches we will focus.

St Michael's, or rather its dedicatee, is the subject of nearly 10,000 words of *De Laude Cestrie*, more text than is devoted to any other church. For Lucian, St Michael, St Michael's church and the South Gate with which it is associated command Cestrians' attention for one principal reason: they provide the entrance to heaven. As he says,

> In hac porta quasi stantes et statu glorie resplendentes benigni angeli ad nos clamant, dignanter uocant et feruidis ex caritate uisceribus ad secretum tante suauitatis inuitant

> (From this gate the benevolent angels, as if standing and rejoicing in their glorious status, call to us with great honour and out of the goodness of their hearts lovingly invite us to their haunt of great sweetness.)[25]

According to Henry Bradshaw, the 'mighty minster' of St Michael was destroyed in the great fire of 1180, so the building where Lucian heard Mass may have been built only recently.[26] The advowson of the new parish church, like the old *monasterium*, probably belonged to the Augustinian canons of Norton Priory, some thirteen miles north-east of Chester.[27] By visiting St Michael's to hear Mass therefore, Lucian was visiting a space with affiliations to neither St Werburgh's nor St John's. The presignifica-tions of St Michael's were therefore complex: it was one of the few parish churches in Chester not controlled by St John's or St Werburgh's and had been recently rebuilt, a testimony both to the havoc fire might cause in the city – even supposing St Werburgh's intercession[28] – and also to the resilience of the townspeople to such adversity. In *De Laude Cestrie*, as we saw, Lucian emphatically associates St Michael with the heavenly role of its patron. On the memorable day he describes, hearing Mass in the church gave him 'temporalis negocii certitudinem' ('the confidence to conduct [his] earthly business'). The recent history of the church, its spir-itual lesson to Cestrians, and its peculiar personal importance to Lucian this Sunday have almost nothing in common.

Lucian's description of the emotional impact of his visit to St John's is much fuller, and reveals the complex ways in which Lucian's spatial hermeneutic influences his conduct within the city. *De Laude Cestrie* praises St John's through a lengthy encomium to John the Baptist, who is associated with the East Gate. John is lauded as the man who announced Christ's birth to the world and thus first heralded the prospect of salvation. Lucian additionally honours St John's by first interpreting *Cestria*, 'cis tria' or 'threefold', to refer to Chester's 'literatum ... episcopum, liberalem archdiaconum, lucidum clerum' ('learned bishop, generous archdeacon and shining clergy'), thus placing the cathedral at the very centre of Chester's identity.[29] Lucian's praise of the canons accords well with what we know of the cordial relations between the monks and the canons in the late twelfth century evident, for example, in their agreement to preserve their respective burial privileges. The canons, like the monks, played a prominent role in Cestrian society, witnessing charters and every Sunday making a formal procession from the nearby *monasterium* of St Mary to St John's.[30] They remained, moreover, strongly associated with the bishop of Coventry, who like his archdeacon retained a residence within the precincts of the cathedral.[31] The church itself remained an architectural work-in-progress.

In his itinerary, Lucian describes himself visiting St John's to take advantage of the Baptist's particular power of intercession, a power which seems here, as in the spiritual topography of *De Laude Cestrie*, to derive from John's unique relationship with Christ. Yet the most seminal event that Sunday happens outside the church.

Lucian exits St John's to the precincts of the cathedral ('in atrio'), evidently a memorable space for Lucian since he is prompted to recall his boyhood education in the cathedral school. This recollection prompts a more general reverie on the relationship between the past and the present and on fate and fortune. These thoughts are interrupted when Lucian sees and greets a priest hitherto unknown to him. The priest's cordiality and intellectual generosity overwhelm Lucian, intoxicating him with a profound sense of collegiality and community and help him to forget his worries about his impending business at the castle. The liminal space of the precinct provides an opportunity to see and be seen. A layman approaches the priest and (Lucian does not explain why) begins to talk in a flattering way. Lucian's patron walks away. Two monks, standing nearby, see this behaviour and are powerfully affected. Lucian's joy originates from the appropriateness of his patron's actions, from finding a clerk who behaves wholly in accordance with scriptural and classical precedent. Lucian delights in the typological resonance of his behaviour, suggesting:

> Et fortasse non errat si quis dixerit quod, familiaritate contubernii, saporem hunc in uiscera editui sui, non arundo luti set amicus sponsi, Baptista transfudit. Qui,

suis temporibus, gaudium et gemitum terrenorum equa lance pensauit, et telas aranearum fauores et furores hominum reputauit. Qui preuenit suum Dominum per ordine humilitatis, ipse te instituit suum famulum ad semitam sanctitatis. Eius tu minister in domo, qui tibi magister in Domino.

(Perhaps one does not err if one says that, with the intimacy of comradeship, the Baptist (not the reed in the mud, but the friend of the bridegroom) seasoned the vitals of his priest with this flavour. In his time, John weighed the ups and downs of worldly people with an unbiased scale, and valued the fortunes and misfortunes of men as he would cobwebs. John, who anticipated the Lord in his humility, made you his servant on the path of holiness. You are his servant in the cathedral ['in domo']; he is your teacher in the Lord ['in domino'].)[32]

Lucian's patron, a secular cleric at St John's, behaves exactly as St John the Baptist himself did, their behaviour as close as the pun on *domo* and *domino*. Lucian finds in this homology the same harmony and proof of the coherence of the Christian *uniuersitas* that he is constantly showing his readers.

Lucian couches his emotional trajectory that day in a series of binaries: nuisance / consolation, pride and pomposity / integrity and affection, salt sea / maternal love. While these binaries undoubtedly echo the ancient preference for *otium* over *negotium*, the way in which Lucian develops the associations of the cathedral is unexpected. His tableau in the precinct casts the clerk as superior to the chatterbox layman and the lax monks. His description of his own emotional response attributes to the cathedral consolation and community, benefits more usually associated with the monastic life. Lucian's text reserves the right for places to be polyvalent.

Lucian revisits this seminal day later in *De Laude Cestrie*, at another key moment of transition:

Ago autem gratias omnipotenti Deo indultum michi tempus et diem, quo primum accepisse tuam merui nocionem. Spero enim ex dulcedine pectoris tui, facilius ferre fastidium fumi, qui ex mundanis ueniens ingrate solet intelligentium faucibus et oculis importari. Et utinam subeat memoriam tuam, qualiter per occasionem temporis uisenti michi basilicam uenerandi baptiste et domini precursoris, apte ac consequenter gustum prime sinceritatis optuleris. Nempe simul in atrio illo tunc conuenisse uisi sunt, et dies dominicus et diuinus locus et dignationis affectus. Hec uestri cordis et corporis uultum michi prius aperuerunt. Dies materiam, locus leticiam, occasio gratiam contulerunt. Ignotus stabam, set ignotus diu stare non poteram. Expressit innata benignitas claram in sui occursus hilaritate naturam. Accessisti, et humane salutatum ac deductum, retenta per gratiam Spiritus Sancti benedictionis memoria, dimisisti. Officium transiit, affectum continuit. Semel actum, semper est nouum. Hinc litera pandit, quod literatus impendit. Pro loco et tempore liberalitas claruit actionis tue. Quid

enim aliud faceret clericus habitator monaco extraneo, quem ad maiores impe-
rium pro causis et utilitatibus monasterii non leuitas et euagatio set necessitas
excussit et ratio.

(I thank the almighty God for the day he gave me, when I merited first to make
your acquaintance. For I, spreading my wares in front of worldly people, accustomed to be conveyed thanklessly before the maws and eyes of intelligent
beings, hope to imitate your innate aversion to windy praise. Let the occasion
of my visit to the church of the venerable Baptist, precursor of the Lord, when
you fittingly gave me a taste of your honesty, sink into your memory. It seems
a lordly day, a divine place, and fitting feeling all converged in those precincts
that day. The appearance of your body and true heart had already revealed
these things. The day brought the means, the place brought happiness, the
occasion brought goodwill ['graciam']. I was standing unrecognized, but I
could not stand unrecognized for long. Your innate kindness pronounced your
excellent upbringing in the cheerfulness of our meeting. You approached, and
humanely greeted and diverted, you allowed me to go on, I retaining through
the grace of the Holy Spirit a memory of the blessing. The obligation passed,
its influence lingered. Performed once, it is always fresh. Here my work
advertises what you, a learned man, did. Your generosity was evident in your
actions in that place and at that time. How else should a clerkly inhabitant act
towards an alien monk, whom not pleasure and waywardness but necessity
and prudence cast out into the empire of the mighty to advocate the causes
and needs of the monastery?)[33]

These reflections allow Lucian to begin discussing the proper relationship
between clerks and monks, before focusing on the appropriate internal
organisation of the monastery, which proves, like Chester, to be an appropriate microcosm for the Christian universe. Here the encounter is between
just Lucian and his patron. He emphasizes again his joy at his patron's
manners, but particularly their absolute appropriateness to a moment when
'a lordly day, a divine place, and a fitting feeling all converged'. This triad
echoes the opening words of Lucian's text – 'tempus et locus et rerum
lapsus sensato cuique tribuunt suadibilem, etiam sine literis, lectionem'
('the state of the times, the location of things and the occurence of events
offer persuasive, unwritten instruction to each intelligent being')[34] – and
thus emphasizes that this moment is an example of how God can engineer
conjunctions of circumstances which are conducive to spiritual learning.
The fitting behaviour of the clerkly 'habitator' towards the alien monk
stands as a practical example of the communal spirit which Lucian wants
to inculcate in the city as a whole. Lucian's itinerary is a powerful illustration of the joy an individual can draw from studying the world around him.
But it is also a testament to the capacity of space to be unpredictable, for

one space to affect an individual's emotions in unexpected ways and for profound events to occur in unusual locations like the *atrium* of St John's Cathedral.

Itinerary II: The Peripatetic Composition of De Laude Cestrie

One of the most remarkable features of the autograph manuscript of *De Laude Cestrie* is a series of marginal notes in the bottom margins of several pages of the text. These notes are in the hand which supplied the marginal apparatus for the rest of the text, a hand which conceivably belongs to Lucian.[35] They appear to record the composition or performance of portions of the text at Easter in 1195 or 1206:[36]

Guntramii regis die [fol. 89v]
Apud *Nouio*[. . .] Passio secundum Marcum [fol. 90r]
Armogasti die apud Neutonam [fol. 90v]
Passio Domini secundum Lucam. Breue uenit tunc a domno abbate ad
      Auliennum [fol. 91r][37]
In cena domini apud Elfstanessfeld ante seruicium [fol. 91v]
Has duas paginas ante altare benigni Petri [fol. 92r] (Figure 8)
Die sanctorum Donatiani et Rogatiani has tres paginas. Tunc monachi sancti
      Petri subdiurnabant [fol. 124v]

(On King Gunthrum's Day [fol. 89v]
At Novio[. . .]. The passion according to Mark [fol. 90r]
On Armogast's Day at Newton [fol. 90v]
The Passion according to Luke. A letter came from the lord abbot for Evelyn [?]
      [fol. 91r]
On Holy Thursday at Alstonefield before the service [fol. 91v]
These two pages in front of the altar of the blessed Peter [fol. 92r]
These three pages on the feast day of Saints Donatian and Rogation; the monks
      of St Peter's then stayed [fol. 124v].)[38]

The dating of these notes presents no problems. King Gunthrum's Day is March 28, the Passion according to St Mark is the gospel for Tuesday of Holy Week, St Armogast's Day is March 29, the Passion according to St Luke is the gospel for Wednesday of Holy Week, and *cena domini* is another name for Holy Thursday.[39] If, as seems fair, we take the notes to be in chronological sequence and take the notes on fols 89v and 90r as a pair, and the notes on fols 90v and 91r as another pair, then Easter Sunday in the year the notes were written must have fallen on 2 April, as it did in both 1195 and 1206.[40] The Easter Table at the beginning of *De Laude Cestrie* also begins in 1195 and it is therefore likely the marginal notes come from this year.[41] The feast day of St Donatian and Rogatian is May 24.

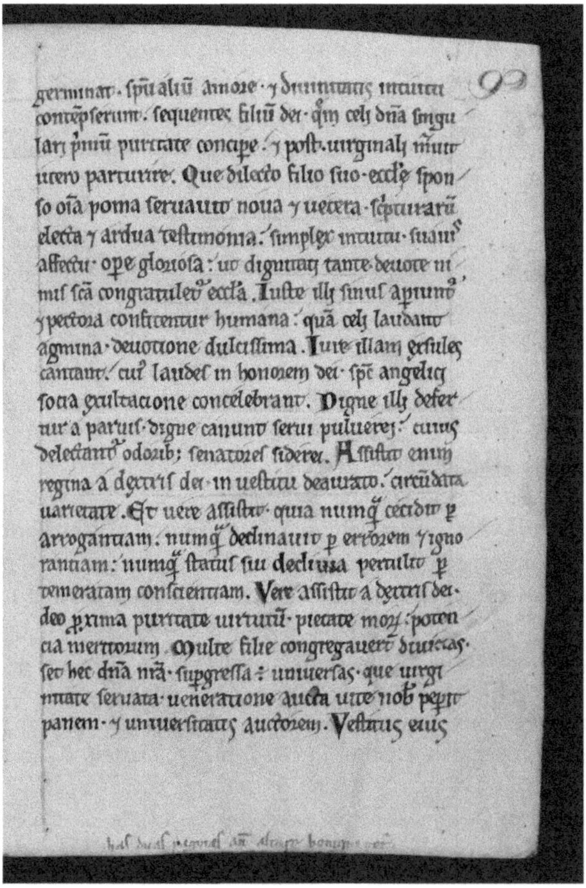

Figure 8. MS Bodley 672 (Lucian, *De Laude Cestrie*), fol. 92r, used by permission of the Bodleian Library.

The references to 'these pages' ('has duas paginas', 'has tres paginas') make it clear that the marginalia record some aspect of the history of *De Laude Cestrie*. It is possible that the notes refer to production of this, the fair copy of the text, though it is difficult to imagine Lucian carrying everything necessary to produce a manuscript from place to place.[42] This leaves us to consider whether they refer to the composition or performance of the text. Several factors make the former more likely: first and foremost, the portions of text described – several pages from the opening of

Lucian's section praising the Virgin Mary (fols 89v–92r) and a comparison of clerks and monks (fol. 124v) – would not readily make good Easter sermons; second, Lucian is unlikely to have preached 'before the altar' ('ante altare'); third, he is unlikely to have preached 'before the service' ('ante seruicium'). We may take it then that these marginal notes record the text's steady composition over Easter 1195.

It is possible to identify some of the places mentioned. Taylor suggested that 'Ventona' was Winchester and proceeded on the assumption that the other places must be within a day's ride of the city, tentatively identifying *Novio[magus]* as Chichester, 'Ankennus' as Alkington in Gloucestershire or Alkerton, near Stroud and 'Elfstanessfeld' as Stonefield in Oxfordshire. However, what Taylor took as 'uentona' almost certainly reads 'neutona' (i.e. Newton), undermining the basis of her deductions. In fact, 'Elfstannessfeld' can be identified securely as Alstonefield (Staffordshire), an appropriated church of the Cistercian abbey of Combermere which was dedicated to St Peter.[43] With this in mind, it seems likely that 'neutona' is Newton in Ashbourne (Derbyshire), presented to Combermere by Robert de Ferrers soon after the foundation of the abbey.[44] It is conceivable that 'Novio[. . .]' is a Latinised form of Newton. Lucian therefore spent Wednesday 29 March 1195 at Newton in Ashbourne, perhaps having arrived there the preceding night. On Holy Thursday, he was at the church of St Peter in Alstonefield, all the time working on *De Laude Cestrie*. By May, having composed another thirty folios, he wrote three more pages at his home monastery before some monks from a monastery dedicated to St Peter visited.[45]

This itinerary, while rather obscure in its details, is exceptionally intriguing. It seems to show Lucian at work composing *De Laude Cestrie* piecemeal, snatching time away from his other duties to write several more pages of text. It seems to show him composing mostly in estate churches, like Alstonefield. It seems to show him desiring to record the precise temporal and spatial inspiration for particular sections of the text, just as he pays so much attention to mapping his emotional trajectory in the first itinerary, as this essay discussed. Lucian's means of marking time and space are particularly interesting. Events are dated with reference to the *temporale* ('On Holy Thursday'), the *sanctorale* ('On King Guntrum's Day'), the liturgical lections ('The Passion according to Mark'), or personal events ('a letter came'). Lucian's references to the *sanctorale* are particularly obscure: while the SS Donatian and Rogation appear in several English litanies, King Guntrum (a Frank) and St Armogast (a Vandal) seem to have been obscure even on the continent. While most English calendars are empty for March 28 and 29, Lucian does seem to have been something of an expert in obscure continental saints to judge from his catalogue ninety virgins and the cities in which they were martyred.[46] Lucian recalls space with reference to the names of places ('Newton') and to particular churches ('before the altar of the blessed Peter').

Lucian's thoroughness in recording the way he composed this portion of the text is revealing in one final way, as conceivably the best clue to his own biography. Hitherto, it has been plausibly assumed that Lucian was a monk of St Werburgh's abbey; however, his presence on the Combermere estates of Alstonefield and Newton suggests that he may in fact have been a monk of Combermere.[47] There is no direct evidence that Lucian was a monk of St Werburgh's,[48] and several features of the text which suggest he was not. While there it is beyond the scope of this essay to discuss where Lucian was a monk, it is worth noting how much of what he writes about Chester betrays an outsider's gaze.[49]

Conclusion: Reading Space / Feeling Space

In *The Production of Space*, Henri Lefebvre questions:[50]

> Does it make sense to speak of a 'reading' of space? Yes and No. Yes, inasmuch as it is possible to envisage a 'reader' who deciphers and decodes and a 'speaker' who expresses himself by translating his progression into a discourse. But no, in that social space can in no way be compared to a blank page upon which a specific message has been inscribed (by whom?). Both natural and urban spaces are, if anything, 'over-inscribed': everything therein resembles a rough draft, jumbled and self-contradictory. Rather than signs, what one encounters here are directions – multifarious and overlapping instructions.

Contrast this with the very first sentence of Lucian's *De Laude Cestrie*:[51]

> Tempus et locus et rerum lapsus sensato cuique tribuunt suadibilem, etiam sine literis, lectionem.

> (The state of the times, the location of things and the occurrence of events offer persuasive, unwritten instruction to each intelligent being.)

Lucian avers here that space has a language that can be decoded, and can yield a reading ('lectionem') even though it is not a text ('etiam sine literis'). For Lucian, there was 'a blank page upon which a specific message has been inscribed', the blank page of the *universitas* on which God inscribed creation. Using a range of techniques from monastic psychology, biblical hermeneutics and Neo-Platonic philosophy, space could be read and its messages transmitted.

As recent critics have recognized, Lucian is often to be found imposing order on 'over-inscribed' city space, exaggerating particular features and downplaying others, to create a deceptively narrow picture of Chester which emphasizes its Christian heritage in defiance of its history and the ecclesiastical routine of the city at the expense of its social and commercial life. Yet for all this inevitable selectivity, space never quite behaves in the way Lucian's reading predicts. As the discussion of the two itineraries has shown, Lucian felt his thought to be anchored very precisely to his location in and around the city. Yet these thoughts could often run contrary to what he might expect from his earlier readings of places. It is not St John's church that proves revelatory on that given Sunday, but Lucian's personal encounter with his patron in the precincts. As with the London itineraries Strohm describes, the inspiration occurs 'as a result of a visitation, a conversation, a shared task, or other socially inflected exchange'.[52]

In *De Laude Cestrie*, then, space can be read, but its meanings are multiple and often unpredictable. Lucian's foregrounding of both his epiphanic encounter with his patron and the spatial and temporal circumstances of the composition of the section concerning the Virgin Mary, reveal his belief that an individual's experience of space could be idiosyncratic: Chester remained a *representational space* inspite of its pre-existing *spatial practice* and Lucian's *representation of space*.

Notes

[1] John T. Appleby (ed.), *Cronicon Richardi Divisensis De Tempore Regis Richardi Primi/the Chronicle of Richard of Devizes of the Time of Richard the First* (London, 1963), p. 66.

[2] *DLC*, fol. 12v.

[3] Ibid., fol. 11v.

[4] Ibid., fol. 113v.

[5] Ibid.

[6] Philip Morgan, 'Cheshire and Wales', in Huw Pryce and John Watts (eds), *Power and Identity in the Middle Ages: Essays in Memory of Rees Davies* (Oxford, 2007), p. 197.

[7] Henri Lefebvre, *The Production of Space*, Donald Nicholson-Smith (trans.) (Oxford, 1991), esp. 36–46.

[8] Paul Strohm, 'Three London itineraries: aestheic purity and the composing process', p. 15.

[9] J. A. Burrow, *The Poetry of Praise* (Cambridge, 2008), pp. 6–20.

[10] D. A. Russell (ed.), *Quintillian: The Orator's Education*, 5 vols (Cambridge, Mass., 2001), vol. 2, pp. 114–115 (3. 7. 27).

11 Marina Passalacqua (ed.), *Prisciani Caesariensis Opuscula, Sussidi Eruditi*, 40, 48, 2 vols (Rome, 1987-), vol. 1, p. 44, lls. 3–7. Translation mine.

12 For full discussion, see Laurent Pernot, *La Rhétorique De L'éloge Dans Le Monde Gréco-Romain*, Collection Des Études Augustiennes: Série Antiquité 137, 2 vols (Paris, 1993), vol. 1, pp. 178–215.

13 'You once nourished me during my first years, and when I was unable to distinguish between opposite propositions, you taught me with letters' ('me olim in primis annis aluisti et cum nequirem discernere inter opposita, literis instituisti'): DLC, fol. 87r. *Opposita*, which could mean 'opposite term or proposition' (Dictionary of Medieval Latin *opponere* 13), perhaps suggests Lucian learnt formal logic at St John's.

14 On the genre, see J. K. Hyde, 'Medieval descriptions of cities', *Bulletin of the John Rylands University Library of Manchester*, 48 (1966), 308–40; Carl Joachim Classen, *Die Stadt: im Spiegel der Descriptiones und Laudes Urbium in der antiken und mittelalterlichen Literatur bis zum Ende des zwölfen Jahrhunderts*, Beiträge zur Altertumswissenschaft Band 2 (Hildesheim, 1980).

15 James Cragie Robertson (ed.), *Materials for the History of Thomas Becket, Archbishop of Canterbury*, Rolls Series 67, 7 vols (London, 1875–1885), vol. iii, p. 2; translated by H. E. Butler, 'A description of London by William Fitz Stephen', in F. M. Stenton (ed.), *Norman London: An Essay*, Historical Association Leaflet 93/94 (London, 1934), 25–35.

16 See Antonia Gransden, 'Realistic observation in twelfth-century England', *Speculum*, 47 (1972), 29–51.

17 For analysis of Fitz Stephen's purpose, see John Scattergood, 'Misrepresenting the city: genre, intertextuality, and William Fitz Stephen's Description of London (*c.*1173)', in Julia Boffey and Pamela King (eds), *London and Europe in the Later Middle Ages*, Westfield Publications in Medieval Studies 9 (London, 1995), pp. 1–34; John M. Ganim, 'The experience of modernity in late medieval literature: urbanism, experience and rhetoric in some early modern descriptions of London', in, James J. Paxson, Lawrence M. Clopper and Sylvia Tomasch (eds), *The Performance of Middle English Culture: Essays on Chaucer and the Drama in Honor of Martin Stevens* (Cambridge, 1998), pp. 77–96; Catherine A. M. Clarke, *Literary Landscapes and the Idea of England, 700–1400* (Cambridge, 2006), pp. 92–8.

18 M. D. Chenu, *Nature, Man and Society in the Twelfth Century: Essays on New Theological Perspectives in the Latin West*, Jerome Taylor and Lester K. Little (trans.), Medieval Academy Reprints for Teaching 37 (Toronto, 1997), pp. 1–48. On the implications of the Neo-Platonic world view for urban history, see Keith D. Lilley, *City and Cosmos: the Medieval World in Urban Form* (London, 2009), esp. pp. 7–12 .

19 *De operibus sex dierum*, prol (*Patrologia latina* vol. CLXXIX, cols 1515–1516), trans. M. D. Chenu, *Nature, Man and Society*, p. 9.

20 *Notae super Johannem secundum magistrum Gilbertum* (London, Lambeth Palace Library MS 360, fol. 32rb), ed. and trans. M. D. Chenu, *Nature, Man and Society*, p. 40: 'De artificialibus quaeritur utrum a Deo facta sunt, sicut caseus,

et sotulares, et hujusmodi quae dicuntur esse opera hominis non Dei. – Omnia quidem a Deo facta sunt tanquam ab auctore . . . Unus ergo omnium auctor Deus, diversae tamen operandi rationes, et auctoritatis et ministerii, quorum alterum homo dicitur auctor, alterum uero Deus. Similiter usualiter dici solet de aliquo divite quod multa fecit edificia, quae eadem singulariter fecit et carpentarius.'

[21] *DLC*, fol. 13rv.

[22] See Faulkner, 'Place and Identity in Lucian's *De Laude Cestrie*' at *www.medievalchester.ac.uk* (accessed 30 September 2009). We might particularly compare Eph. 2:19 where Paul describes Christians as no longer 'strangers and foreigners' ('hospites et advenae') excluded from the Jewish temple, but 'fellow citizens with the saints and domestics of God' ('ciues sanctorum et domestici Dei'). See also Lucien Cerfaux, *The Church in the Theology of St Paul*, Geoffrey Webb and Adrian Walker (trans.), second edn (New York, 1959); Paul S. Minear, *Images of the church in the New Testament* (London, 1961); Robert Banks, *Paul's Idea of Community: The Early House Churches in their Historical Setting* (Exeter, 1980).

[23] J. B. Harley, 'Maps, Knowledge and Power', in Denis Cosgrove and Stephan Daniels (eds), *Iconography of Landscape: Essays on the symbolic representation, design and use of past environments* (Cambridge, 1988), pp. 277–312.

[24] *DLC*, fols 5v–6r.

[25] DLC, fol. 72r (unedited).

[26] Henry Bradshaw, *Life of St Werburge*, Catherine A. M. Clarke (ed.) at *www.medievalchester.ac.uk* (accessed 30 September 2009), ll. 1637–9.

[27] *VCH Ches*. 5. ii. p. 146; *Calendar of the Charter Rolls Preserved in the Public Record Office*, 6 vols (London, 1903–27), vol. 4, pp. 123–5 (Edward III's *inspeximus* and confirmation of Henry II's charter in favour of Norton Priory).

[28] For Lucian's description of St Werburgh's decisive intervention, see *DLC*, fol. 54v.

[29] *DLC*, fol. 8v.

[30] *VCH Ches*. 5. ii. 125–7; *DLC*, fols 111v–12r.

[31] *VCH Ches*. 5. ii. 125–6; James Tait (ed.), *The Chartulary or Register of the Abbey of St Werburgh Chester*, Chetham Society New Series 79+82, 2 vols (Manchester, 1920–3), vol. 2, pp. 299–302.

[32] *DLC*, fol. 6v.

[33] Ibid., fols. 115v–16r (unedited).

[34] *DLC*, fol. 2v.

[35] Palaeographically, it is not possible to be certain the text script and the informal script of the marginalia are identical. However, it is likely they are identical because the marginal hand makes substantial, apparently authorial, additions to the text proper, most spectacularly on fols 166v–7r.

[36] The marginalia have been printed and discussed by M. V. Taylor (ed.), *Extracts from the MS. Liber Luciani De laude Cestrie written about the year 1195 and now in the Bodleian Library, Oxford*, Record Society for the publication of original documents relating to Lancashire and Cheshire 64 (Chester, 1912), pp. 1–78, pp. 75–8. I differ from Taylor in several readings and in the interpretation of the notes. I would like to thank Jane Laughton and Alexander Rumble for their help in identifying the places mentioned in these notes.

[37] *Auliennum* is uncertain. Placing uncertain readings in square brackets, we might transcribe it *a[u/n][k/li]e[nnu/nti/omu/tin][m/n]*; *Auelinnum* may possibly be the personal name *Auelinum* (i.e. Evelyn). Alexander Rumble (personal communication) has suggested identifying it as Alkmonton, Derbyshire (*Alchementune* DB, *Alk(e)munton* 1243, *Aukmonton* 1629), in which case we should probably read *Aukeomunton*, expanding the common mark of abbreviation as -*nton*. Alkmonton belonged to William II, Lord Ferrers in the 1190s, who married a sister of Randulf, earl of Chester, in 1192 and whose grandfather and father, Robert II and William I, had presented the estate of Newton in Ashbourne to Combermere Abbey. The identification is therefore plausible, if not wholly acceptable palaeographically. For the Ferrers family, see *The Complete Peerage of England, Scotland, Ireland, Great Britain, and the United Kingdom, extant, extinct, or dormant by G. E. C.* New edn, 13 vols in 14 (London, 1910–1959), vol. 4, pp. 190–203. For Newton in Ashbourne, see *VCH Ches.* 3, p. 151.

[38] The reading *monachi* is very uncertain, and a further uncertainty about whether we should read *subdiurnabant* or *subdiurnabam* complicates the reconstruction of what Lucian meant. Though Taylor and Richard Sharpe (personal communication) would read *subdiurabam*, I am convinced the word ends **āt** and that we must read *subdiurnabant*. The word transcribed here as *monachi* consists of four minims with a superscript **o** after the second minim, and thus might be interpreted as *n°n*, *m°i*, *i°m*, *iiii°* etc. Neither *m°i*, a normal abbreviation for *modi* nor *iiii°*, Lucian's standard abbreviation for *quatro*, give good sense. Taylor read *monasterii*, but this does not give us a subject for *subdiurnabant*. Kathrin Korn, of the Dictionary of Medieval Latin, suggested (personal communication), reading *monachi* which gives good sense, and is adopted here. It should nonetheless be noted that the abbreviation *m°i* is nowhere else recorded as meaning *monachi* or *monasterii*. I would like to thank Hugh Doherty, Kathrin Korn, Ralph Hanna and Richard Sharpe for their help in transcribing this note.

[39] For the gospel lections, see *The Sarum Missal*, John Wickham Legg (ed.) (Oxford, 1916), pp. 99–108.

[40] It would also be possible to take the notes on fols 90rv as a pair, and those on fols 91v and 92r as a pair, implying that Easter Sunday fell on 3 April, as it did in 1149, 1211 and 1222. However, the correlation between the Easter Table and the notes suggests 1195 is the correct date.

[41] It should be noted that the traditional dating of *De Laude Cestrie* is problematized by Lucian's reference to two deceased priests, Andrew and Walter (*DLC*, fol. 27v), who apparently appear as witnesses to a charter usually dated *c.*1225: Wm. Ferguson Irvine, 'Notes on the history of St Mary's Nunnery, Chester', *Journal of the Architectural, Archaeological and Historic Society for the County and the City of Chester and North Wales*, New Series 13 (1907), 98–9.

[42] The manuscript is usually dated 1195 since the Easter table at the beginning of manuscript begin with this year, though Lucian seems to have continued to work on the manuscript for a number of years, at least until 1200. If, as I argue, the marginal notes refer to the text's composition in 1195 and the Easter table can be taken as evidence that the manuscript too was begun in 1195, then either Lucian

finished the second half of the text in less than a year, or began producing his fair copy with the composition of the text still ongoing.

[43] Hugh Malbank, second baron of Wich Malbank, presented the church when he founded Combermere in 1133. The foundation charter is printed by William Dugdale, *Monasticon Anglicanum*, 8 vols in 6 (reprinted Farnborough, 1970), vol. 5, pp. 323–4.

[44] *Calendar of the Charter Rolls Preserved in the Public Record Office*, 6 vols (London, 1903–1927), vol. 1, p. 428 and vol. 4, p. 204.

[45] I have not been able identify which monastery of St Peter is meant.

[46] *DLC*, fols. 49r–50r (unedited).

[47] Jane Laughton has suggested that Lucian may have been visited Alstonefield while touring St Werburgh's estates around Weston-on-Trent. This is certainly possible, but there is no direct evidence in favour of this conjecture.

[48] The only evidence which Taylor cites is Lucian's statement that he is 'uirginee . . . regionis alumpnus' ('a foster-son of the county of the virgin' *DLC*, fol. 53v (inedited): Taylor, *Liber Luciani*, p. 10, n. 2.

[49] Lucian's outsider's gaze seems to go beyond the detachment conventional in urban encomia. I hope to make the case that Lucian was a monk of Combermere in a future publication.

[50] Lefebvre, *Production of Space*, p. 142.

[51] *DLC*, fol. 2v.

[52] Strohm, 'Three London itineraries', p. 5.

6

'3e beoð þe ancren of Englond . . . as þah 3e weren an cuuent of . . . Chester': Liminal Spaces and the Anchoritic life in Medieval Chester

LIZ HERBERT MCAVOY

In her account of mapped views of the world, commentator Irit Rogoff argues that such views are, in fact, merely 'meditations on issues of boundaries and definitions and the interactions between the two'.[1] In her study, Rogoff demonstrates how geographical narratives, which aim to pin down the apparent specificity of place, help to shape our own concepts of representation and meaning. For Rogoff, the geography of the land is ultimately the geography of spatial construction which, in turn, becomes a geography of the mind itself.[2] This is a concept which has also recently been explored in the context of medieval literature by Christopher Cannon who, drawing upon the Hegelian notion of thinking as mediated through objective materialities, suggests that 'the unique object assembles a singular combination of ideas'.[3] Such ideas, which are formulated out of material realities surrounding the thinker within any given culture therefore find their way from the landscape and the material world around us, into our cognitive processes themselves, rematerializing in the ways in which we envisage our world, its societies and what they signify.

Such cognitive processes, as Cannon has also argued, are clearly at play in the early thirteenth-century guidance text written specifically for female anchorites, *Ancrene Wisse*, which provides a primary focus for his discussion. However, whilst Cannon's interest lies in the ways in which the

English landscape and contemporary politics are brought to bear upon the text's imagistic patterns and hermeneutics, he overlooks the anonymous author's more specific allusions to geographic location found in a revised version of the original text extant in CCC MS 402.[4] Known as the 'Corpus revision', Part 4 of this revised text contains an authorial interpolation in which the writer compares his expanding audience of female anchorites to religious communities living elsewhere:

> For euch is wiðward oþer in an manere of liflade, as þah 3e weren an cuuent of Lundene ant Oxnefort, of Schreobsburi oðer of Chester. . .

> (For you are all turned toward one another in a single manner of living, as though you were a single community of London and Oxford, of Shrewsbury or of Chester. . .)[5]

Whilst the author's use of the binary 'London and Oxford' is readily explained, their being paradigmatic hubs of learning and religious activity throughout the period,[6] his use of the Marcher towns of Shrewsbury and Chester is not so obvious. This begs the questions as to why the author attempts to map his text and audience in this specific way and what it suggests about the concomitant mapping of minds, if we return to Rogoff's configuration of the effects of geographical narratives upon culture. These, then, are the primary questions I would like to address in this essay within the context of the anchoritic traditions of medieval Chester and its environs.

It is now generally accepted that *Ancrene Wisse* was composed in the late 1220s or early 1230s at the request of three female anchorites who felt in need of further guidance.[7] By the time the author came to revise his text some five years later, this small community had burgeoned from three to 'twenti nuðe oðer ma' ('twenty, now, or more'),[8] virtually a seven-fold increase. Even by the standards documented by Ann Warren in her *Anchorites and their Patrons* which reveal a two-and-a-half-fold increase in female anchorites in England during the thirteenth century,[9] such a sevenfold increase constitutes an extraordinary growth in this particular expression of female spirituality. The place of this text's production and audience was the mid to northern borderland between England and Wales – the Welsh Marches – and at least four of the extant manuscript versions appear to have originated at some point along this axis, with one having its provenance in south Cheshire itself.[10] These Marches, always a hybrid and plastic space during the wars of conquest in the twelfth and thirteenth centuries,[11] formed an area which the *Ancrene Wisse* author himself identifies in the Corpus revision as 'Englondes ende' ('the end of England') towards which 'ower cuuent biginneð to spreaden' ('your community is beginning to spread').[12] Female anchoritism then, is presented in this revised text as organic and fluid, pouring its influence over the contested land towards the similarly organic and fluid border itself.

In the thirteenth century, of course, the region now entitled 'Wales' was deemed to be a dark, uncivilized and irreligious place, the construction of which within popular English imagination tipped over into threatening unknowability. The twelfth-century *Gesta Stephani* configures it as a land 'Angliae proxima uicinitate contermina' ('immediately bordering on England'), going on to bestialize its inhabitants as, amongst other things, 'hominum nutrix bestialium [. . .] fide semper et locis instabilium' ('men of an animal type . . . unstable in their faith and abodes').[13] In his letters, John of Salisbury writes of the Welsh as a godless race which 'aspernatur verbum vitae' ('despises the Word of Life').[14] In these twelfth-century texts at least, the godlessness and inherent instability associated with the Welsh people renders them entirely resistant to the 'civilizing' forces of the Anglo-Normans which might offer them their only chance of reaching full humanity.

Responding to this type of discourse in his study of the monstrous discourses attached to the Welsh borderlands, Jeffrey Jerome Cohen has identified the region as having constituted 'a difficult middle' and 'a complex web of competing gravitational forces', a liminal region where typically 'self-declared advanced culture imagines it discovers a more primitive realm'.[15] Such a hybrid identity therefore left the region and its inhabitants particularly vulnerable to what Rogoff has termed a 'political rhetoric which has served to harden [the arbitrariness of borders] into immutable facts'.[16] Read within this context then, the extraordinary burgeoning of an anchoritic community along the problematic fault line of the Marches as documented by an author fully imbued with the tenets of Parisian scholasticism and a new ecclesiastical pastoral mission, would certainly bear this out.[17] In his allusion to a growing anchoritic audience, the author is mapping out a physical 'territory-of-occupation', one inevitably productive of a 'geography of the mind' or, in other words, a navigable spiritual mindset based upon tangible and physically immediate circumstances. Dotted along these volatile borderlands, such spiritually elite women, who were frequently drawn from the ruling classes, could play a vital role in literally *anchoring* civilized, Christian – and English – values to a terrain with very little stability and one which, more often than not, was likely at any time to explode into a cycle of male-orchestrated insurrection and retaliation. In this sense, the *Ancrene Wisse* author's reminder to his audience at the same point in the text, '3e beoð þe ancren of Englond' ('you are the anchorites of England'),[18] resounds with what can be read not merely as nationalistic pride but even as propaganda – especially in his insistence on the absolute homogeneity of his anchoritic audience as *cuuent*, in spite of their geographical separation from one another. In his emphasis upon the Englishness of his anchorites then, the author imbues them with a strong sense of both religious *and* national identity which co-mingle in a body – and bodies – which stand in for the stability of English borders and English religiosity. And of course, the heavily-policed body of the female anchorite is itself ideally suited to the production of a rhetoric which will harden such border discourses into 'immutable facts' and talk a permeable and shifting geography into some kind of coherent stability.

Another borderlands writer to make good political use of the figure of the anchorite is the frequently identity-confused Gerald of Wales who, more than a century previously, in his *Itinerarium Kambriae* (*Journey through Wales*) had articulated the difficulties of occupying a grey-zone of multiple identities.[19] Gerald, like so many of the primary Marcher figures, was of mixed Welsh and Anglo-Norman parentage and quite evidently caught between both nationalistic rhetoric and discourses of alienation.[20] In his *Itinerarium* Gerald recounts his kaleidoscopic journey through Wales to Chester and back down through the Welsh Marches, a journey undertaken with Archbishop Baldwin in order to win men to 'take the Cross', that is to say for the Crusades. Medieval Chester was a place which, in the words of Cohen, 'incarnates the fluctuating Welsh borderlands' because of its being built, at least according to Gerald's account, upon a river whose banks and fords are perennially unstable,[21] sometimes moving towards Wales, sometimes towards England, depending upon which nation is destined to win the next skirmish.[22] As a liminal, hybrid, out-on-a-limb town, therefore, it is probably inevitable that Gerald chooses to populate Chester with strange, hybrid bodies which serve further to destabilize any sense of this being a solidly English settlement – or solid entity at all. There is, for example, a group of monkey-like dogs who are fatally misunderstood by the town's population and are wrongly destroyed;[23] similarly, there is a congenitally handless woman, an expert seamstress whose legs and feet have adopted the tasks normally allocated to the hands.[24] Far from being depicted in a negative light, however, these inhabitants are a source of wonder, intrinsic to the sense of 'otherness' which Chester embodies for Gerald, but also illustrative of the power of Archbishop Baldwin to win the population over to 'the Cross'. Thus, with its unstable geographical location, along with its unpredictable inhabitants who frequently tended towards the monstrous and caught as they are within the interstices between two competing cultures, the town of Chester therefore called out for an injection of stability from Gerald's partisan pen. No wonder, therefore, that it is to the ideologically and physically stable figure of the anchorite to whom Gerald turns for such a stabilizing discourse. But it is not just any old anchorite: according to Gerald, King Harold himself of England was reputedly one of the first recorded anchorites in the city, having escaped the carnage at Hastings and fled to Chester, taking up residency as a recluse in the cemetery of St John the Baptist's church just outside the city walls.[25] Whatever the origins of this story – and there is no evidence whatsoever to support it – this church does appear to have housed male anchorites in a number of locations in its cemetery throughout the period, at least two of whom were buried *in situ*.[26]

A second Chester anchorite whom Gerald invokes in his text is the Holy Roman Emperor, Henry V, who, supposedly having abandoned Mathilda, his wife (also the mother of England's Henry II), withdrew to Chester to live out a life as a recluse named Godescall.[27] Both monarchs of course, had been closely bound up in the political crises of conquest and continuity which beset the period and their supposed anchoritic vocations and interment at Chester provides Gerald and his audience with a rhetoric not just of elite religiosity, but also of stability and historical continuity as a new order took hold.

Chester, as a particularly elusive 'interspace',[28] between England, Wales and Ireland, is identified as such by a third borderlands writer, a monk of St Werburgh's monastery in Chester, known to us only as Lucian. The text in question is his *De Laude Cestrie,* a lively encomium dedicated to the town and its peoples and written at some stage in the 1190s.[29] In this text, as we might expect, Lucian makes clear those same widely-held cultural attitudes towards the Welsh which we saw articulated in the writing of John of Salisbury. For example, he laments that his much beloved Chester 'collimitetur lividis hostibus' ('is bordered upon by spiteful enemies'),[30] who, because of their inherently bellicose nature, have been left only 'angularem angustiam' ('a narrow corner of land') on which to live.[31] Elsewhere however, Lucian, like Gerald during the same period, destabilizes his own discourse on this subject, recognizing about his fellow Cestrians, 'Britonibus ex uno latere confines, et per longam transfusionem morum, maxima parte consimiles' ('having a common border with the Welsh on one side and, through the long admixture of customs, [they are] similar to a great degree').[32] He also depicts the cordial trade-links between

north Wales and Chester upon which the town is, in part, dependent again
pointing towards a fissure between those official narratives of otherness
and separation between the English and the Welsh with which he has been
engaging and the type of discrete and separate regional coherence which
his text attempts to promote overall. As he later asserts, Chester can best
be defined as 'Hibernis receptoria, Britannis vicina, Anglorum summin-
istratur annonam' ('harbour of the Irish, neighbour of the Welsh [and]
afforded the provisions of the English').[33] In effect, the town *was* a quasi-
autonomous space full of free citizens, a place which, as Lucian explains,

> quadam a ceteris Anglis privilegii distinctione sit libera, et per indulgentias
> regum atque excellentias comitum magis in cetu populi gladium principis quam
> coronam regni consuevit attendere.
>
> (by a certain distinction of privilege . . . is freed from certain English customs,
> and through the indulgence of kings and the excellencies of its earls the popular
> assembly is more accustomed to attend the sword of the earl rather than the
> crown of the king.)[34]

If, as Henri Lefebvre has argued, space is created by means of those social
practices which are enacted within it, as well as by the meanings and
implications attached to those practices,[35] then Chester was clearly a space
spinning away from the rest of England because of its marginal geographic
location and the relative emancipation from feudal control which it had
begun to enjoy. Indeed, this reading of medieval Chester and its environs is corroborated by James A. Alexander who, in his biography of Earl
Ranulf III of Chester (to whom I will return later) claims: 'Whatever one
calls Cheshire, it was not a normal English county', adding, moreover,
that within the affairs of this quasi-independent region, 'kings of England
did not apparently think it politic to interfere.'[36] Quite evidently aware of
this movement towards independence and the celebration of difference,
Lucian frequently depicts Chester in terms of a hybrid, feminine otherness,
free-floating, ethereal, an ambiguous maternal body feeding her citizens
and neighbours with her teats ('ubera'),[37] a woman who is both 'Mater
et Domina' ('Mother and Mistress')[38] and whose four gates ('portas quattuor') correspond to the four winds ('ventis quattuor').[39] Although such
allusions constitute generically recognizable literary *topoi*, nevertheless
Lucian's treatment of them is offered weight, momentum and singularity
by the fact that the town is built upon an unstable tidal river where nothing
ever remains as it first appears:

> Aliquis delicates aut durus, nesciens naturam maris, credere fortasse contemp-
> neret, si non orbis astrueret, oculus comprobaret.

(Someone frivolous or uncouth, not knowing the nature of the sea, may perhaps disdain to believe what the eye confirms.)[40]

Lucian exploits the city's inherent elusiveness to the full, configuring it in terms governed by powerfully feminine aesthetics:

Habet preterea nostra Cestria ex Dei munere, ditantem atque decorantem amnem secus urbis muros pulchrum atque piscosum [. . .] Preterea reumate cotidiano non cessat eam revisere maris patentissima plenitude, quam apertis et opertis latissimis harenarum campis, indesinenter grate vel ingrate aliquid mittere vel mutauare consuevit, et suo accessu vel recessu afferre quippiam vel auferre.

(God has given our Chester an enriching and beautifying river which follows the line of the city walls and teams beautifully with fish . . . The daily tide does not cease to render a very generous bounty from the sea, which from both known and hidden ports grants or loans things both pleasant and unpleasant and by its ebb and flow brings things forth and takes them away.)[41]

For Lucian, the river's softly undulating curves draw the city towards it and its boundaries meld themselves to its fecund, unstable and shifting contours, adding to the sense of feminine unfixedness and instability. Like the mother-woman too, the river is presented as the harbinger of both life and death, 'nunc existens aqua, nunc arida' ('one moment water, the next dry land')[42] and for those fishermen who once greedily attempted to over-drain her to appropriate her maternal productivity, 'dum fretum exhaurire volunt, fluctibus absorti sunt' ('when they wanted to drain it further, they were engulfed in waves').[43] If, as Irit Rogoff has asserted, 'female bodies as sites of geographical ambivalence . . . provide a possibility for critically thinking through official narratives . . . of cultural belonging',[44] in Lucian's text a female-bodied river gives undulating form to an ethereally feminized Chester in order to work through, in part, the official narrative of its being a somewhat anomalous frontier town situated on the liminal threshold of three unsettled nations in a time of turbulent warfare.

Such a claim is further supported by the fact that Lucian, as we might expect within a text of this type, draws copiously upon the patron saint of his own monastery, Saint Werburgh, reshaping the ontology of her body to render it synonymous with Chester itself, this time as its primary figure of protection. For Lucian, she may be a member of the 'weak sex' ('infirmo sexu'), but she is also:

firmissimam sanctitate, laudabiliter et letissime providit ex suo munere, que puellari virtute et preclara virginitate refulgens, civem tuendo, civitatem tenendo contra adversa omnia, suis sufficiat meritis incolas obumbrare. Nam regis filia et sponsa regis regionem secundum nomen suum tuetur ab emulis, quia convirginalis Virginis Matris votis suis dulciter inclinat viscera Salvatoris. Et ideo facile tuetur urbem quia sponsum habit orbis auctorem. Cui nihil arduum vel difficile, salvam et incolumem gloriosis precibus asserrare, et supplicem familiam gregis sui et humilem fidem simplicis populi. Quod si pravitas nostra provocat ulcionem ad prima flagella penitentibus nobis, sanctitas illius avertet sentenciam iudicis.

(most firm in her sanctity, gleaming with maidenly virtue and preeminent virginity, to protect the city, to support the population and to suffice to defend the inhabitants by her merits against all hostilities. For the daughter of a king and the bride of a king protects the region from rivals according to her name, because the fellow virgin of the Virgin Mother sweetly bends his Saviour's flesh to her intercessions. And therefore she easily protects the city because she has as a husband the creator of the world. To her to protect this city, the suppliant household of her flock and the honest faith of the ordinary people safe and unharmed with glorious prayers, is not at all arduous or difficult. For, if our depravity provokes retribution, her sanctity averts the judge's sentence before the first lashes against our sins.)[45]

Like Lucian's beloved city, Werburgh's body is a site of ambivalence: it is weak, vulnerable and unstable in its femininity but yet it is in possession of a sacred seal which perpetually re-inforces its intactness and thus serves to stabilize it. Such sealed stability is able then to be superimposed upon the town itself to render it similarly inviolable. Countering and supplanting the discourses of militarism, aggression and incursion which elsewhere punctuate Lucian's text and thus acting as antidote to the 'depravity' of humanity, Werburgh's body functions as a representational strategy in the text which mobilizes both her gender and sexual status to establish what Rogoff has termed 'a new visual language anchored at the level of the body – for the dominant ideology'.[46] Whilst this 'dominant ideology' in Lucian's text is essentially a male, monastic one, nevertheless within his 'visual language', Werburgh's body takes centre stage, embracing the town with hands and feet which reach out to the city's 'guardian churches': St Peter's at the west gate, St John's at the east gate, and St Michael's at the south gate. As such, she undergoes the same startling transformation as does the protagonist in that most lyrical of texts written specifically for a female anchoritic audience and closely associated with *Ancrene Wisse,* the poem known as *Þe wohunge of ure Lauerd* (*The Wooing of Our Lord*).[47] Here, at the culmination of this poem, the female anchorite cries out to Christ, uniting with him synecdochally as crucified body and merging with her cell as animated cross:

Mi bodi henge with thi bodi neiled o rode, spered querfaste with inne fowr wahes. And henge I wile with the and neauer mare of mi rode cume tilt h[at] I deie [. . .] A Iesu, swa swet hit is with the to henge, forhwen th[at] iseo o the th[at] henges me biside, the muchele swetnesse of the reaues me fele of pine.

(My body hangs with your body nailed to the cross, enclosed on all sides within four walls, and I will hang with you and never again come off my cross until I die [. . .] Oh Jesus, it is so sweet to hang with you, for when I see you hanging beside me, your great sweetness totally frees me from pain.)[48]

In Lucian's text, there is a similar conflation of woman, enclosure and salvation: Werburgh's body as symbol of the city is mapped onto the 'cross' of its streets, anchoring it not only to the land – but also to God himself:

Habet etiam plateas duas equilineas et excellentes in modum bendicte crucis, per transversum sibi obvias et se transeuntes, que deinceps fiant quattuor ex duabus, capita sua consummantes in quattuor portis, mistice ostendens atque magnifice, magni Regis inhabitantem graciam se habere.

(Chester also has two excellent, equally straight streets in the manner of the blessed cross, by means of their intersection exposed to and crossing each other, which thereafter become four from two, their ends finishing at the four gates, secretly and marvellously showing themselves to have the inherent grace of the great King.)[49]

In view of Lucian's arresting use of feminine imagery and feminized bodies to configure – perhaps somewhat paradoxically – both instability and stability in his writing, it is of particular interest to learn that soon after the production of his text, the records begin to reveal other enclosed female bodies housed within the town and its immediate vicinity. The rapid appearance of a number of female anchorites during the course of the next hundred years would, I argue, not only serve a similar purpose within their local communities as anchoring and stabilizing mechanisms but also introduce the same type of purifying element alluded to by Lucian in his contrasting of Werburgh's sanctity with the 'depravity' of ordinary humanity quoted above. Moreover, whereas all recorded male anchorites connected to Chester lived outside the city walls (at St John's; on the Isle of Chester; on Hilbre Island), those anchorites recorded as having been attached to churches *inside* the city walls were all female. BL Harley MS 2162, for example, records that Cecelia, maidservant of the female anchorite attached to St Chad's church in the town, was involved in a quit-claim lawsuit in the year 1300.[50] Other female anchorites of the city seem to have been imbued with an important enough status to have attracted the attention of both noble and royal patrons during the late thirteenth century. In 1284, for example, Queen Eleanor gifted the sum of £6 3s. ½d for building a home and a chapel for the female recluse of St Martin's Church within the city walls, as well as contributing towards her maintenance: 'ad quamdam capellam et quamdam domum ad opus Recluse ecclesie sancti Martini Cestrie' ('for a certain chapel and residence [and] for the works of the recluse of Saint Martin's church, Chester').[51] This again is something certainly worthy of note since, as Warren's findings clearly demonstrate, royal support for anchorites throughout the rest of England appeared to wane rapidly upon the accession of Eleanor's husband, Edward I, in 1274.[52] We must therefore conclude that those recluses recorded as having been supported by Edward and Queen Eleanor were more than ordinarily important to them. Edward of course, was also Earl of Chester and both he and the queen, who had also accrued considerable lands in Cheshire,[53] seem to have had a particular loyalty to those anchorites who lay in the earldom.

In 1280, Edward is recorded as having bestowed 2 marks upon the recluse of St James's church at Christleton, a small village just outside Chester itself,[54] much of whose lands had been in the possession of the Chester nunnery since 1160 when one Mathilda de Roges brought them with her upon taking the veil.[55] According to Lucian, Christleton was known as the 'Village of Christ' because it lay directly to the east of Chester and, lying between the roads to the Old Ford (Aldford) to the south and the sinister Valley of Demons (Hoole) to the north. In Lucian's estimation, the road to Christleton was therefore the only road to be taken by the traveller who wished to remain safe from the dangers which lay on the roads to either side:

[I]ntendat Cestrie habitator, exeunti portam orientalem qualiter ei trinus viarum trames aperitur [. . .] Nam progressus paululum a civitate si directus incedit, statim a fronte venientem locus explicit, quem nominant Villam Christi.

(The inhabitant of Chester remembers how, exiting the east gate, a threefold branch of streets is revealed to him, and . . . having progressed a short distance from the city, if he continues as directed [there is], at once a place in front, which they call the Village of Christ, will relieve the journeyer.)[56]

Attached umbilical-cord-like to the town of Chester which, as mentioned, Lucian in the same breath has characterized as a feeding mother, for this writer Christleton and its church form part of a sacred female geography which can 'relieve the journeyer'. This journeyer, after all, is not simply the physical traveller but the spiritual pilgrim too and the presence of a documented female anchorite supported by the king himself in this Village of Christ less than ninety years after Lucian was writing, would attest to the continued importance of the sacred female body to Chester, its supporters and associated communities. Thus, in 1283 three years after offering support to the Christleton anchorite, we find Edward I also offering simple protection for two years to Emma de Le 'inclusa de medio Wychio' (recluse at Middlewich), a village again directly to the east of Chester, this time by some twenty miles.[57] Some years earlier, in 1274, he had similarly offered support to two others, one at Macclesfield[58] and the other at Frodsham, a village ten miles from Chester.[59] Edward's gift of a penny a day to this latter anchorite named Winmark, from 1274 until she died in 1278, suggests she was an anchorite of particular renown since her original sustenance had formerly been established 'for life' by the powerful Marcher lord, Ranulf III of Chester, some time before his death in 1232. At some stage in the intervening period, however, the payment had evidently fallen into arrears. Edward now ordered not only that the arrears be made up in full but that Winmark should be paid the said amount for the remainder of her life. The king clearly felt an enhanced sense of responsibility to maintain Winmark in the manner to which she had become accustomed during the reign of his father; indeed, for Winmark's former patron, Ranulf III, the amount of 1d a day for life which *he* had originally pledged had been a hugely generous gift, one which matched royal rates for anchoritic support and which, in fact, constituted the most expensive single benefaction of his life.[60] We can then, only conclude that Winmark must also have been an especially important figure for Ranulf, for Henry III, for Edward I and for the wider community. Interestingly too, the very name Winmark, with its Anglo-Saxon echoes of purity and borders (*win* and *mearc*) connotes much of what I have been arguing here. As an idealized figure of purity and bodily containment, she no doubt served to reify the same type of elite spirituality which Lucian wished to present as so characteristic of the region. Like Werburgh too, the anchorite's closing and sealing of her own female bodily borders helped to solidify and stabilize the shifting boundaries between pure and impure, pious and impious, same and other and, in so doing, consolidate the position and identity of all who came into contact with her in an otherwise unpredictable physical and spiritual geography.

   The importance of the figure of the female anchorite within border politics however, was not restricted to Chester and its environs. The thirteenth and fourteenth centuries saw a veritable explosion of activity all along the fault line between England and Wales which, I argue, became intrinsic to the identity – self-hood, even – of the region during the period. Here I concur entirely with Cannon in his assertion regarding *Ancrene Wisse* and associated texts that,

> the idea of the self in [these] texts borrows the materiality of exterior objects in order to fashion an interiority that is a made thing.[61]

If, therefore, as Rogoff argues, 'The body which marks the soil gives evidence of the human power executed in the land,'[62] and if the meanings attributed to that marked soil conversely serve to forge an interior 'self', then the *Ancrene Wisse* author's instruction to his borderland anchorites 'þet meast grið is among, meast annesse' ('that most peace is among, most unity')[63] that they should 'schrapien euche dei þe eorðe up of hare put þet ha schulen rotien in' ('each day scrape up the earth of their graves in which they will rot')[64] takes on a new, politicized resonance as a behest to mark the unstable and contested soil with her own, sacred body in order to assert the power it too executes in the land. In the liminal and shifting soil of Chester and the Welsh Marches, an anchoritic impulse for women was engendered which spread rapidly throughout England, offering individual women, many of whom hailed from the ruling classes, a stake in consolidating the discourses of nationhood and civilized Christian values which were so central to the borderland conflicts of the area. Little wonder then that *Ancrene Wisse* and *De Laude Cestrie*, both in their ways urgent, hyperbolized texts, should have emerged from within the hybrid maelstrom of the Welsh-English borderland geography and culture.

Notes

[1]   Irit Rogoff, *Terra Infirma: Geography's Visual Culture* (London and New York, 2000), p. 98.
[2]   Ibid., p. 96.
[3]   Christopher Cannon, *The Grounds of English Literature* (Oxford, 2004), p. 9. Here Cannon draws upon Hegel's *Philosophy of Right* in which Hegel asserts that the 'universe' of the mind is simultaneously the 'universe' of nature, arguing: 'the content of what is thought receives, indeed, the form of something existing, but this existence is occasioned by our activity and by it established. These distinctions of theoretical and practical are inseparable; they are one and the same; and in every activity, whether of thought or will, both these elements are found.' See G. W. F. Hegel, *Philosophy of Right*, S. W. Hyde (trans.) (Kitchener, 2001), pp. 29–30.
[4]   This text has recently been edited by Bella Millet as *Ancrene Wisse: A Corrected Edition of the Text in Cambridge, Corpus Christi College, MS 402 with Variants from Other Manuscripts*, 2 vols EETS OS 325 (Oxford, 2005). All quotations are

from this edition. Unless otherwise stated, translations of the Middle English are taken from *Anchoritic Spirituality*, Anne Savage and Nicholas Watson (eds and trans) (Mawah, 1991), references to which appear in parenthesis after the Middle English citation.

⁵ *Ancrene Wisse*, pp. 96–7 (p. 141). Here I have altered Savage and Watson's translation of *cuuvent* as 'convent' to 'community' in the light of my argument in this essay. In this I concur with Bella Millett's reading of this passage in '"He speaks to Me as if I was a public meeting": Rhetoric and Audience in the *Ancrene Wisse* Group', in *Rhetoric of the Anchorhold: Place, Space and Body in the Discourses of Enclosure*, Liz Herbert McAvoy (ed.) (Cardiff, 2005), pp. 50–65, pp. 54–5.

⁶ On medieval London see, for example, Caroline M. Barron, *London in the Middle Ages: Government and People 1200–1500* (Oxford, 2000), esp. pp. 302–7. For a useful history of the city of Oxford, see Ruth Fasnacht, *A History of the City of Oxford* (Oxford, 1954).

⁷ On the debate surrounding the dating of this text, see Bella Millett, *Annotated Bibliographies of Old and Middle English Literature: Ancrene Wisse, the Katherine Group and the Wooing Group* (Cambridge, 2006), esp. p. 12. Here Millett refers to 1230 as an 'anchor date' for the *terminus ante quem* of the original version, and a *terminus a quo* for the revised version of the text.

⁸ *Ancrene Wisse*, p. 96.

⁹ Ann K. Warren, *Anchorites and their Patrons in Medieval England* (Berkley, 1986), p. 38.

¹⁰ Millett, *Annotated Bibliographies*, pp. 19–20. The Cheshire version is extant in BL MS Cotton Titus D.xviii, and has been adapted sporadically for a male audience (Millett, *Annotated Bibliographies*, p. 53). I am grateful to Ralph Hanna for pointing this out to me.

¹¹ For a detailed history of the Welsh Marches see, for example, Gerald Davies, *Lordship and Society in the March of Wales* (Oxford, 1987).

¹² *Ancrene Wisse*, p. 97 (p. 141).

¹³ *Gesta Stephani*, K. R. Potter (ed. and trans.) (Oxford, 1976), pp. 14–15.

¹⁴ John of Salisbury, *Letters*, W. J. Mellor and H. E. Butler (eds) (London, 1955), Letter 87, pp. 135–6.

¹⁵ Jeffrey Jerome Cohen, *Hybridity, Identity and Monstrosity in Medieval Britain: On Difficult Middles* (New York and Basingstoke, 2006), pp. 82, 84 and 101.

¹⁶ Rogoff, *Terra Infirma*, p. 98.

¹⁷ On the intellectual and literary traditions to which the author was subject, see in particular Bella Millett, 'The Genre of *Ancrene Wisse*', in Yoko Wada (ed.), *A Companion to Ancrene Wisse* (Cambridge, 2003), pp. 29–44.

¹⁸ *Ancrene Wisse*, p. 96 (p. 141).

¹⁹ Giraldus Cambrensis, 'Itinerarium Kambriae', in James F. Dimock (ed.), *Opera* (London, 1868), Liber II, cap. ix, pp. 1–227. For a useful full-length study of Gerald of Wales see Robert Bartlett, *Gerald of Wales* (Oxford, 1982).

²⁰ Cohen also focuses on Gerald's writings on Wales in *Hybridity*, pp. 80–4 and 90–104.

²¹ Cohen, *Hybridity*, p. 103. Gerald himself refers to the Dee as '*fluvio transcurso*' in *Itinerarium*, p. 139.

[22] According to Gerald, the outcome of the next skirmish could be ascertained according to which side the river was currently veering towards, the Welsh or the English. *Itinerarium*, p. 139.

[23] *Itinerarium*, p. 141.

[24] Ibid.

[25] *Itinerarium*, p. 140. Whilst this story has no shred of evidence to support it, it was taken up in the fourteenth century by Ranulf Higden, a monk of St Werburgh's Abbey in Chester, in his *Polychronicon*. See C. Babington and J. R. Lumby (eds), *Polychronicon Ranulphi Higden, Monachi Cestrensis: together with the English Translations of John Trevista and of an Unknown Writer of the Fifteenth Century*, Rolls Series 41, 9 vols (London, 1879–86), vol. vii, p. 244.

[26] Their remains were uncovered in about 1770, for which see Daniel and Samuel Lysons, *Magna Britannia* (Institute of Historical Research, 1814), vol. 2, p. 624, as cited in 'Religious Houses: Introduction', in *VCH Ches*. 3, pp. 124–7, n. 18.

[27] *Itinerarium*, pp. 139–40. 'Religious houses: Introduction', *VCH Ches*. 3, pp. 124–7.

[28] I borrow this term from Cohen, *Hybridity*, p. 103.

[29] All references to Lucian's *De Laude Cestrie* will be taken from the M. V. Taylor edition and cited by folio and page reference. The English translations are taken from that of Mark Faulkner (*DLC*) with the occasional modification. For other discussions of Lucian in this volume, see Doran, pp. 57–77 and Faulkner, pp. 78–98.

[30] *De Laude Cestrie*, fol. 9r., p. 42.

[31] Fol. 12v., p. 45.

[32] Fol. 114r., p. 65.

[33] Ibid.

[34] Ibid.

[35] For Lefebvre, the city, for example, is 'a space which is fashioned, shaped and invested by social activities during a finite historical period'. See Henri Lefebvre, *The Production of Space*, Donald Nicholson-Smith (trans.) (Oxford, 1991), p. 73.

[36] James A. Alexander, *Ranulf of Chester: A Relic of the Conquest* (Athens, Georgia, 1983), p. 61.

[37] *De Laude Cestrie*, fol. 114r., p. 66.

[38] Ibid., fol. 105v., p. 62.

[39] Ibid., fol. 12v., p. 45.

[40] Ibid., fol. 13r., p. 46.

[41] Ibid., fol. 12v., p. 46.

[42] Ibid.

[43] Ibid.

[44] Rogoff, *Terrra Infirma*, p. 147.

[45] *De Laude Cestrie*, fol. 9r., p. 42.

[46] Rogoff, *Terra Infirma*, p. 144.

[47] The term 'Wooing Group' was first coined by W. Meredith Thompson as a means of identifying the links between four lyrical meditative poems on Christ and the Virgin Mary, all of which are closely connected with *Ancrene Wisse* and its associated texts: *On Ureisun of ure Louerde*; *On Lofsong of Ure Lefdi*; *On Lofsong*

of ure Louerde; *Þe Wohunge of ure Lauerd*. For an account of provenance and manuscript traditions, again see Millett, *Annotated Bibliography*, esp. p. 39. Here Millett points out the dearth of scholarly attention received by this group at the time of writing, although that has now been rectified in part by a most useful volume of essays devoted to the Wooing Group works: see Susannah M. Chewning (ed.), *The Milieu and Context of the Wooing Group* (Cardiff, 2009).

48   *Þe Wohunge of ure Lauerd*, ll. 590–602.

49   *De Laude Cestrie*, fol. 13r, pp. 46–7.

50   BL Harley MS 2162, fol. 61v. The use of servants by anchorites is well documented and, in some cases, a servant would follow her mistress into the anchorhold after her death. See Warren, *Anchorites and their Patrons*, especially p. 26.

51   *Tribute to an Antiquary*, Frederick Emmison and Roy Stephens (eds) (London, 1976), p. 117.

52   Warren, *Anchorites and their Patrons*, p. 167. Here Warren attributes the lack of evidence for extensive support of anchorites by both Edward I and Edward II as 'essential indifference' which, however, did not amount to 'total disregard': ibid., p. 168.

53   Eleanor had, for example, been granted 'the manor of Macclesfield with its hundred and forest' by Edward in 1270 (CPR 1266–72, p. 459). Macclesfield is recorded as housing a female anchorite in 1301 in *The Cheshire Sheaf*, Series 3, vol. 43 (1948), p. 12.

54   CCR 1279–1288, p. 32.

55   *Journal of the Chester Archaeological Society*, New Series xiii, pp. 93–5 and pp. 97–8, cited in 'House of Benedictine Nuns: The Priory of Chester', *VCH Ches*. 3, pp. 146–50, n. 22.

56   *De Laude Cestrie,* fol. 112v., p. 63.

57   CPR 1281–92, p. 74.

58   CCR 1272–9, p. 209.

59   Ibid.

60   Alexander, *Ranulf of Chester*, p. 44.

61   Cannon, *Grounds of English Literature*, p. 168.

62   Rogoff, *Terra Infirma*, p. 135.

63   *Ancrene Wisse*, p. 96 and p. 141.

64   Ibid., p. 46. The translation here is my own, since Watson and Savage's translation dilutes the impact of the statement by omitting the explicit reference to the earth as a grave.

7

Sanctity and the City: Sacred Space in Henry Bradshaw's *Life of St Werburge*

LAURA VARNAM

> Reioyse Chestre / reioyse ye religious
> And thanke your maker of his beniuolence
> That hath you gyuen suche treasure preciouse,
> Aduocatrice / in your most indigence![1]

This apostrophe to the city of Chester and its religious appears in an anonymous ballad appended to the 1521 printing of Henry Bradshaw's *Life of St Werburge*. The author describes St Werburgh as a precious treasure and, employing a term most commonly used of the Virgin, as '*aduocatrice*'. The idea of Werburgh as the city's advocate or intercessor is central to the socio-political context in which Bradshaw composed the *Life* in the early sixteenth century. Bradshaw was a Benedictine monk at the abbey of St Werburgh in Chester and his text is not only a record of the life, death and miracles of a seventh-century Anglo-Saxon saint but also, in the tradition of Lucian, a paean to the city of Chester itself. But it is a portrait of a city whose topography is being re-mapped along sacred coordinates in order to demonstrate the dependence of urban life upon the protection of the abbey, the centre of the city's sacred power.

This essay will explore the relationship which Bradshaw establishes between the sacred, the saint and the city within the *Life of St Werburge* and in the text's sixteenth-century context. The first section will explore the terminology with which Bradshaw constructs the sacred in relation to Mircea Eliade's formulation in *The Sacred and Profane*.[2] The second will examine two categories of miracle discernable in the *Life*, the natural and material, and the final section will locate the urban miracles of St Werburgh in their socio-political context and argue that Bradshaw presents Werburgh as a potent icon for the abbey's campaign for autonomy and sovereignty in the city.

1. Defining the Sacred

In *The Sacred and Profane*, Mircea Eliade declares that the sacred 'transcends this world but manifests itself in this world'.[3] This duality characterises the paradoxical nature of the sacred, that while it reaches beyond the world and opens a channel of communication with the divine, its manifestation is necessarily terrestrial and tangible. The sacred becomes incarnate in the landscape and in the bodies of the saints who traverse that landscape. The sacred as embodied in the saint and their relics is mobile and contagious, it is both dependent upon but unrestrained by material artefacts and boundaries.

Eliade employs the term *hierophany* to define the sacred. He states that a hierophany is 'an irruption of the sacred that results in detaching a territory from the surrounding cosmic milieu and making it qualitatively different'.[4] The notion of 'irruption' captures the spontaneous, unexpected but tectonic quality of the sacred. Miracles dramatically alter our conception of space and place and as a result, our behaviour towards them becomes 'qualitatively different'. Once the sacred has manifested itself, most commonly in the form of a miracle, it demands a communal response. Ritual veneration, faith and conversion all form a part of the sacred practice which affirms and recreates the significance of the hierophany.

The sacred also 'founds the world': 'in the homogeneous and infinite expanse, in which no point of reference is possible and hence no *orientation* can be established', Eliade argues, 'the hierophany reveals an absolute fixed point, a centre'.[5] This definition is especially resonant for Bradshaw's *Life* because the sanctity of Werburgh is the major mode through which the primacy and autonomy of the city and, more importantly, its abbey, is established. Her miracles mark out Chester as the sacred centre of Britain, a fixed point by which readers of the *Life* can orient themselves.[6] 'What is to become "our world"', as Eliade states, 'must first be "created"'.[7] Bradshaw's sacred mapping creates the city of Chester and as readers of his text demands our personal allegiance. As Katherine Lewis states, the *Life* is 'a call to the people of Chester to identify with the monastery and its version of both past and present'.[8]

Bearing in mind Eliade's notions of manifestation, irruption and orientation, the first part of this essay will consider Bradshaw's definition of the sacred. I will treat his sacred lexicon in three groups: words which apply to miracles, those which apply to Werburgh as sacred icon and those which represent the ecclesiastical response to the sacred.

Miracles of Nature

Eliade's notion of manifestation resonates with Bradshaw's *Life* as he frequently collocates the term with instances of miracles. He declares for example, that Werburgh's great holiness 'by sygnes and myracles / were dayly manyfest' (I: 2821). The manifestation is the visible, external evidence of personal sanctity and Bradshaw makes the link between external miracle and internal merit explicit when he states:

Her mertyes were / moche more commendable
Than were her miracles – / manyfest and playne:
For why by her merytes / famous and notable
Sygnes and myracles / were shewed full playne (I: 2606–9)[9]

Her merits, 'manyfest and playne', are the direct cause for the 'showing' of miracles. The virtue of the saint is the conduit for the sacred to be 'shown' in the world. The verb *to show* is frequently used in the *Life* to highlight the role of the sacred as a sign and a public revelation. When converted sinner Alnotus becomes an anchorite and is martyred, for example, the lord 'shewed many myracles / affyrmynge his holynes' (I: 2773). Miracles both enact and affirm sanctity.

Werburgh's miracles play a primary role in her public recognition as a saint and healer:

The excellent fame of this glorious lady
Dilated was through all this region,
Manifest by myracles full honorably:
Therfore from diuers partes came many a person
For helth of body and gostly conuersacion,
Some to be cured from payne intollerable
And some of olde sores that were incurable (II: 905–11)

The manifestation of miracles encourages wider devotion and pilgrimage to the saint. The use of the word 'diuers' is also significant here because Bradshaw begins the *Life* by lamenting the diversity of men's conditions and the 'great vnstedfastnes / of this wretched worlde' (I: 8–9). The diversity of miracles rehabilitates the word as sacred abundance rather than human frailty.

Miracles also glorify God and his house on earth. They signify God's omnipotence because they represent a fracture in the natural order and demonstrate God's divine power to reorder his creation. As Michael Goodich has shown, by the later Middle Ages the dominant theological understanding of miracles was that of Aquinas, who categorised them as *supra naturam*, *contra naturam*, and *praeter naturam*.[10] In the *Life*, Bradshaw seems to take an unusual interest in the relationship between miracles and nature which seems reminiscent of attempts by theologians such as Aquinas to understand precisely how the power of God was at work in the world. Bradshaw places a considerable emphasis on the sacred 'transcendynge nature', which we might see as Aquinas's *praeter naturam*.[11]

Werburgh's major miracle in medieval and later tradition, and the miracle for which she is commemorated in the Chester Cathedral misericords, concerns a flock of wild geese which she tames and throughout the episode the events are interpreted according to the laws of nature. When Werburgh discovers that the geese have been laying waste to the crops she tells a servant to command the geese to come to her house 'there to be pynned / and punysshed for theyr trespace' (I: 2632):

> The messanger merueyled / and mused in his mynde
> Of this straunge message / stode styll in a study,
> Knowynge it well / it passed course of kynde
> Wylde gees for to pynne / by any mannys polycy,
> Syth nature hath ordeyned / suche byrdes to fly;
> Supposynge his lady / had ben vnreasonable
> Commaundynge to do / a thynge vnpossyble (I: 2633–9)

The obedience of the geese is presented as a miracle 'transcendynge nature'. The geese behave 'as yf they had reason naturall' and when they reach Werburgh's house they 'with hye voices (as yf it were) on her dyd call / for grace and pardon / of theyr offence' (I: 2652, 56). The geese, whose natural state is wildness, act and indeed almost speak as though they were human. In a parody of confession the geese declare their sins to Werburgh and crave absolution.

The episode continues with a second miracle after a servant takes and cooks one of the geese. The birds fly over Werburgh's hall and make their supplication: 'why suffer ye suche wyckednes / done for to be / anendes our felawe / agaynst all ryght and charyte?' (I: 2687–8). That which is normative, the eating of geese, has become redefined as an act of wickedness due to the initial miracle. As a result of Werburgh's commandment, it is now their 'maner & kynde' to be loyal to their fellowship and reveal the sin which has been committed against them (I: 2686). The accepted place of humans above animals in the natural hierarchy has been reversed. Werburgh resolves the episode by retrieving the bones of the said goose and 'by the vertue / of her benedyccyon' (I: 2720) the goose is 'restaured / and flewe away full soone' (I: 2703). Oddly perhaps, Bradshaw does not dwell on this incident as a miraculous resurrection. Indeed, in the final stanza of the chapter he undermines the episode's miraculous tenor entirely:

> The foresayd wylde gees / attempten by no way
> To hurte theyr fruytes / ne lyght in that possessyon.
> No merueyll it is / remembrynge the deuocyon
> And true loue she had / to god omnypotent:
> For vnto vertue / all thynge is obedyent (I: 2706–10)

When viewed in the light of Werburgh's devotion to God, the incident cannot be read as a marvel because 'all thynge is obedyent' to virtue, even above the laws of nature. Werburgh's obedience to God is imitated by the geese's obedience to her. As St Chad declares earlier in the *Life*, 'all thynge possyble is / to a faythfull persone / that perfytely byleuys' (I: 1112–13, recalling the biblical text of Mark 9: 23).

Spectacle and Exemplarity

The vocabulary of nature is also employed to construct sacred exemplarity in the *Life* and to establish the saint as part of a network of hereditary holiness. Werburgh's mother Ermenilde is described with the conventional epithet 'floure of chastite' (I: 322) but Bradshaw later extends this image:

> Suche syngular confort / of vertuous doctryne
> In her so dyd water / a pure perfyte plante,
> Which dayly encreased / by sufferaunce deuyne,
> Merueylously growynge / in her fresshe and varnaunt,
> With dyuers propryties / of grace exuberaunt,
> As sobrynes / dyscrecyon / and mekenesse vyrgynall,
> Obeydyence / grauyte / and wysedome naturall (I: 603–9)

Ermenilde's virtues grow marvellously within her like a perfect plant. Her wisdom is natural, her virtuous doctrine is 'varnaunt' (flourishing, blooming). Natural growth is a metaphor for lineage as well as spiritual development in the *Life*. Drawing on the natural imagery employed by Goscelin of Saint-Bertin in his *Vita Sancte Werbvrge*, Bradshaw also uses such organic metaphors to describe the birth of his saintly heroines.[12] Of Ermenilde, he states:

> Euery tree or plante / is proued euydent
> Whyther good or euyll / by experyence full sure,
> By the budde and fruyte / and pleasaunt descent;

A swete tree bryngeth forth / by cours of nature
Swete fruyte and delycyous / in tast and verdure:
Ryght so to Ercombert / by his quene moost mylde
Brought graciously forth / the swete Ermenylde (I: 610–16)

Ermenilde is the sweet fruit brought forth by the union of King
Ercombert and St Sexburge. That the fruit should prove the quality of
the tree is a common biblical metaphor but in the case of Werburgh, her
nature transcends both her parentage and her saintly lineage. 'A newe plant
of goodnes / in her dayly dyd sprynge' (I: 716) which causes her parents
'moche merueylynge' (I: 718). Bradshaw redefines Werburgh's virtue with
the related natural metaphor of a rose proceeding from a briar (I: 724–5)
but he then goes further and suggests that Werburgh passes 'aboue the
cours of nature' like 'Phebus in his heuenly regyon' (I: 735, 733). This classical image figures Werburgh as not only surpassing her parents but also as
transcending terrestrial space. She inhabits a sacred space outside time and
place and this paves the way for her sanctity to transcend the boundaries
of the temporal and material world. In Goscelin's *Vita* Werburgh 'derives
high lustre' from her ancestors and is figured as a 'morning star' which
'may the more clearly be observed as if by the light of those foregoing
stars', but in Bradshaw's *Life* rather than a star illuminated by her saintly
predecessors, she is likened to the sun which eclipses them all.[13]

The language of exemplarity is inextricably linked to the material
however. Werburgh is referred to as a 'spectacle of vertue' on two occasions in the *Life* in relation to her profession at Ely (I: 3285, II: 1783), in
the first case when the narrator addresses female readers of the *Life*:

Sekynge for pleasures / ryches and arayment,
Blynded by your beaute / and synguler affeccyon,
Consyder this vyrgyn / humble and pacyent:
A spectacle of vertue / euer obeydent:
Beholde how she hase / clerely layde away
Her royall ryche clothes / and is in meke aray (II: 1780–5)

The imperative 'beholde' encourages us to visualize Werburgh as a spectacle of sacred virtue but paradoxically, her 'meke aray' can only be
constructed in direct contrast to the visual display of the implied audience of courtly ladies and Werburgh's own rich array as a member of the
Mercian royal family.[14] Bradshaw continues to apostrophize courtly ladies
and to exploit the reliance of the sacred upon the material:

[Y]our garmentes now be gay and gloryous
Euery yere made / after a new inuencyon,

Of sylke and veluet / costly and precyous,
Brothered full rychely / after the beest facyon,
Shyngynge lyke angels / in your opynyon (I: 1786–90)

The terms 'gloryous', 'precyous', and most especially 'inuencyon', are
commonly found together within the hagiographical lexicon in relation
to relics and here they are employed as a critique of costly clothing.[15]
Bradshaw encourages such ladies to take Werburgh as a 'pleyne exsample'
and to imitate her in renouncing 'pleasures' for 'penaunce and prayere' (I:
1793–7) but perhaps ironically the language of display displaces the spectacle of virtue through its use of decorative and ornate terms.

In the anonymous *Balade to the Auctour* at the end of the *Life*, the author
states that 'theffect [of the *Life*] is manifest':

All vices surely it confoundeth.
Shewynge the legende of this mayde pure,
Her shenyng lyfe eche – where redoundeth.
Suche steppes folowyng / we hope in them tendure (ll. 35–40)

Werburgh's role as a visual sign of exemplarity is spatialised in this metaphor as the reader is urged to follow in her sacred footsteps. It is perhaps
not coincidental that the steps remind us of the ending of Chaucer's *Troilus
and Criseyde* where the narrator's 'litel bok' is urged to 'kis the steppes
where as thow seest pace / Virgile, Omer, Lucan, Stace'.[16] In Bradshaw's
own conclusion to the *Life* he tells his 'litell boke' to 'submytte the' to
'maister Chaucer / and Ludgate sentencious', to 'preignaunt Barkley' and
'inuentiue Skelton' (II: 2020–5). His anonymous continuator replaces the
steps of ancient poetry with the sacred footsteps of Werburgh, offering the
Life not as subject to literary tradition like Chaucer's *Troilus* but as a new
sacred *auctorite* which the reader must consciously emulate. Moreover,
the continuator appropriates the language of miraculous revelation,
'shewynge' (l. 36), to describe the work which Bradshaw's *Life* performs.
The text 'shews' the legend of St Werburgh and the *Life* itself becomes the
sacred spectacle which manifests her virtue.

Translation

The term *translate* is fundamental to the vocabulary of sanctity. It is used
both of the translation of the text from one language to another and for the
physical and geographical translation of the body of the saint. In the *Life
of St Werburge* the term, even more so than usual, also has connotations of
ecclesiastical and political power. In the prologue to the *Life*, Bradshaw
states:

I purpose to wryte / a legende good and true
And translate a lyfe / into Englysshe doubtles (I: 93–4)

Bradshaw's separation of 'wryte' and 'translate' encourages the spatial meaning of the latter to come into play. The linguistic translation of saints' lives often also involved their relocation to a landscape familiar to their audience. In the *Life,* the text clearly anchors the sacred power of Werburgh in the city of Chester, placing considerable emphasis on her role as the city's 'chyef protectryce' (I: 101) which is especially significant given that Werburgh had no association with Chester during her lifetime.

Translation is the official ecclesiastical confirmation of sanctity. In Chapter Thirty-One the heading declares that 'for her [Werburgh's] myracles shewed þᵉ couent of Hambury purposed to translate her body' (p. 118). Werburgh's miracles attract pilgrims and as a result they decide to 'exalte' her further through translation:

The couent, consyderyng suche great company
From diuers partes / resortynge to theyr place
In pylgrimage to Werburge / for helpe and remedy,
Entended to translate this glorious abbasse,
To exalte her body replet with great grace
To her great honour / comfort to eche creature –
Pite that suche a relique shulde lye in sepulture (I: 3343–9)

Translation elevates the resting place of the saint beyond a mere 'sepulture' to a sacred space honoured by communal veneration.[17]

The word *translate* is also used in the *Life* to denote the transformation of a building. When King Wulfer repents his sins, St Chad urges him 'the temples of paganes / to translate to the honour / of god almyghty' (I: 1284–5). On the surface this aligns translation with transformation: the pagan temples will become Christian churches. But implicitly, while the dedication of the temples has changed, the sacred and material coordinates remain the same. Since Pope Gregory's letter to Augustine, the Christianisation of pagan temples has been read as a strategy of appropriation.[18] The conversion of pagan sacred sites is a deliberate move to reinvest their sanctity in the new religion and rather than offering Christianity as an alternative, to redirect the population's devotions to a new deity in their existing sacred space.

The rearrangement of the diocesan sees is also represented through the metaphor of translation. Bradshaw states that:

Kynge Offa translated / as sayth Polycronycon,
By myghty power / the see of Canterbury

Vnto Lychefelde chyrche / with famous oblacyon,
For euer to contynu / confyrmed by auctoryte (I: 253–6)

Here translation collocates with a vocabulary of power ('auctoryte',
'myghty power'). The translation of the Canterbury see is directly associated with Offa's consolidation of his political power as Bradshaw mentions
it immediately after his description of the king subduing the 'kynges of
Westsaxons / Northumberlande & Kent' (I: 247). The repositioning of
the see from southern England to the Midlands relocates the centre of
ecclesiastical power nearer to Chester and its patron saint. Translation is
a powerful socio-political as well as sacred practice which expresses and
confers authority and status through the use of space.

2. Manifest by Miracles

Sanctity is made manifest by miracles in the *Life of St Werburge* and as
my investigation of Bradshaw's sacred lexicon has suggested, they fall
into three broad categories: the natural, the material and the urban. In
Book I, a considerable number of the miracles take place outside, in the
forest or wilderness, and involve animals or trees. The natural environs
are sanctified and this paves the way for the construction of the city in
the midst of a *locus amoenus*, an idealised space appropriate for the ideal
city and its saint. Throughout the *Life* material culture is transformed by
St Werburgh's miracles and physical objects function as a proof of sanctity. In this section I will focus on two of the *Life*'s natural and material
miracles, before turning to Werburgh's urban miracles in part three. The
natural miracle which is most resonant for a consideration of sacred space
concerns Werburgh's oak tree sanctuary. This miracle is a rewriting of the
Daphne and Apollo narrative from Ovid's *Metamorphoses* and it demonstrates the ability of the saintly body to create sacred space.

In the Ovidian narrative Apollo is chasing Daphne through the forest
and she prays to her father, the river god Peneus, to save her from his
advances. Peneus grants his daughter's wish and she is metamorphosed
into a laurel tree.[19] In the *Life* Werburgh is also pursued by an unwanted
lover but when she prays to God to defend her, a miracle occurs:

She ranne for socour / to a great oke-tree.
By grace the sayd tree / opened that same season,
Sufferynge this mayde / to haue sure and fre entree;
Wherby she escaped his / wycked tyrannye.
Whiche tree to this day / endurynge all the yere
By myracle is vernaunte / fresshe / grene / and clere (I: 2803–8)

Rather than being metamorphosed into a tree, Werburgh finds refuge inside an oak which opens up to receive her like a sanctuary. Werburgh's prayer to God results in the miracle but her presence there causes further miracles. The tree becomes evergreen and, like Werburgh herself in the passage discussed above, it becomes 'vernaunte'. The tree is 'fresshe' and 'clene': it assumes a virginal state in imitation of the saint it protected.

The sanctity of the space is then foregrounded when Bradshaw reports the subsequent life of the oak:

Of the sayd oke-tree / is a famous opynyon:
That no man may entre / the sayd concauyte
In deedly synne bounden / without contrycyon;
But in clene perfyte lyfe / who-soeuer he be,
May entre the sayd oke / with fre lyberte.
And nygh to that place / a chyrche is now dedycate
In honour of god / and werburge immaculate (I: 2809–15)

The oak gains a reputation as a testing ground for virtue: only those with a 'clene perfyte lyfe' like St Werburgh may enter the space. Sacred space distinguishes between saint and sinner and offers the virginal Werburgh as an example to which her local community should aspire. The importance of the site is confirmed by the building of a church near to the tree. Church building often functions as the official recognition of sacred space in hagiography. Churches are frequently built near miraculous springs, for example, but here the spatial dynamic is inflected with a gendered significance. The focus on sin and contrition aligns the space with confession but the tree's location outside the church and its status as an enclosed space which protects the virginal body from penetration gestures towards the anchorhold. The use of the word 'concauyte' is resonant in this context as it is an anatomical word most commonly used of bodily cavities such as the womb.[20] The oak tree contains and symbolises Werburgh's inviolate virginity. The sacred space which the presence of the saint engenders both embodies and reproduces her physical sanctity and looks forward to Werburgh's further enclosure within the monastic cloister.

The second group of miracles which feature in the *Life* are similarly associated with the impression which the sacred leaves on the material world. There is an interplay between the material and spiritual throughout the *Life*, and in medieval hagiography more generally, which is directly related to the incarnation of sanctity in the saint. Sanctity is embodied but, as evidenced by the practice of making contact relics, it can be transferred to another object or person through physical contact. This can be seen in the *Life* when a barren woman prays to St Werburgh for a child and the saint appears in a vision, telling her to go to the abbey and visit her altar:

> Also for to compasse her holy aulter
> With a linen cloth / knelyng on her kne,
> And after for to take the same cloth in-fere
> And compas her wombe about reuerentle (II: 821–4)

The woman performs the ritual, transferring the sanctity of the altar into
the cloth and enabling her to conceive a child. The parallel movement of
'compassing' the altar and womb sets up an analogy between the female
body as vessel for new life and the altar as receptacle for sacred relics. Both
this and the oak tree miracle gesture towards the imagery of anchoritic and
monastic enclosure and the significance of the relationship between inner
and outer in female spirituality. The woman's ritual performance must
also be carried out properly if it is to be efficacious: she must compass her
womb 'reuerentle' and kneel beside the altar. These gestures and inten-
tions symbolise the respect which is due to the sacred, which is especially
relevant here as the laity would not ordinarily have access to the altar as
the chancel was reserved for priests. After the woman has given birth to
the child she performs a ritual of thanksgiving:

> And after the tyme of her purificacion
> Of the same faire cloth she made an oblacion,
> Richely set in syluer / well wrought in compas
> With many riche enormentes she sende to this place.
> After came her-selfe vnto the monastery
> With many of her neyghboures / there nye dwellyng,
> Praysyng and laudyng this glorious lady (II: 831–7)

The woman's successful conception results in the cloth itself being viewed
as a sacred object and therefore the woman transforms it physically into
an object resembling a relic. She decorates, 'compasses' it, with rich orna-
ments and sets it in silver, forming the linen's quotidian appearance into
a sign of sanctity. The woman also makes a pilgrimage to the monastery
with her neighbours and locates her personal praise within a communal,
and perhaps implicitly female, devotional context. Public recognition
of the sacred was central to its memorialisation within a culture and the
woman calls upon her neighbours to bear 'true witnes' to the miracle (II:
839). The miracle is both claimed by the neighbourhood and relocated at
Werburgh's shrine, its sacred origin.

3. Sanctifying the Sixteenth-Century City

Michael Goodich states that 'the religious cult and its trappings had become one of the major expressions of social and political unity in the later Middle Ages'.[21] In the *Life*, Henry Bradshaw marshals the cult of St Werburgh to both express and create a unity which not only withstands the threat of Danish invasion but also strengthens Chester's identity as a sacred city. In sixteenth-century Chester, however, the abbey of St Werburgh and the city's civic authorities were competing for control of the city and Bradshaw additionally uses the *Life* to locate the source of the city's sanctity firmly upon the abbey where Werburgh's relics were enshrined. The effect of this realignment of power structures justifies the abbey's autonomy in the city and sends a clear message to their detractors that Chester's sacred status is entirely due to the abbey's patronage and protection.

According to Jane Laughton's recent book on Chester, although Werburgh's shrine was rebuilt in the 1340s, it was never finished and 'it seems that Werburgh did not command much devotion within the city'.[22] Laughton does include evidence of bequests to the shrine in 1489 and 1506 however, which perhaps demonstrates an increased interest in the cult of Werburgh in the late Middle Ages.[23] It was in the abbey's personal and financial interests to encourage such devotion and within this context we might see Bradshaw's text as an advertisement for the benefits which St Werburgh could confer upon devotees.[24] Bolstering the reputation of the saint could strengthen the reputation of the abbey at a time when relations between St Werburgh's and the city authorities were fraught with tensions. The abbey's jurisdiction over their tenants and the abbot's rights over pleas during the Midsummer Fair were a major cause of resentment for the urban community and as Laughton points out, the abbey came to be viewed as a 'serious threat to social harmony'.[25] There is evidence to suggest that the townspeople deliberately antagonised the abbey in order to challenge their privileges and in 1506 when the abbey lost their Midsummer Fair rights to the mayor and sheriffs, a marginal note in the Mayor's Book reports the city's reaction in a joyous tone: 'nota nota nota bene. Pro libertate nostra contra abbatem tempore nundinarum' ('on behalf of our liberty against the abbey at fair time').[26] We might read a miracle in Book II of the *Life* in this context, in which an innocent man is arrested and hanged by the 'officers and rulers' of Chester and miraculously freed by the intercession of St Werburgh (II: 951). The man's 'tortuous turmentours' who 'cessed their tyrranny' (II: 980) reflects the abbey's hope that Chester's civic authorities finally concede defeat in the face of St Werburgh's sacred power.[27]

When Bradshaw was writing his *Life of Werburge* in the confines of the abbey, he was writing against a backdrop of long-running conflict with a city that was doing its utmost to keep the abbey's authority well within the walls of its own precinct. Tim Thornton argues that the abbey was recovering from a period of decline and that the completion of the abbey's west front demonstrates that 'economically and politically the abbey was reasserting its place in the region'.[28] Architectural development was one mode through which a foundation might seek to advertise its increased confidence and bolster its reputation but literary endeavour could also be marshalled to such a purpose. According to Thornton, the other extant text which may have been authored by Bradshaw, the *Life of St Radegunde*, was also written at a time of turbulence when the Cambridge nunnery of which Radegunde was patron was under threat of being turned into a college and 'losing connection' with the saint.[29] We might then see the *Life of St Werburge* as Bradshaw's literary riposte to a hostile urban community. The text clearly anchors the sanctity of the city within the abbey, the guardians of Werburgh's shrine, and attributes the safety and protection of the city to the saint and her canons.

The clearest evidence for this argument can be found in the third to last section of the *Life* in which a refrain is introduced at the end of each of the eighteen stanzas: 'wherfore to the monasterye be neuer vnkynde' (II: 1761). The section attributes the success of various groups in the city to the protection and help of St Werburgh and threatens vengeance for those who refuse to acknowledge the role which the abbey has played in the defence of the city:

> There was neuer man of high nor lowe degree,
> Lorde / baron / knyght / marchaunt / and burges,
> Attemptyng to infringe their rightes and liberte,
> Remaynyng in the same malice and wyckednes,
> But if they repent shortly theyr busynes
> Askyng absolucion to theyr conscience blynde,
> Vengeance on them doth lyght, doutles:
> Wherfore to the monastery be neuer vnkynd (II: 1842–9)

Tim Thornton argues that the refrain is targeted especially at Cardinal Wolsey, whose protracted conflict with abbot John Birchenshawe led to the abbot's forcible removal in 1523.[30] Read in the light of the city's increasing autonomy, culminating in the 1506 Great Charter, the refrain also functions as a warning to the wider readership of the *Life* that those who threaten the monastery's 'speciall franches and liberte' (II: 1778) will receive 'sharp punycion' at the hands of the saint (II: 1856).

When Bradshaw first introduces St Werburgh in the *Life*, this political context surfaces in his choice of diction. He describes her firstly as 'chyef protectryce of the sayd monasterye' and then as 'protectryce of the Cytee', the order of reference establishing the *Life*'s internal hierarchy (I: 101, 103). But more importantly, he describes her as 'specyall prymate / and pryncypall president, / There rulynge vnder / our lorde omnypotent' (I: 104–5). The use of the word 'prymate', given Birchenshawe's feud with Wolsey, is telling as while primate can denote a 'person of first rank, dignitary, noble' in Middle English, its more precise meaning is 'the pre-eminent official of an ecclesiastical province' and as such it is often used of bishops and archbishops.[31] The saint as primate, whose superior is God himself, is, I would argue, more than a match for Wolsey and the city authorities.

Werburgh's role as 'protectryce' of the city is demonstrated in three miracles which occur in relation to one of the major topographical features of Chester, the city walls. In the first miracle, when Werburgh is translated to Chester, the entire urban community welcomes her and addresses her as 'our refuge' and 'our speciall defence' (II: 323, 325). When the Welsh then attack the city, Werburgh's shrine becomes a sacred fortification when the canons of the abbey 'set it on the towne-walles for help and tuicion' (II: 711).[32] The word 'tuicion' means 'protection from enemies, defence' and is often used in militaristic contexts.[33] The shrine on the city walls is a symbol of Werburgh's protection of Chester, the sanctity of her shrine seeps into the walls and encloses the city within a sacred force field. When one of the Welshmen throws a stone at the shrine and damages it, a 'great punysshement vpon them all lyght':

> The kyng and his host were smytten with blyndnes,
> That of the cite / they had no maner of sight;
> And he that smote the holy shryne, doubtles,
> Was greuously vexed with a sprite of darknes,
> And with hidous payne expired miserably –
> The kynge was sore-adred / and all his company (II: 716–22)

The attack on the shrine is an attack on the city and it results in an appropriate punishment: the besieging army can no longer see the city and therefore cannot attack. The shrine as the material embodiment of Werburgh's sanctity protects the city's defences from being breached. A similar attack by the Danes and Scots is foiled when the canons place the shrine at the North Gate (II: 773), another key locus of the city's identity and a controversial space in sixteenth-century Chester.[34] When one of the attackers throws a stone at the 'riall relique' one of its corners breaks off.

Here the shrine becomes the city's surrogate: it is damaged and broken so that the city can remain whole.

The shrine also protects the city from other threats to its material fabric, including a great fire which threatened to engulf the city. Bradshaw elevates the status of Chester by comparing the situation to the two great classical cities, Troy and Rome, 'all flamyng as fire' (II: 1627). But with Werburgh as its patron saint, the city is not 'remedeles' like its classical forebears (II: 1632). The abbot and brothers of the monastery process the shrine around the city, creating a sacred enclosure to ward off the fire:

> [they] toke the holy shryne in prayer and deuocion,
> Syngyng the letanie bare it in procession,
> Compasyng the fyre in euery strete and place,
> Trustynge in Werburge for helpe, aide and grace (II: 1650–3)

Sacred space is created not only through the sacred material object but also through the canons' sacred practice. They sing the litany and pray while 'compasyng' the city and sanctifying its diverse spaces. Earlier in Book II, Bradshaw describes the monastic precinct of St Werburgh's as 'the great compas of the sayd abbay' (II: 97) and here he again employs the language of enclosure as the canons 'compass' the city, linking Werburgh's virginal body, the walled city and the monastic cloister. Shari Horner comments that 'the female religious body itself comes to symbolise not only the "walls" of an enclosure but that which is enclosed within it' and here the 'compasyng' of the streets cements the conflation of saint and city in the *Life*. The protective enclosure of the virginal, monastic body encompasses the walled body of urban space, warding off both physical and spiritual invasion by association with the patron saint.[35]

Bradshaw describes the shrine's procession as 'procedyng in stacion' (II: 1655) and the term 'stacion' is frequently used of the sacred spaces of pilgrimage, most especially in Rome.[36] The term maps out a sacred pathway through the city. When the litany is complete, the fire ceases and the people then make their own spatial performance by processing to the shrine in thanksgiving, in imitation of the canons and recognition of their role in the miracle. The people say 'full sadly' that 'we shall neuer able be / the place to recompence for this dede of charite' (II: 1680–1). This is precisely the attitude which Bradshaw aims to foster in readers of the *Life* in his contemporary Chester. The miracles of St Werburgh's shrine which protect the city from foreign invasion and natural disaster refocus the city's attention on the abbey and demonstrate its importance within the urban landscape.

In this essay I have explored the ways in which Henry Bradshaw defines, manifests and makes use of sacred space in his *Life of St Werburge*. The literary text is part of what Etienne Balibar and Pierre Macherey have called the 'ensemble of social practices' which a community employs to establish its identity and negotiate social conflict.[37] Bradshaw's *Life of St Werburge* was just such a social practice for the embattled Benedictine abbey of St Werburgh as it tried to reassert itself as the sacred centre of late medieval Chester.

Notes

[1] 'An other balade [to the author]', appended to Henry Bradshaw, *The Life of Saint Werburge of Chester*, Carl Horstmann (ed.), EETS OS 88 (London, 1887), ll. 9–12, p. 201. All quotations refer to this edition.

[2] Mircea Eliade, *The Sacred and Profane: The Nature of Religion* (Orlando, 1987).

[3] Eliade, *The Sacred and Profane*, p. 202.

[4] Ibid., p. 26.

[5] Ibid., p. 21.

[6] Bradshaw also constructs Chester as a sacred centre in Book II: 421–62 in which he suggests that the city has been the only place of continuous Christian religious practice since the conversion of the Britons.

[7] Eliade, *The Sacred and Profane*, p. 31.

[8] K. J. Lewis, 'History, historiography, and re-writing the past' in S. Salih (ed.), *A Companion to Middle English Hagiography* (Cambridge, 2006), pp. 122–40, p. 140.

[9] Bradshaw is responding to Goscelin of Saint-Bertin here who states: 'perhaps now we are wearying the reader in holding back from an account of her miracles. Far greater than miracles are the merits by which those same miracles come about, because merits can be perfect without signs, but signs are nothing without merits', Rosalind C. Love (ed. and trans.), *Goscelin of Saint-Bertin: The Hagiography of the Female Saints of Ely* (Oxford, 2004), pp. 25–51, p. 39.

[10] Michael Goodich, *Miracles and Wonders: The Development of the Concept of Miracle 1150–1350* (Aldershot, 2007), pp. 19–21.

[11] Bradshaw may have encountered these ideas while at Gloucester College, Oxford.

[12] See Love, *Goscelin of Saint-Bertin*, pp. 30–3.

[13] Ibid., pp. 30–1.

[14] See Catherine Sanok, *Her Life Historical: Exemplarity and Female Saints' Lives in Late Medieval England* (Philadelphia, 2007), esp. chapter 2, pp. 24–49.

[15] 'Invention' was used of the discovery of the true cross and the bodies of saints, see MED s.v. '*invencioun*' 1b).

[16] Larry D. Benson (ed.), *The Riverside Chaucer* (Oxford, 1987), p. 584.

[17] Werburgh's tomb is indeed a sacred *space* as after the Danish invasion her body dissolves into powder, leaving an empty tomb (II: 3470–6).

[18] See J. McClure and R. Collins (eds), *Bede: The Ecclesiastical History of the English People* (Oxford, 1999), pp. 56–7.

[19]   A. D. Melville (ed.), *Ovid: Metamorphoses* (Oxford, 1998), pp. 14–18.

[20]   MED s.v. *concavite* 1).

[21]   Michael Goodich, *Miracles and Wonders*, p. 14.

[22]   Jane Laughton, *Life in a Late Medieval City: Chester 1275–1520* (Oxford, 2008), p. 68.

[23]   Ibid.

[24]   Cf. Robert W. Barrett, Jnr, *Against all England: Regional Idenity and Cheshire Writing, 1195–1656* (Notre Dame, 2009), pp. 27–51.

[25]   Ibid., p. 130.

[26]   Ibid., pp. 130–1.

[27]   Barrett, however, reads such textual efforts as 'ineffectual fantasies' on the part of the abbey, p. 49.

[28]   Tim Thornton, 'Opposition drama and the resolution of disputes in early Tudor England: Cardinal Wolsey and the Abbot of Chester', *Bulletin of the John Rylands University Library of Manchester*, 81 (1999), 25–47, p. 29.

[29]   Thornton, 'Opposition drama', p. 38.

[30]   Thornton, 'Opposition drama', pp. 31 and 44.

[31]   MED s.v. *primate* a) and b).

[32]   For a discussion of the historical background to this episode, see A. T. Thacker, 'Early Medieval Chester 400–1230' in *VCH Ches*. 5. i, pp.16–33, p. 24.

[33]   MED s.v. '*tuicioun*' 1).

[34]   See Jane Laughton, *Life in a Late Medieval City*, p. 130.

[35]   Shari Horner, *The Discourse of Enclosure: Representing Women in Old English Literature* (New York, 2001), p. 16.

[36]   See for example, Frederick J. Furnivall (ed.), *The Stacions of Rome*, EETS OS 25 (London, 1867).

[37]   E. Balibar and P. Macherey, 'On literature as an ideological form', in *Untying the Text: A Post-Structuralist Reader*, R. Young (ed.) (London, 1981), pp. 79–99, p. 83.

8

Plotting Chester on the National Map: Richard Pynson's 1521 printing of Henry Bradshaw's *Life of Saint Werburge*

CYNTHIA TURNER CAMP

Few vernacular saints' lives participate as vocally in regional politics as Henry Bradshaw's *Life of Saint Werburge*. Composed before
Bradshaw's death in 1513, *Werburge* is 'calibrated to effect change on
the level of local politics',[1] as Robert Barrett and others have shown,
defending the abbey from civic encroachments on its historic privileges. In
Bradshaw's poem, Werburgh becomes 'the embodiment of abbey, city and
region'[2] and Barrett has recently examined *Werburge* and other Cheshire
writings as part of 'the sheer variety of local responses to institutional and
cultural initiatives emerging from the center'.[3] Yet this decidedly regional
saint's life is witnessed solely from the centre. Richard Pynson's 1521
printing of *Werburge*[4] troubles an easy dichotomy between hub and margin
by demonstrating a complex interplay between regional concerns and
national affairs. I wish to reverse the terms of regional literary studies like
Barrett's by asking how and why Chester writing might be deployed in and
for London. Specifically, this essay will address foundational questions
invoked by the printing of *Werburge*. Whose idea was it to print a marcher
saint's life with Pynson? Why was it printed? How could its focus on
regional affairs appeal to metropolitan readers? Most simply, how does the
periphery make itself known to the centre? Bradshaw's poem addresses
more than regional concerns, and the possibility of byplay among the
regional, national and universal facets of *Werburge* arises when one exam-

ines its circulation *outside* palatine borders, among readers less invested in local civic intrigue.

In considering how *Werburge* might play in London, I examine those features proper to its print manifestation: its title page and the anonymous liminary ballads appended to Bradshaw's poem. These paratexts mediated between the metropolitan consumer and the Chester-centric text, shaping readers' expectations and generating a saleable product. Because name recognition alone would not have sold *Werburge*, as it would have a *Katherine* or a *Margaret*, its front matter must first explicitly market *Werburge* to a London audience. Werburgh was primarily a monastic saint, even within Chester,[5] and there is little evidence of a robust London cult. Whatever cult once existed in London had long waned; the parish church on Friday Street, dedicated to Werburgh in 1100, was rededicated in the mid-fourteenth century to John the Baptist,[6] suggesting that devotion to Werburgh was insufficient to weather changes in devotional fashion. It is therefore a key initial concern of this paper to consider how the imprint's paratexts initially encourage metropolitan readers to acquire *Werburge* by situating the imprint within a common discourse of hagiographic production, devotional writing and early print conventions.

Beyond general sales, the liminal pages also construct a relationship between readers and Werburgh. As part of its marketing technique, the front matter tempers the poem's regionalism by inviting the reader to focus on Werburgh's intercessory and exemplary features rather than her Cestrian patronage. Bradshaw's poem does highlight Werburgh's exemplary features, as Catherine Sanok has shown,[7] yet her role as a regional saint dominates the text. While Bradshaw portrays her at times as the protectress of city and shire, she is also the monastery's patron, and the liminary ballads similarly foreground the intimate, occasionally exclusionary, patronal relationship between Werburgh and her monks. The printed form of *Werburge* thus holds in tension its construction of monastic identity with its address to a universal audience. The tensions that arise from *Werburge*'s movement from periphery to metropolis invite a consideration, as do early imprints more broadly,[8] of printing's lack of fixity, its tensions between paratext and text and its negotiations between text and reader.

The dissemination of *Werburge* in London works to put Werburgh and Chester 'on the map', geographically and spiritually, for metropolitan readers. In 1521, the early modern cartographic explosion was a half-century in the future, but readers of early printed books would have been familiar with a verbal map of England, Caxton's *Description of England*.[9]

Derived from Book I of Ranulf Higden's *Polychronicon*, Caxton's *Description* was a best-seller, first printed in 1480, reprinted twice by 1502, then frequently appended to the St Alban's Chronicle. Bradshaw's poem opens with a chorographic description of Mercia, also adapted from *Polychronicon* Book I, and the two imprints' shared source allowed them to interface seamlessly. Once Bradshaw's poem circulated in print, its opening description of Mercia and subsequent conflation of Mercia and Chester would have located these marcher regions on the London readership's spatial-temporal cognitive map of England. By intimately affiliating city and abbey with Werburgh's pre-Conquest sanctity, Bradshaw can elevate Chester's spiritual prominence amidst this received English geography, dotted with other powerful monasteries which took their own authority from early saints like Alban, Edmund and Etheldreda. The Chester monks who then sponsored the 1521 printing, as I show below, capitalize on this chorographic positioning to promote the abbey, in the liminal ballads, as an ancient, austere institution in a climate of declining monastic standards.

This paper treats *Werburge*'s appearance in London in three sections. The first consolidates the paratextual evidence for the conditions under which *Werburge* saw print, demonstrating that the Chester monks worked closely with Pynson to develop an attractive, marketable text. The second section examines how the title page and framing liminal ballads place *Werburge* within a wider devotional context, yet without entirely excusing Werburgh's role as a monastic patron. The third section considers one reason the Chester monks printed *Werburge* in London, some eight years after its author's death – Cardinal Wolsey's desire to reform the religious orders – discussing *Werburge*'s contribution to ecclesiastical concerns about monastic observance. Taken together, these three sections demonstrate how the printed *Werburge* partially assimilates the regional virgin to metropolitan expectations of sanctity and devotional writing in order to map Chester and its abbey as a centre of ancient English holiness and monastic virtue.

1. Seeing Werburge *into print*

In narratives of the early sixteenth-century press, Pynson's decision to print any saint's life is considered unsurprising; religious literature was a perennial best-seller, and Pynson had printed many hagiographical texts.[10] However, when examined in detail, Pynson's printing of *Werburge* in 1521

is not self-explanatory. How did a London printer obtain a poem by a dead
Chester monk? Why was it printed eight years after Bradshaw's death, and
why is he lauded so highly in the accompanying liminary ballads? Most
centrally, what in this text – a poem as much historical as devotional and as
fixated on regional affairs as universal exemplarity – would have appealed
to a metropolitan audience? The manipulation of the print conventions in
which *Werburge* participates – the use of commendatory verse, the deliberate reuse of title-page woodcuts and the printing of saints' lives and
contemporary poetry – not only helps clarify why and how *Werburge*
entered print but also points to deliberate shaping of the text's reception.
The evidence of the liminal poems and other paratextual materials on
balance indicates the Chester monks as having initiated *Werburge*'s appearance in print and suggests that their collaboration with Pynson resulted in
an attractive and saleable volume that would have benefited the reputations
(and pocketbooks) of both parties. I will save the question of the date, title
page and woodcut for sections two and three, focusing on the ballads here.

Early printed saints' lives rarely contain any prefatory texts. Liminary
genres in print worked rather differently than they had in manuscripts as
a result of the shift to large scale book production and the need to move
speculatively printed material.[11] Religious literature, however, had a ready
market,[12] so commendatory verses and author-penned prologues would
be superfluous advertising. Of the twenty-four early printed saints' lives I
have examined, only three are attributed to contemporary writers and only
Bradshaw's *Werburge* and Alexander Barclay's translation of Baptista
Spagnuoli's *Life of St George*[13] contain any prefatory material. Barclay's
George, which contains a dedicatory verse prologue for Thomas, Duke of
Norfolk, and a Latin prose prologue for Nicholas West, bishop-elect of
Ely, is clearly anomalous, a translation of humanist hagiography printed
with the Latin in the margins as proof of its antecedents. The Chester
verses establish *Werburge* as equally anomalous, for unlike other printed
saints' lives whose institutional origins can be only tentatively identified,[14]
Werburge's ballads accentuate its monastic sponsorship.

Before delving into the ballads' details, I need to describe the imprint's
paratexts in order.[15] The title page contains a woodcut of a nun sitting at a
writing desk, with the title 'Here begynneth the holy lyfe and history of
saynt Werburge / very frutefull for all christen people to rede'. The next
two pages (¶1v–¶2) present the first commendatory ballad, 'The prologue
of J. T. in the honour & laude of saint Werburge / and of the prayse of
the translatour of the legende folowynge'; the table for Book I follows
(¶2–¶4). A second title page repeats the woodcut and gives a different

title ('Here foloweth the lyfe of the gloryous virgyn saynt Werburge / also many miracles that god hath shewed for her / & fyrst the prologe of the auctour', A1); the woodcut alone is repeated on the verso. The prologue written by Bradshaw runs from A2–A4, where the text of Book I begins. Book II has its own table (L7–L8) and prologue by Bradshaw (L8v–M2v); the poem ends on S2v and is followed by three more commendatory poems: 'A balade to the auctor' (S2v), 'An other balade' on Werburgh and Bradshaw (S3r–v), and finally 'Another balade to saynt Werburge' (S3v–S4). The colophon reads 'And thus endeth the lyfe and historye of saynt Werburge . Imprinted by Richarde Pynson / printer to the kynges noble grace / with priuilege to hym graunted by our souerayne lorde the kynge. Anno.M.D.xxi.' (S4). Pynson's printer's mark appears on the final verso.

The four commendatory poems[16] are marked by the hands of Chester monks and Bradshaw's associates. Two of the four poems are signed; the opening ballad's author, 'J. T.', has not been identified, but the writer of last ballad has. Curt F. Bühler notes the acrostic 'Bulkley C' in the ballad's last stanza, while Tim Thornton has narrowed the identification to Charles Bulkeley, monk of Chester Abbey and sometime Master of the Works.[17] Bulkeley was one of the Abbot John Birchenshawe's assistants in his ongoing legal disputes, and Thornton finds it likely that Bulkeley was operating as Birchenshawe's agent by publishing *Werburge* with Pynson.[18] Other incidental evidence suggests monastic composition; the first of the closing poems, 'A balade to the auctour', was written in the year of Bradshaw's death (ll. 19–20), while 'An other balade' also laments Bradshaw's death (ll. 23–28). The key point is that all three closing ballads were not composed within the printshop, as was common for non-humanist liminary verse in the 1510s and 1520s,[19] but by individuals who claim to have known Bradshaw in life or are demonstrably associated with his monastery.[20]

Another sign of monastic involvement is the naming and praising of Bradshaw. His name appears as an acrostic in the opening two stanzas of J. T.'s ballad, is repeated in that poem thrice, and reappears in the second-to-last ballad. Henry Bradshaw, of course, was not a name to conjure with in early Tudor London; Pynson would have gained nothing by puffing a dead monk from the marches. Chester Abbey, on the other hand, could have benefited greatly from having one of its members praised as a 'disciple of Tully' who is skilled in 'polysshed termes / and good sence litterall' ('A balade to the auctour' l. 1; 'An other balade' l. 33). William A. Ringler observes that most attributed contemporary verse printed in the early sixteenth century was published at the author's behest, while

anonymous verse was often chosen by the publisher;[21] the prominent
naming of Bradshaw thereby indicates monastic sponsorship. I find it
likely that the unknown 'J.T.' was also associated with Chester because
he, too, repeatedly names Bradshaw and because the language he uses to
describe Bradshaw – an eloquent 'floure' whose pure lifestyle kept him
'As clene as cristall' (ll. 24, 34) – echoes the floral and gemological metaphors Bradshaw uses of Werburgh throughout Book I. Not only had J. T.
read *Werburge*, he had internalized its poetics sufficiently to echo them
in his ballad. Taken together, these indications of monastic sponsorship
demonstrate the involvement of the Chester monks in the printing process.
No other early printed saint's life so loudly proclaims its institutional ties,
so I believe we are justified in reading the ballads as deliberate marketing
of text and abbey, as they strive to invite the metropolitan reader into the
poem while simultaneously extolling the singular merits of this Chester
saint and monastery.

2. Accommodating the reader, advancing the monastery

Werburge's paratexts, like the front matter of any early imprint, mediated
between the reader, the writer, the printer and the text to shape the consumer's reading experience.[22] In addition to marketing the product, the title
page and liminary ballads strive to accommodate the non-Cestrian reader
by assimilating Werburgh to familiar models of exemplarity and sanctity.
Specifically, Werburgh partakes of an early Tudor vision of historicized
holy perfection, as emphasized in the prologues to vernacular legendaries
like the *Kalendre of the Newe Legende of Englande*. The *Kalendre*'s
prologue lauds native saints' 'trewe mekenes, inuyncyble pacyence,
symple obedyence, heuenly wysdome, parfyght charyte', all virtues
explicitly associated with an older, declining but still valued spiritual practice.[23] This form of religious writing shared with contemplative texts a
concern for readerly emulation while also emphasizing the saint's intercessory abilities. By highlighting Werburgh's exemplary and intercessionary
features, these paratexts engage the audience by creating a familiar devotional space for the non-Cestrian reader to praise and venerate Werburgh.
Yet the front matter cannot fully exclude Werburgh's role as the exclu-
sive patron of Chester Abbey. Nor should it, for in presenting her Chester
identity, the ballads also preserve the monks' claim to singular holiness.
These tensions, between Werburgh's local and national appeals, are the
product of the multiple and somewhat contradictory ends of the imprint.

Werburgh's sanctity elevates the monastery amidst contemporary religious affairs; as her caretakers and devotees, the monks participate intimately with her ethical heritage and benefit from her intercession. The imprint must also, however, render *Werburge* attractive to a metropolitan audience familiar with devotional literary conventions, if not with Werburgh. The former goal cannot be met unless the poem is read widely, but it would not be so read without engaging a broad readership. The ballads thus capitalize on Werburgh's potential for universal appeal in order to promulgate widely her *Life* and regional authority.

The process of finding *Werburge* a wide audience begins with the title page, as its woodcut associates the printed *Werburge* with devotional literature emanating from Syon Abbey. The woodcut[24] depicts a female nun, St Bridget, writing at a desk, an angel on her shoulder and meditative images surrounding her. Pynson used this woodcut two other times: to open the 'Life of St Bridget' appended to the *Kalendre of the Newe Legende* and for the 1526 *Pylgrimage of Perfection*[25] by William Bonde, monk of the Bridgettine Syon Abbey. Martha Driver has identified this woodcut as modelled on a cut of Bridget receiving her Revelations, used frequently by de Worde.[26] In the hands of de Worde, as Driver has demonstrated, this woodcut was used exclusively for texts originating from Syon Abbey; she suggests that the 'woodcut functions as an imprimatur, a seal of approval, and bookplate, assuring the reader of the authenticity of the textual contents'.[27] Pynson's other two uses of his version of the cut are similarly linked to Bridget and / or Syon, making his use of the image for *Werburge* its only non-Bridgettine appearance. Surely this is not a factotum deployment of the woodcut; Pynson's use of his Bridget cut here seems a deliberate attempt to market *Werburge* as the type of text that would appeal to readers of Syon-sponsored texts.[28] The title too, heralding *Werburge* as 'very frutefull for all christen people to rede', highlights its universal and ethical productiveness, perhaps echoing Syon-affiliated texts with horticultural titles, like the *Orchard of Syon*[29] and the *Fruyte of Redempcyon*.[30] Before turning a page, the London reader is asked to associate *Werburge* with spiritual writing authorized by one of England's most respected religious institutions. Such an association between a Mercian abbess and a continental visionary is tenuous at best, highlighting the gap between text and paratext opened by the front matter's attempt to disseminate *Werburge* widely, but it also illustrates the care with which this marketing was pursued.

This assimilation of *Werburge* to devotional literary conventions continues, if less univocally, in the liminal ballads. As the first text the bookstall-browser would encounter, J.T.'s opening ballad would shape readers' expectations of the poem. Werburgh's Chester affiliation is never mentioned in the opening two stanzas; rather, they praise those features of her sanctity lauded in the print legendaries. Her virginity is early established ('intact / as pure as cristall', l. 3), as is her singular holiness in life ('None was the lyke / wydowe / mayde / ne wyfe', l. 7) and her effectiveness as an intercessor, a 'Relefe to all synners' (l. 4):

> By diuyne grace / to *vs* a ryche present,
> Reioyce *we* may / in Werburge *one and all*,
> A gemme of vertue / a virgin resplendent,
> Dilect of *our* lorde (in ioye and blis eternall
> Surely she is set) to intercede and call,
> Her mouth nat cessyng / *for them* to call and crye
> *And in her trust* / of synne to haue mercy (ll. 8–14, emphasis added).

The inclusive use of the first person plural draws the reader into the community of those who rejoice in divine benefits available through Werburgh, and her role as heavenly advocate is open to any who 'in her trust', making the position of petitioner available to all readers. The title page and initial stanzas of the imprint thereby open a devotional space for non-Cestrian readers by highlighting Werburgh's universal benevolence within a print tradition of historicized hagiography.

This expansive move is continued by certain aspects of the three closing ballads. Coming after the *Life* proper, these poems function as a form of 'exit counselling' to guide concluding reflections on the text. Although all the closing ballads invite this universal appreciation of *Werburge*, the final, Bulkeley ballad offers the most open – and the most problematic – space for the non-Cestrian reader to voice his or her devotion. The five-stanza poem is phrased as a first person prayer asking Werburgh to help reform the speaker's life. By voicing the prayer and accepting the implied subject-position of the praying *I*, the reader enacts the prayer's sense of repentance, desire for an austere lifestyle and overall devotion to the saint. The mode of repentance and veneration is in no way Chester-specific: in subsequent stanzas, the *I* requests help 'Aydynge my fraylete and lyfe vacillaunt' (l. 2), lauds Werburgh's holy and catholic parentage, praises Werburgh's virtue and 'doctrine celicall' in life (l. 18), rejects worldliness and asks for Werburgh's succour and finally begs Werburgh to 'Be nowe beniuolent / whan I shall on the call' (l. 33). The way the praying *I* constructs the speaker's performance of the prayer's remorse ensures that the title's promise is met; the poem's morally generative abilities are executed as the *I* asks Werburgh to preserve him or her from vice and cupidity. The frame begun by the title page and J.T.'s commendatory prologue is completed by the closing ballad as it firmly establishes *Werburge*'s ability to engender repentance and ethical action, not just within a closed group of privileged, Cestrian devotees, but among 'all christen people'.

Despite these deictic openings for a non-Chester readership, the ballads cannot sustain their expansiveness. Each returns, decisively, to the singularity of the relationship between Werburgh and the Chester monks, reserving her intercession for them. The opening, J.T. ballad, while it does highlight Cestrian singularity, maintains the most inclusivity; after the opening stanzas broadly lauding Werburgh, the poem narrows its focus to the now-dead author, praising his literary skills and his virtue in life. Bradshaw is elevated to a quasi-saintly status, as the ballad recycles Bradshaw's own images to describe both Bradshaw and Werburgh. Just as Werburgh is 'pure as cristall' (l. 3), Bradshaw is 'clene as cristall' (l. 34); Werburgh is a 'gemme of vertue' (l. 10) while Bradshaw is a now-lost 'treasure' (l. 22). This ethical elevation of Bradshaw, 'sometyme monke in Chester' (l. 17), hints at Chester Abbey's spiritual superiority as a result of its patronal relationship with Werburgh, the subject of and inspiration for Bradshaw's poem. In lamenting his death, the poem acknowledges the loss to Chester, but also makes space for non-Cestrian readers:

> Alas, of Chestre / ye monkes haue lost a treasure,
> Henry Bradsha / the styrpe of eloquence!
> Chestre, thou may wayle / the deth of this floure;
> So may the citezens / alas! for his absence,
> So may many other / for lacke of his sentence (ll. 22–6)

The ballad broadens its circle of mourners, from the Chester monks, to the Chester citizens, to those 'many others' knowledgeable of Bradshaw's 'sentence' in his poetry. *Any* reader is thereby envisioned as mourning alongside Cestrians, assimilating for a moment the metropolitan reader to the regional perspective. The second closing poem, on the other hand, forecloses the possibility of an expansive community of devotees. Although lines 6–8 seem to offer Werburgh's merits to all readers, the following lines limit her favours to a strictly monastic audience:

> Reioyse Chestre / reioyse ye religious
> And thanke your maker of his beniuolence
> That hath you gyuen suche treasure preciouse,
> Aduocatrice / in your most indigence! (ll. 9–12)

The expansive invocation of all readers' 'spirituall hertes' (l. 4) in the previous stanza is quickly curtailed; now, it is the 'religious' of Chester, addressed in the second person, who claim Werburgh as their advocate and intercessor. The 'gemme of virtue' available to all in J.T.'s ballad here belongs solely to Chester Abbey, and Werburgh becomes the representative solely of her monastic community.

The closing ballad by Charles Bulkeley most strongly demonstrates just how tenuous are the imprint's efforts to make room for the metropolitan reader and why such accommodations might not be in the sponsoring monks' best interests. As long as the *I* of the closing ballad remains an empty deictic marker, to be filled by the speaker, the poem invites any reader to inhabit its penitent position. However, because the poem is signed, the *I* can also refer specifically to the writer of the poem, the monk Charles Bulkeley. In this reading, the poem becomes a monastic cry to Werburgh for assistance in refusing worldly temptations and embracing a more austere life. The poem opens with Bulkeley adopting a posture of repentant abjection:

> Renegate and contumace in all obstinacion,
> Bewrapt with all synne / detestable and recreaunt (ll. 3–4).

After praising Werburgh's heritage and doctrine, Bulkeley continues to petition Werburgh

> Wordly felicite [to] abiect from my courage;
> Enuy and pride / with lustes voluptuous
> Rancorous cupidite myn hert sore do aswage (ll. 25–26).

Werburge is still morally productive in this reading, but now it is the monk Bulkeley called to contrition, aware of human 'fraylete' (l. 2) as a threat to his observance of monastic rigours. His requests are all particularly appropriate to a monastic *I*, as when he asks that Werburgh 'Rancorous cupidite myn hert sore do aswage' (l. 27). The narrowing of the audience to the monastic community at Chester coalesces in this reading, in the line 'Gouerned by grace / were thy disciples all' (l. 23); the knowledge that this line is voiced by a Chester monk highlights not the expansive potential of an ever-widening circle of Werburgh's 'disciples', but rather the narrow identification of the historical members of her community.

Unlike the other ballads, which oscillate between appeals to a universal audience and promotion of a unique Werburgh-Chester bond, Bulkeley's ballad is perpetually suspended between them, simultaneously available to both monastic and metropolitan readers. The capacity for this double reading enacts the unresolved tension between two of the imprint's envisioned communities of Werburgh's devotees – the savvy Londoner conversant with printed devotional material and the regional monk taking his institutional identity from the saint. These paratexts attempt no resolution (indeed, the irresolution is strongest at the book's conclusion) because any resolution would undermine the imprint's advancement of Chester Abbey. The universalizing appeals function to elevate Werburgh, and hence Chester Abbey, within a familiar devotional discourse of intercession and spiritual renewal by using the tools of metropolitan print culture. Why the ballad writers should then so carefully emphasize their distinguishing relationship with their patron – especially when Bradshaw's poem already isolates that relationship – can be uncovered by turning to this essay's last outstanding question: why 1521? Examining reasons behind the publication's timing helps explain why the Chester monks might wish to emphasize their Werburgh-derived singularity to a national readership.

3: Monastic Reform and the 'Primitive Church'

Literature under the first two Tudor kings, as Alistair Fox and Andrew Hadfield have demonstrated, was inseparable from political engagement,[31] and in this way Bradshaw's *Werburge* – in both its pre-1513 and 1521 manifestations – was the product of its time. Where Bradshaw's poem originally addressed tensions between city and monastery, the printed form reframes the poem's participation in political affairs, speaking to affairs at the centre of English politics, especially concerns about spiritual authenticity, welling up in 1520–1. Tim Thornton has shown how the printing defends the abbot's jurisdictions against legatine interference,[32] while Barrett reads the printing as part of the royally sponsored attack on Lutheranism.[33] To these contexts I wish to add a third: Cardinal Wolsey's proposed Benedictine reform. To defend the abbey's spiritual integrity, *Werburge*'s monastic sponsors drew readers' attention to the abbey's continual observance of traditional monastic virtue, heightening its spiritual centrality within a broader chorography of England. The net result offers a London readership more than a defence of monastic rights; it demonstrates how an appeal to regional, institutional antiquity and traditional monasticism could function as a progressive response to contemporary issues.

Both Bradshaw's poem and the Chester ballads portray Chester Abbey as a site of ancient and pure monastic observance, suggesting that *Werburge*'s 1521 printing may have been a Chester response to Cardinal Wolsey's efforts, in his role as papal legate, to reform the English Benedictines.

That effort began in 1519 with preparations for a 1520 convocation of the monastic orders, apparently to propose a reversion to a narrower interpretation of the Rule with an emphasis on austerity and regular observance.[34] Religious reform, including reform of the regular orders, was in the wind in the fifteenth and early sixteenth centuries,[35] and many Tudor reformers desired a return to the austerity of an earlier age. In 1519, for example, the reforming Richard Fox, Bishop of Winchester, wrote to Wolsey lamenting the loss of 'omnia quae ad antiquam cleri et praecipue monachiae integritatem' ('everything belonging to the ancient integrity of the clergy, and especially of the monastic life'),[36] while that same year John Longland, Bishop of Lincoln, exhorted the Westminster monks to attain the high standards of their predecessors by renewing their dedication to poverty, chastity and obedience.[37] Wolsey's 1520 convocation occurred within this climate of reform, although the details of his proposed Benedictine reform are unavailable – he circulated a book of statutes, probably before the 1520 meeting, which is unfortunately lost. Some of the abbots who did read it, however, produced an extant document objecting to Wolsey's statutes and hinting at their contents.[38] The reforms are undesirable, the abbots claim, because black monks nowadays do not desire to observe the Rule's stringencies; imposing such rigorous change will only drive away current monks and limit recruits. These objections reveal both a deep-seated debate over the best form of contemporary monasticism and the reformers' nostalgia for the 'ancient integrity' (in Bishop Fox's words) of monastic life. The 1519–20 interest in monastic change was received by some abbots as a threat to their autonomy and lifestyle, even as the idea of retrograde reform was common among, and attractive to, influential ecclesiasts.

Werburge's printing a year after this council met may have been Chester Abbey's contribution to reform discussions by positioning the abbey as long observing these 'ancient' monastic values. Bradshaw's poem strongly resonates with the reforming bishops' emphasis on traditional monastic virtues, as it highlights the spiritual austerity of Werburgh's community. On her deathbed, for example, Werburgh stresses to her nuns the value of poverty, charity, obedience and temperance (I: 3012–39) and exhorts her nuns to regular observance and to embrace those actions lauded by the reforming bishops:

> In deuyne seruyce / loke ye contynu;
> Obseruynge pacyence / mekenes / and chastyte. (I: 3006–7)

Moreover, early in Book II Bradshaw presents his vision of the English 'primatiue churche' of Werburgh's day (II: 151); then, even nobles eagerly embraced the austerities later disdained by the Tudor abbots when they took religious vows,

> Professed obedient, chaste, without propurte,
> Vertue to encrease / true loue and charite. (II: 153–4)

Although the purity of this 'primatiue' English church is lost with time (II: 162–8), it inheres in Werburgh, her relics and her later community. Her relic translation to Chester in the seventh century imbues the city and its clerics, Bradshaw claims, with a renewed religious fervour:

> Diuine seruice was obserued deuoutly
> Euery day, encreasyng with feruent adoracion . . .
> Preistis and clerkes with pure meditacion
> Obseruynge their dutie gaue vertuous example
> Of great perfection to the comon people (II: 562–8)

Throughout *Werburge*, Bradshaw portrays the saint and her community as perpetuating traditional monastic values and fervent spiritual devotion. Distributing this text in the reforming climate of the early 1520s would portray the Chester monks as already demonstrating the integrity of ancient monasticism that Fox, Longland and perhaps Wolsey were advocating. Bradshaw's *Werburge* thereby maps Chester Abbey as central to this reform discourse, offering place and community as examples of proper monastic observance and defending them against reproach by claiming to be always, already reformed.

The way Bradshaw's poem can be read as a ready-made response to Wolsey's propositions suggests to me that this may be a pivotal reason for the 1521 printing; moreover, the paratextual emphasis on the singular relationship between Werburgh and her abbey reinforces the poem's portrayal of Chester Abbey as rigorously observant. The woodcuts' implicit association with Syon Abbey, for example, links the imprint to one of the orders universally recognized as still upholding a more stringent observance.[39] The opening ballad's quasi-sanctification of Bradshaw works similarly. Beyond assimilating him to Werburgh's virginal sanctity, it also highlights Bradshaw's rejection of 'Enuy and wrath' and 'Auarice and glotony' while embracing 'Chastite / obidience / and wylfull pouerte' (ll. 30, 32, 35). Not only does the dead poet's spiritual probity authorize his poem, but it also allows him to stand in metonymically for his community: surely a monastery that could produce such a holy writer must be scrupulous itself. The closing Bulkeley ballad also portrays the monastery as a place of ongoing spiritual renewal and adherence to traditional monasticism. When voiced by an abject monkish *I*, the poem depicts Chester Abbey as continually performing these revalued traits. Yet the poem exceeds the reforming bishops' vision of renewal by casting traditional monastic virtues not as static values to be legislated, but as states of being maintained through a process of repentance and regeneration. Bulkeley's ballad more sensitively portrays the challenges of austere monasticism than can episcopal nostalgia, while not rejecting that lifestyle as impractical or inappropriate. And over the entire process stands Werburgh, patron of Chester, who can offer the contrite monk a 'memoriall' of 'Knowlege effectuall of thy lyfe pure' – that is, her *Life* – to help him 'Euer in purite [his] lyfe to contynue' (ll. 35, 36, 38). In this context, not only is the Bulkeley-voiced poem witness to the continuing efforts of Werburgh's monks to maintain the high moral standard sought by the reforming bishops, but *Werburge* becomes 'very frutefull' not only for 'all christen people', as its title proclaims, but particularly fruitful for the monastic life, within and beyond Chester Abbey.

The 1521 printing positions *Werburge* within early print conventions of religious writing while identifying the monks as privileged participants in Werburgh's sanctity and 'primitiue' English spirituality. The imprint strives to put Chester on London readers' cognitive map, both topographically, via Bradshaw's opening geographical description, and culturally. The repackaging of this regionally focused saint's life not only opens *Werburge* to a universalizing and exemplary reading of the kind Sanok has suggested, but also highlights the Chester monks' contribution to contemporary religious discussions. Their distinctive relationship with Werburgh and her idealized monastic observance allows them to portray their community as participating in an ancient monastic tradition, rooted in the very foundation of English spiritual history. If living on the margins can enable cultural and spiritual authority, as Kathy Lavezzo suggests,[40] then Chester Abbey's location on the kingdom's periphery enhances its exemplary potential. In the ballads, the quasi-saintly Bradshaw and the penitent Bulkeley both act as current exemplars of Chester monastic virtue to stand alongside the pre-Conquest examples of Werburgh and her nuns. The printed *Werburge* thereby proclaims the Chester monks' long-standing centrality to the question of traditional monastic observance being debated at the heart of English ecclesiastical life. The periphery offers itself to the centre as a monastic model and a promulgator of contemporary devotional literature, combining the two in the Bulkeley ballad to characterize Chester spirituality, grounded in Werburgh, as responsibly pursuing spiritual purity.

How metropolitan readers responded to the dual programme outlined here is, of course, a largely unanswerable question. Although many probably consumed *Werburge* like any other saint's life, London readers familiar with Chester's obdurate abbot, its legal squabbles and its internal conflicts may have been sceptical of the picture of monastic virtue constructed by the paratexts. Among this readership would have been many who worked in ecclesiastical administrative offices, those whom the Chester monks would have wanted to impress with their supposedly ancient observance. These readers were also those likely to know that the 'C. Bulkeley' of the closing ballad was a monk of Chester Abbey, and so associate the ballad's penitence with renewed monastic observance – whether or not they conceded the larger point concerning Chester Abbey's ancient spiritual purity. The fact that five copies of the 1521 *Werburge* are extant, while many printed saints' lives exist only in single or fragmentary copies, does demonstrate the esteem accorded it by some. Moreover, we do know that some readers valued *Werburge* for its chorographic description of Mercia's place within England's spiritual history. Readers of the British Library copy of *Werburge*[41] heavily annotated the poem, noting key dates and figures of English religious history alongside supposedly early religious practices – including Werburgh's 'obedyence', 'chastyte', and 'pouerte', all heavily underlined by one reader (I: 1749–50, fol. 2r). For these readers, the 1521 *Werburge* was indeed a 'map' to Chester's place in an ancient spiritual tradition, Mercian history and the geography of England, past and present.

Notes

1 Robert W. Barrett, *Against All England: Regional Identity and Cheshire Writing, 1195–1656* (Notre Dame, 2009), pp. 44–51, p. 47; Tim Thornton, 'Opposition drama and the resolution of disputes in early Tudor England: Cardinal Wolsey and the abbot of Chester', *Bulletin of the John Rylands Library*, 81 (1999), 25–47, pp. 37–44.

2 Katherine J. Lewis, 'History, historiography and re-writing the past', in Sarah Salih (ed.), *A Companion to Middle English Hagiography* (Woodbridge, 2006), pp. 122–140, p.136.

3 Barrett, *Against All England*, p. 17; Clarke in this volume.

4 In this essay, early books and woodcuts will be referred to by Short Title Catalogue (STC) and Hodnett numbers, respectively. See A. W. Pollard and G. R. Redgrave (eds), *A Short-Title Catalogue of Books Printed in England, Scotland and Ireland, and of English Books Printed Abroad 1475–1640*, second edn (London, 1991), and Edward Hodnett, *English Woodcuts 1480–1535*, second edn (Oxford, 1973). Bradshaw's *Life of St Werburge* is STC 3506. The most recent complete edition is Henry Bradshaw, *The Life of Saint Werburge of Chester*, Carl Horstmann

(ed.), EETS OS 88 (London, 1887); for a detailed discussion of *Werburge* and its contents, see Catherine A. M. Clarke's introduction to her selective edition of *Werburge* on the 'Mapping Medieval Chester' website *www.medievalchester. ac.uk* (accessed 30 September 2009).

⁵ A. T. Thacker, 'Later medieval Chester 1230–1550: Religion, 1230–1550', in *VCH Ches*. 5. i, pp. 80–9, pp. 87–9.

⁶ B. W. Kissan, 'An early list of London properties', *London and Middlesex Archaeological Society*, New Series 8 (1940), 56–69, pp. 60, 62, 65. The shift in name can be traced through London wills; compare the changes recorded in Roll 63 (97), Roll 77 (86), and Roll 84 (66) in Reginald R. Sharpe (ed.), *Calendar of the Wills Proved and Enrolled at the Court of Hustings* (London, 1889–90), vol. 1, pp. 406, 596, 690–1.

⁷ Catherine Sanok, *Her Life Historical: Exemplarity and Female Saints' Lives in Medieval England* (Philadelphia, 2007), pp. 83–110.

⁸ See especially William Kuskin, *Symbolic Caxton: Literary Culture and Print Capitalism* (Notre Dame, 2008), and the essays he edited in *Caxton's Trace: Studies in the History of English Printing* (Notre Dame, 2006).

⁹ STC 13440.

¹⁰ Stanley Howard Johnson, 'A study of the career and literary publications of Richard Pynson' (unpublished Ph.D. thesis, University of Western Ontario, 1977), pp. 160–3; H. S. Bennett, *English Books & Readers 1475–1557* (Cambridge, 1952), pp. 65–76.

¹¹ Michael Saenger, *The Commodification of Textual Engagements in the English Renaissance* (Burlington, 2006), esp. pp. 8–10; A. S. G. Edwards and Carol M. Meale, 'The marketing of printed books in late medieval England', *The Library*, 6th series 15 (1993), 95–124; Russell Rutter, 'William Caxton and literary patronage', *Studies in Philology*, 84 (1987), 440–70. The full apparatus of preliminaries becomes ubiquitous in the 1550s: Arthur F. Marotti, *Manuscript, Print, and the English Renaissance Lyric* (Ithaca, 1995), pp. 291–302.

¹² Mary C. Erler, 'Devotional Literature', *The Cambridge History of the Book in Britain*, vol. 3 (Cambridge, 1998), pp. 495–525; H. S. Bennett, *English Books & Readers 1475–1557* (Cambridge, 1952), pp. 65–76.

¹³ Pynson 1515, STC 22992.1. William Nelson (ed.), *The Life of St George*, EETS OS 230 (London, 1955). Print legendaries, on the other hand, all contain prologues.

¹⁴ The *Life of Joseph of Arimathea* in rhyme royal (Pynson 1520, STC 14807), one of several possible examples, bears all the hallmarks of Glastonbury sponsorship without the clear paratextual links of *Werburge*; see Valerie M. Lagorio, 'The evolving legend of St Joseph of Glastonbury', *Speculum*, 46 (1971), 209–231, pp. 229–30.

¹⁵ Throughout, I will cite parenthetically the ballads and texts of *Werburge* by line number from Horstmann's edition; here only, to demonstrate the position of the paratexts within the book, I cite by signature from Pynson's printing.

¹⁶ The classic study is Franklin B. Williams, Jr., 'Commendatory verses: the rise of the art of puffing', *Studies in Bibliography*, 19 (1966), 1–14.

¹⁷ Curt F. Bühler, 'Note on the "Balade to Saynt Werburge"', *Modern Language Notes*, 68 (1953), 538–9, p. 539; Thornton, 'Opposition drama', p. 44.

[18] Thornton, 'Opposition Drama', p. 44–5.

[19] Julia Boffey, 'Early printers and English lyrics: sources, selections, and presentation of texts', *Papers of the Bibliographic Society of America*, 85 (1991), 19–20; Helen Phillips, 'Aesthetic and commercial aspects of framing devices: Bradshaw, Roos and Copland', *Poetica*, 43 (1995), 37–65; Mary Carpenter Erler (ed.), *Robert Copland: Poems* (Toronto, 1993), pp. 11–15; David R. Carlson, *English Humanist Books: Writers and Patrons, Manuscript and Print, 1475–1525* (Toronto, 1993), pp. 148–9; Williams, 'Commendatory verses', pp. 1–4; Saenger, *Commodification*, pp. 72–6.

[20] J. W. Saunders has suggested the ballads were composed while the poem circulated in manuscript, then were printed accidentally from loose papers 'slipped in' to the exemplar: 'From manuscript to print: a note on the circulation of poetic MSS in the sixteenth century', *Proceedings of the Leeds Philosophical and Literary Society, Literary and Historical Section*, 6 (1951), 507–28, p. 515. Although 'A balade to the auctour' and 'An other balade' were certainly composed during the now-lost exemplar's manuscript circulation, accidental printing is unlikely.

[21] William A. Ringler, Jr., *Bibliography and Index of English Verse Printed 1476–1558* (London, 1988), p. 9. More generally, see A. S. G. Edwards, 'From manuscript to print: Wynkyn de Worde and the printing of contemporary poetry', *Gutenberg-Jahrbuch* (1991), 143–148; and Boffey, 'Early printers'.

[22] Heidi Brayman Hackel, *Reading Material in Early Modern England: Print, Gender, and Literacy* (Cambridge, 2005), pp. 85–125; Marotti, *Manuscript, Print*, pp. 222–3, 293.

[23] Pynson 1516, STC 4602. Manfred Görlach (ed.), *The Kalendre of the Newe Legende of Englande* (Heidelberg, 1994), pp. 44, 65–7. Sanok, *Her Life Historical*, pp. 110–12 discusses the *Kalendre*'s exemplary focus.

[24] Hodnett 1349.

[25] STC 3277.

[26] Hodnett 457.

[27] Martha W. Driver, 'Nuns as patrons, artists, readers: Bridgettine woodcuts in printed books produced for the English market', in Carol Garrett Fisher and Kathleen L. Scott (eds), *Art into Life: Collected Papers from the Kresge Art Museum Medieval Symposia* (East Lansing, MI, 1995), pp. 249–52, p. 250; Driver, 'Pictures in print: late fifteenth- and early sixteenth-century English religious books for lay readers', in Michael G. Sargent (ed.), *De Cella in Seculum: Religious and Secular Life and Devotion in Late Medieval England* (Cambridge, 1989), pp. 229–44, pp. 243–4. On Syon's involvement with printing, see J. T. Rhodes, 'Syon Abbey and its religious publications in the sixteenth century', *Journal of Ecclesiastical History*, 44 (1993), 11–25.

[28] See Sanok, *Her Life Historical*, p. 115 for another interpretation of the woodcut's reuse.

[29] de Worde 1519, STC 4815.

[30] Two imprints predate *Werburge*: de Worde 1514, STC 22557 and de Worde 1517, STC 22558.

[31] Alistair Fox, *Politics and Literature in the Reigns of Henry VII and Henry VIII* (Oxford, 1989); Andrew Hadfield, *Literature, Politics and National Identity: Reformation to Renaissance* (Cambridge, 1994).

[32] Thornton, 'Opposition Drama', pp. 44–5.

[33] Barrett, *Against All England*, pp. 51–8.

[34] Peter Gwyn, *The King's Cardinal: The Rise and Fall of Thomas Wolsey* (London, 1990), pp. 270–1; David Knowles, *The Religious Orders in England, Volume III: The Tudor Age* (Cambridge, 1959), pp. 159–60; William H. Pantin (ed.), *Documents Illustrating the Activities of the General and Provincial Chapters of the English Black Monks*, vol. 3 (London, 1937), pp. 117–18.

[35] Hubert Jedin, *A History of the Council of Trent*, Ernest Graf (trans.), vol. I (London, 1957), pp. 5–165; Gwyn, *King's Cardinal*, pp. 338–51.

[36] Richard Fox, *The Letters of Richard Fox, 1486–1527*, P. S. Allen and H. M. Allen (eds) (Oxford, 1929), p. 115, my translation.

[37] Margaret Bowker, *The Henrician Reformation: The Diocese of Lincoln under John Longland, 1521–1547* (Cambridge, 1981), pp. 17–18; Gwyn, *King's Cardinal*, pp. 333–4.

[38] Gwyn, *King's Cardinal*, pp. 273–4; Pantin, *Documents*, vol. 3, pp. 123–4.

[39] Knowles, *Religious Orders III*, pp. 212–21 and Pantin, *Documents*, vol. 3, pp. 124.

[40] Kathy Lavezzo, *Angels on the Edge of the World: Geography, Literature, and English Community, 1000–1534* (Ithaca, 2006), esp. pp. 38–44.

[41] Shelfmark C.21.c.40; Clarke discusses these marginalia further at pp. 214–15 below.

9

The Outside Within: Medieval Chester and North Wales as a Social Space

HELEN FULTON

From a modern perspective, one of the central ideas about medieval Chester is its image as a border city, marking the difference between the English and the Welsh. Politically and geographically, this was the case: the political border between England and Wales in the north was the river Dee, so when travellers from Wales came into Chester they crossed the bridge over the Dee from the south and entered both Chester and England by the Bridge gate at the south-west corner of the city.

Socially and experientially, however, the border was imagined differently from the subject positions of English and Welsh. Neither group, identified by linguistic and cultural practices as well as by significant legal and administrative factors, treated the political border as a 'hard barrier' between two separate spaces, but each appropriated the landscape in different ways. In this essay, I will use the evidence of late medieval Welsh poems which refer to Chester – one of the few Welsh language sources of information about Welsh attitudes to the English in north Wales and Chester – to suggest that in many respects the city and its western neighbourhood formed a single social space. Within this shared space, however, English and Welsh defined themselves in opposition to each other and understood the space differently. The evidence of the poems suggests that the Welsh interpretation of Chester as a social space was in many respects at odds with that of the English and that the uses made of Chester by Welsh people was to a large extent transgressive of the English hegemonic order.

The documentary records for Cheshire and north Wales are almost entirely those of the English royal administration, written in French or

Latin, occasionally capturing some Welsh place names or personal names, along with regular complaints about the rebellious Welsh and what should be done about them. As for the Welsh themselves, they are silent – except for the large body of semi-formal court poetry addressed to the Welsh gentry after the conquest of north Wales by Edward I in 1282.[1] Among this body of poems, dating from the fourteenth to sixteenth centuries, there are at least twenty-five which mention Chester as a significant loca-tion.[2] The majority are religious poems, praising churchmen such as John Birkenshaw, the abbot of St Werburgh's in Chester in 1493–1524 and again in 1529–38, or in praise of the holy cross at Chester, the gilt and wood cross in the collegiate church of St John the Baptist which was a major pilgrim destination for the whole region around Chester.[3] A few poems describe military campaigns relating to the Wars of the Roses and several others have a satirical purpose. These poems provide the best evidence we have for the relationship between medieval Chester and the people of north Wales, as seen by the Welsh themselves.

Transgression and the 'outside'

Poststructural theories of space and identity have suggested ways in which we can view topographical or geographical space as 'always already' constituted as social space, that is, as a place or places which have specific meanings constructed by social practice.[4] In other words, geographical space, whether empty or occupied, is constantly being reconfigured as 'place', somewhere that is imbued with institutional meaning. An empty landscape, containing only trees and fields, can be read in various ways as institutionally-constructed 'place' – as economically-productive farmland, as the estates of the nobility, as the scene of peasant oppression and so on. Individual users of a space, according to Michel de Certeau, construct for themselves a specific spatial experience which may escape or transgress the institutional panoptic gaze (though I would argue that individuals and their practices are themselves institutionally produced).[5] Thus, the Welsh in Chester, who were not officially recognized as legitimate users of the city (that is, as citizens), found ways to transgress its limits, for example by occupying the religious space of the church of St John the Baptist where they worshipped the holy cross.

Implicit within this concept of geographical space as semiotically-defined 'place' is the notion of borders: without these, institutional 'places' lack definition and therefore cannot be easily controlled by hegemonic

power. Borders themselves, whether physical (like the river Dee) or representational (a line on a map) are semiotic constructs whose authority of
meaning rests solely upon a hegemonic consensus regarding the status of
the places on each side of the border. The social geographers Wolfgang
Natter and John Paul Jones have described the work done by borders
and boundaries in constructing artificial binary opposites of 'inside' and
'outside'. They show that, like all binary opposites, one side tends to
be privileged over the other, creating a hierarchy in which 'inside' the
boundary is a more powerful place than 'outside'. Yet crucially, as they
describe it, the boundary itself is contingent:

> The constitutive outside is a relational process by which the outside – or 'other'
> – of any category is actively at work on both sides of the constructed boundary,
> and is thus always leaving its trace within the category. Thus, what may appear
> to be a self-enclosed category maintained by boundaries is found in fact to
> unavoidably contain the marks of inscription left by the outside from which it
> seemingly has been separated . . . The outside of any category is already found
> to be resident within, permeating the category from the *inside* through its trace-
> able presence-in-absence within the category.[6]

This process, by which the constructed outside inevitably leaves traces
of itself on the inside, thus revealing the partial and mythical nature of
the boundary itself, is amply illustrated in the history of English colonization of Wales. If Wales was (and still is) constituted as 'outside' Chester,
through a hegemonic discourse of borders and exclusion, medieval Wales
nonetheless left its traces within and upon the city, inscribing itself as a
'presence-in-absence' through textual and material representation. At the
same time, Chester itself, and the dominant power which it represented,
overflowed into Wales, inscribing itself there through the processes of
urbanization and governance. Various kinds of interactions worked to
expose the limits of Chester's walls as anything more than a semiotic
boundary, while political, economic and cultural practices spilled over
from one side to the other. In many significant ways, Chester and north
Wales formed a single social space in which dichomotized identities, such
as Welsh and English, town and country, inside and outside, were denatu-
ralized and decentered.

The relative geography of north Wales and Chester

The subjectivities of English and Welsh are characterized by different
mental maps of Britain. From the English point of view, Chester has a

key location on an east-west axis marking a clear boundary between two very different nations, England and Wales. From the Welsh point of view, however, the boundary with England has always been compromised by the multilingualism and multiculturalism of the March and Chester was a Marcher city with the same kind of diversity. The historian Philip Morgan has come close to recognizing this with his description of Chester as 'ethnically diverse', but he also refers to what he calls the 'Welsh version' of Cheshire history: what he means by this is not a version of Cheshire history produced by the Welsh, but a version of the Welsh produced by English writers of Cheshire history who have constructed a self-image of Chester as 'a bastion against Wales' wherein the Welsh are marginalized and humiliated.[7] According to Morgan, this 'Welsh version' constructs a myth of Chester's hostility towards the Welsh which conflicts with the reality in which both city and county offered assimilation and tolerance towards the Welsh. This 'Welsh version' also conflicts with the actual uses made by the Welsh of Chester as a shared social space, since the Welsh often resisted offers of 'assimilation and tolerance' and instead appropriated the 'place' of Chester as part of a specifically Welsh spatial experience of the city.

Morgan is right to point to the evidence of Welsh settlement in the border lands of Cheshire as an example of assimilation and there are certainly cases of men of Welsh descent becoming part of the Chester elite by the fifteenth century, holding senior offices such as that of mayor. What this points to is a degree of assimilation which extends beyond Chester and the western boundaries of Cheshire into the eastern lands of Wales, eliding the political boundary between the two countries.[8] To the west and south of Chester were neighbourhoods belonging to a common culture of the March in which Welsh and English lived as neighbours, united by geography but divided by a regional and linguistic identity differently experienced.

There is a further dimension to these very different mental maps of the same terrain. From the English point of view, Chester was the border between England and Wales; but from the Welsh point of view, the true borderland of the northern frontier, the location of a hybrid culture accommodating both Welsh and English, was not Chester or Cheshire, but Flintshire. Following his conquest of north Wales in 1282, Edward I divided the traditional Welsh territories of the north along a typically English east-west axis. Those lands to the west of the river Conwy, Llywelyn ap Gruffudd's former realm of Gwynedd, were put under the jurisdiction of a justice of north Wales, based at Caernarfon. In the east, the old native lands of Tegeingl and Maelor Saesneg were combined into an expanded county of Flint, under the jurisdiction of the justice of Chester.[9] In other words, the north-east of Wales became part of an English administrative structure, while the north-west, like other parts of native Wales further south, were left on the margins as outlying provinces of the English empire.

Flintshire after 1284 was therefore a contested space, technically in Wales but extensively colonized by English settlers and dominated by the English borough town of Flint. Around it, to the west and south, were Marcher lordships created by Edward I, in Denbigh, Dyffryn Clwyd and Bromfield and Yale: Welsh lands given by Edward to aristocratic families in exchange for military service. The Welsh population of these areas was largely displaced, removed to the least habitable parts of the lordships or otherwise encouraged to leave by the imposition of taxes. An inventory of the lands owned by the lord of Denbigh, Henry de Lacy, Earl of Lincoln, on his death in 1311, lists a number of commotes held by free Welsh tenants who not only paid rent to the lord of Denbigh but also their customary legal payments such as *amobr*, the fee paid to the lord when a woman was given in marriage:

> Et dicu't qd. p'des. Comes h'uit apud Caymerth de r. ass'io libor. ten. Wallens' xx li. viij.d. o' ad festa Natal. Dni. Aplor . . . Et de r. assi'o nativor. Wallens' ibid'm lxiij.s. iiij.d ad eosde. t'minos . . . & est ibide' q^cdam consuetudo que vocat^r Amobr' que val. p. annu' xl.s. pli'ta & p'quisit. Cur. Wallens'.

> (And they say that the said Earl had in Cinmerch, from the rents of free Welsh tenants, twenty pounds, and eight pence halfpenny, at the feasts of Christmas [and] of the Apostles . . . And from the rent-charges of Welsh natives there, sixty-three shillings and four pence at the same seasons . . . And there is a certain custom called Amober, which is worth forty shillings per annum, and the fees and perquisites of the Welsh court.)[10]

As in many parts of Wales after 1284, particularly in the north, Welsh tenants found themselves subject to English lords, paying both English and Welsh taxes and in many cases removed from their patrimonial lands. The legacy of colonization was resentment and distrust, as R. R. Davies has noted:

> The native Welsh proprietors who were expelled from their lands to make room for the colonists were often, though by no means invariably, compensated with land elsewhere in the lordship; but the lands so given to them frequently lay in remote and infertile upland districts. What might be construed mathematically as fair exchange must often have been regarded by native Welshmen as virtual internal exile and brazen dispossession. It was to leave a bequest of bitterness which soured relationships between natives and settlers in north-east Wales throughout the fourteenth century.[11]

Given this pattern of colonization, in which displaced Welsh farmers and labourers and a few remaining Welsh landowners were forced to give way to English lords and their tenants, it is not surprising that the north-east was the focus of a major Welsh rebellion in 1400, led by Owain Glyndŵr.[12] Owain was a hereditary Welsh lord living on his family lands in Glyndyfrdwy in Merioneth; a dispute over land with his neighbour, Sir Reginald Grey of Ruthin, an English Marcher lord, escalated into a full-scale rebellion against royal control in Wales. It came at a critical time, only a year after Henry IV had deposed Richard II to seize the throne for himself. A number of English lords, led by the Earl of Northumberland and his son Henry Percy (or Hotspur), used the Welsh rebellion to join forces with Owain Glyndŵr and challenge the legitimacy of Henry IV's kingship. Hotspur died in battle in 1403, his father in 1408, and royal authority was fully re-established by 1415, by which time Owain himself was missing, presumed dead.

During the rebellion, particularly from 1400 to 1408, the main focus of Owain's campaigns had been the English towns of Wales. From Conwy and Caernarfon in the north to Cardiff and Newport in the south, Owain and his supporters attacked and vandalized these visible symbols of the English presence in Wales. Though Owain was ultimately unsuccessful in his bid to reclaim Wales for the Welsh under his rule, his rebellion clearly identified the root cause of Welsh resentment, namely the colonial towns, founded first by the Normans and then increased by the Edwardian settlement; towns whose fortified walls and administrative authority were the price the Welsh had to pay for a market economy and greater access to consumer goods. The English had overflowed into Wales, ignoring the political border between the two countries while establishing new boundaries in the form of city walls; but the Welsh were strongly discouraged from flowing in the opposite direction, into the English towns of Wales and the March.

The city of Chester and its symbolic meaning for its Welsh neighbours has to be seen in this context of Welsh relations with English towns in general. It is almost an irrelevance that Chester was an English town in England; from the perspective of the Welsh who lived in its shadow, it was merely one of a number of English towns in the region, like Flint or Denbigh or Ruthin or Holt, whose very existence signified the administrative and economic subordination of the Welsh.[13] There is no doubt that Chester was considerably larger and more important than the English colonial towns to the west and south on the Welsh side of the border: it had a large jurisdictional area (extending into Wales), its status as a royal earldom gave its courts the authority to hear cases reserved for the King's Bench and it was a major religious centre. Nevertheless, the Welsh regarded Chester with much the same ambivalence as they regarded other English towns on the Welsh side of the border, since all were equally symptomatic of Welsh oppression by English authority.[14]

The reality of this oppression and the role of the towns in orchestrating direct discrimination against the Welsh, can be reconstructed from the numerous proclamations and statutes initiated by urban authorities against the native Welsh population in and around the English towns. The plantation towns of the Edwardian settlement in the late thirteenth century were given a monopoly of wholesale trade in their regions, effectively excluding the Welsh from becoming burgesses and enjoying the commercial advantages of urban life. The Welsh themselves were legally obliged to buy and sell their goods as retailers only within the English towns and were therefore subject to urban tolls.[15] Tentative efforts by the Welsh during the fourteenth century to infiltrate the English towns as burgesses were regularly undermined by various proclamations demanding that the Welsh should all leave, especially in times of social unrest and tension. This urban legislation is an example of writing the 'outside' into the towns themselves: even as the burgesses attempted to exclude the Welsh from their towns, the presence of the (largely absent) Welsh was written in to their urban records.

Anti-Welsh legislation in the early years of the Glyndŵr rebellion was particularly punitive: the burgesses of the Flintshire town of Hope, whose charter of 1351 was the first in north Wales explicitly to exclude Welshmen, stipulated in 1401 that 'no Welshman can or ought to acquire to himself or his heirs. . .any English land. . .for any price, so long as an English burgess is willing to buy and hold it'.[16] In September 1403, following his victory in the battle of Shrewsbury against the forces of Owain Glyndŵr and Henry Percy, the Prince of Wales and future Henry V, who was also the Earl of Chester, expelled the Welsh from Chester. They could only enter the city during the hours of daylight, they were not allowed to hold any meetings in the city (including drinking with friends in a tavern), and they had to leave any weapons or armour at the city gate, apart from a knife to cut their food.[17] This particular proclamation is perhaps related to a curious little poem about Chester composed by an unknown Welsh poet in the fifteenth or sixteenth century:

> Od ai di i Gaer, arch i'r maer roi imi gyllell;
> O gollwng ddim i ti,
>   I ddiawl geniog;
>   Ni feddai groes i ymgroesi
> Pe cawn Caer a'r maer i mi.

(If you go to Chester, ask the mayor to give me a knife;
if he doesn't allow you anything,
he can go to hell for a penny;
he wouldn't have a cross to cross himself with
if I owned Chester and the mayor.)[18]

A knife was the kind of gift which a poet might request from a patron, along with gloves, a sword, a horse and other accessories.[19] Nonetheless, the mention of a knife in relation to the mayor of Chester may well be an ironic reference to the fact that at one time the Welsh were not allowed to bring anything into the city except a knife and if that was refused, the Welshman would go hungry. The bold assertion in the last line – 'if I owned Chester and the mayor' – along with the discourse of bargaining seems to bridge the gap between north Wales and Chester, suggesting however ironically, that these are part of the same space and that the Welsh are empowered to negotiate with the (English) civic government. Along with the humour, the poem is challenging and subversive, denying the political border between the two territories and claiming equal rights of ownership of the city.

Chester as a religious site

The English towns of Wales and the March were a particular focus for Welsh oppression and Welsh resentment and Chester was one such town, part of a mapping of economic and political dominance which disregarded the official border between the two countries. It was true, as Philip Morgan argues, that Chester was 'far from being an alien city to the Welsh', who visited frequently and in many cases took up residence there as servants, labourers and tradespeople.[20] There is some evidence from personal names in the city records that men of Welsh background were beginning to infiltrate the city elite, as aldermen or occasionally as mayor, once the disturbance of the Glyndŵr rebellion had been settled but these were generally men of anglicized families such as John Walsh and his son of the same name who appear as mayor and sheriff during the first three decades of the fifteenth century.[21] So although Chester was not an 'alien' city to the Welsh, they were invariably regarded legally as 'aliens' by the English burgesses and officials of Chester and the treatment handed out to the Welsh was often less favourable than that applied to English foreigners or aliens who lived outside the city.

Perhaps the most positive way in which the Welsh interacted with Chester was in the form of pilgrimages to Chester's various religious sites.

This was also one of the main ways in which Welsh people transgressively claimed a religious experience that was also a spatial experience, in defiance of the institutional 'place' of Chester as an English town.

A considerable number of the medieval Welsh poems about Chester are concerned with the holy cross of St John's, the miracle of its arrival at Chester, washed up by the tide, and its healing properties, all of which are appropriated by the Welsh into their own language and their own experience. When Maredudd ap Rhys, composing around the middle of the fifteenth century, describes his cure by the *crog drugarog*, the 'merciful cross', he embraces the image of Christ on the cross as a symbol of redemption which is available to everyone who comes to Chester:

> Gwir a brau 'mod ger bron
> Gŵr llawir o Gaerlleon
> Y grog drugarog, wiwrym,
> A fu, Dduw gwiw, feddyg ym.
> Urddasol arwydd Iesu
> Urddedig o feddyg fu.
> Miragl Duw a gymerais –
> Mae'r glun heb y nemor glais.
> Llun Duw yng Nghaerlleon deg,
> Lle rhoed ym allu rhedeg,
> Yn yr un modd y'i rhodded
> Ar bren croes i brynu Cred.
>
> (True and free am I in front of
> a generous man from Chester.
> The merciful cross, fitting its strength,
> was, dear God, a doctor to me.
> A dignified symbol of Jesus,
> it was a high-ranking doctor.
> I received a miracle of God –
> my knee has hardly a bruise.
> An appearance of God in fair Chester,
> where I was given the power to run,
> in the same way that he was given
> on a wooden cross to redeem Christendom.)[22]

'Caerlleon deg', 'fair Chester', is placed in parallel to '*Cred*', 'Christendom', implying that the two are mapped on to each other as part of the same space, a trope that dissolves the borders between Chester and the rest of Christendom (including Wales) and challenges the hegemonic consensus that these borders are real and natural. There is no hint in this poem that Chester is in England rather than in Wales, that it lies across any particular kind of border: the Welsh pilgrims overflow into Chester as a matter of right, undermining English efforts to keep them in their place. In a fifteenth-century poem by Tudur Aled in praise of John Birkenshaw, the abbott of Chester, the poet translates the main religious foundations of Chester into Welsh – *Sain Werbwr* (St Werburgh), *Sain Safiwr* (St Saviour), *Sain Bened* (St Benedict) – while the title of the poem addresses the abbott himself as 'Siôn Byrchinsha'.[23] This linguistic appropriation is an act of subversion, a clear denial that English is the only vernacular that may be used to name the religious spaces of Chester.

Welsh poems to religious monuments in parish churches and towns are quite common, so poems like those to the cross of St John's do not necessarily imply a distinctive relationship between the Welsh and Chester. A poem ascribed to the fourteenth-century poet, Dafydd ap Gwilym, for example, describes a painting on wood of Christ and some of his followers, displayed in a parish church.[24] Holy wells and springs were often praised as pilgrimage sites, such as the well of *Gwenfrewi* or Winifred.[25] A poem to the town of Brecon (*Aberhonddu*) by Ieuan ap Huw Cae Llwyd in the late fifteenth century praises the church there as a second Jerusalem, the Constantinople of Wales, a place as worthy of pilgrimage as Rome itself.[26] Though Chester was clearly important as a site of worship and drew Welsh pilgrims from as far as Caernarfon and Anglesey, the principle of visiting towns, both English and Welsh, for the purpose of religious worship was widespread in Wales. This meant that there was a specifically Welsh experience of urban worship which expressed itself not only in the Welsh language but in the assumption that the 'places' designated as holy by a hegemonic English church were mapped on to a wider Welsh topography of religious space.

Satire and urban culture

Very few Welsh names appear as members of guilds, that is, as burgesses who were able to conduct wholesale trade in the city, though Welsh people certainly came into Chester to sell their goods at the market. One such person was Alicia, wife of 'Hoell' (*Hywel*) of Holyhead who was charged in 1456 with forestalling and regrating – these were misdemeanours by which 'foreigners', that is, outsiders who were not members of the Chester gild merchant, bought up goods on the way to market and then sold them in the market at a higher price.[27] Similarly, two brothers with the Welsh

name of Pellyn (W. *pellynt*, 'far-reaching, travelling far'), William and
Henry, were cappers who were indicted in 1498 as 'foreigners' illegally
practising their trade within the liberties of the city.[28]

Given the status of the Welsh in Chester as 'aliens' from the point of
view of commerce and legal practice, it is not surprising to find that the
Welsh experience of Chester as an urban and commercial space was very
different from that of other townspeople. While the English towns in Wales
and the March were important to the Welsh as centres of trade and religion, they were also the objects of a disempowered resentment which was
articulated through the mode of satire. A couple of the Welsh poems about
Chester make fun of the Franciscan friars there, as part of a wider tradition of anti-clerical satire.There is also a sustained satire of the city and its
English inhabitants by the fifteenth-century poet Lewys Glyn Cothi. As far
as we can judge from his poetry and in the absence of any other records
about the poet's life, it seems that Lewys tried to move into Chester as a
resident, possibly by marrying a widow of the town. This did not go down
well with the citizens of Chester who retaliated by vandalizing his possessions and running him out of town. Having described this assault on his
property and poured insults on to the heads of every person in Chester, the
poet ends with this vindictive backlash:

> Tref yw Caer Lleon mewn tir afiach,
> tref nid gwehelyth byth na bo iach,
> tref ddig Wyddelig, feddalach – na'i phwys,
> tref ddwys yn cynnwys gwerin Connach.
>
> tref y saith bechod heb neb dlodach,
> tref gaerog fylchog heb neb falchach,
> tref Sieb glothineb, glwthenach – eu pryd,
> tref lle cyfyd llyd a phob lledach.
>
> Llawer cell yn hon ddiffaith bellach,
> llawer ffau ellyll, llawer ffollach,
> llawer cyw wythryw cyfathrach – dan lwyn,
> llawer twyn o frwyn a chyfrinach,
>
> llawer mab dan gist a fydd tristach,
> llawer bron gwiddon a fydd gweddwach,
> llawer gwraig maelier gwamalach – wrth gâr,
> llawer cymar wâr anniweiriach.
>
> Anniweirion blant, anwiredd – a wnânt
> yn wŷr ac yn wragedd.
> Am a wnaethan' â'm hannedd
> cânt hwythau glapiau gan gledd. (ll. 73–92)

(Chester is a town in an unwholesome land,
a town whose pedigree has never been good,
an angry Irish town, weaker than its importance,
a depressing town containing folk from Connacht,

a town of the seven sins where no-one is poorer,
a fortified turreted town where no-one is prouder,
a town with a Cheap of gluttony, their faces more guzzling,
a town where desire grows and everyone is low-life.

Many a room now run-down,
many a goblin hole, many a short fat person,
many the offspring of eight kinds of intercourse in the bushes,
many a mound of sadness and secrecy,

many a boy in a coffin will be sadder,
many a widow's breast will be more bereft,
many a merchant's wife more wanton with a lover,
many a tame partner more unfaithful.

Unfaithful children, they will tell lies
as men and women.
For what they did to my property,
they will sing to the beats of the sword.)[29]

The poet makes his feelings about Chester fairly plain – it is a city which is unwelcoming to the Welsh while full of despised Irish, but it is a city where no-one would want to live anyway because it is so run-down and its people are so unlikeable. Despite the exaggeration of Lewys's invective, he has managed to capture something of the reality of medieval Chester as a trading centre and a major commercial port, attracting its fair share of unsavoury characters while promoting a ruthless consumerism in its large market places which drew in dealers from the surrounding countryside and from across the sea. But we must also read the poem in its Welsh literary context.

This type of satire, based on a string of colourful insults directed at a specific object or person, was very much part of the bardic repertoire, styled in part to show off the poet's skill with metre and rhetorical word-play. There are a number of other satires directed towards the English towns of Wales and its borders, including a famous satire on the city of Flint and its burgesses, a poem attributed to the fifteenth-century poet Tudur Penllyn. The poet goes to the town looking for work as a musician and singer, but is beaten to a job playing at a wedding by an English piper who makes a dreadful noise with his bagpipes. The poet turns his back on the town in disgust and ends with a curse on Flint and its people:

Ei ffwrn faith fal uffern fydd,
A'i phobl Seisnig a'i phibydd.

(May its burning be as long as hell, both its English people and its piper.)[30]

To some extent then, we have to read Lewys's satire on Chester not as a literal rejection of a hated English town but rather as an example of a popular poetic genre which Welsh poets were expected to perform. Chester is not singled out because it is a city in England, on the English side of the border: rather it is grouped together with all the other major towns of Wales and the March which were established, settled and owned by the English conquerors of Wales. The effects of that conquest in 1282 were felt much more strongly in the north of Wales than elsewhere, because that was the last major territory of an independent Welsh prince to fall to the English. The cities of Chester and Flint, of Hope and Ruthin, of Holt and Denbigh were part and parcel of the Welsh sense of political and economic disempowerment in the wake of conquest. Yet Lewys's brutal satire of Chester inscribes a map of the city which contains the traces of the 'outside' already present inside the city itself, which is described from an outsider's point of view. The shabby streetscape and the decadent 'Cheap', or market, represent a Welsh experience of Chester as an institutional 'place' and this description of the city throws out a challenge both to its complacent self-identity and its hegemonic power.

The politics of war

During the Wars of the Roses in the fifteenth century, the bitter factionalism of Yorkists and Lancastrians undermined the neighbourhood of north Wales and Chester. The city of Chester, as an earldom of the crown, was solidly Yorkist during the reign of Edward IV; much of north Wales, on the other hand, supported the Lancastrian faction led by Jasper Tudor on behalf of the exiled Henry VI. What this meant for the region is expressed in a number of Welsh political poems of the period, including one attributed to Tudur Penllyn in praise of Rheinallt ap Gruffydd. The son of Gruffydd ap Bleddyn and his wife Gwerfyl, Rheinallt ap Gruffydd was a Lancastrian supporter and part of the rebel garrison at Harlech which carried out military campaigns against Edward IV. Harlech, held since 1460, finally surrendered to the Yorkist leader, William Herbert in 1468, by which time Rheinallt was dead. Marginal notes in a number of manuscript copies of the poem record Rheinallt's death in 1465, when he was 'not yet 27 years old'.[31]

A year or so before he died, Rheinallt was attacked by a mob of Chester men near Mold (*Yr Wyddgrug*), his home town. The attack followed a proclamation by Edward IV in 1464 requiring the mayor and sheriff of Chester to announce that the defenders of Harlech would be put to death unless they submitted by 1 January 1465.[32] Rheinallt himself was found guilty of treason and told that his lands would be forfeit to the Crown unless he took an oath of loyalty before Ascension Thursday that year (1464). The men of Chester took this to be an invitation to start plundering Rheinallt's lands around Mold and Rheinallt retaliated with a brutal attack on them which took place on *Dydd Calan*, New Year's Day 1465, Edward's deadline for the surrender of Harlech. In one of a number of violent assaults on that day, Rheinallt seized Robert Bryne (or Byrne), a former mayor of Chester (who had held office in 1462), and executed him by hanging.[33] Further retaliation by the men of Chester in later weeks resulted in the burning down of Rheinallt's fortified house, *Y Twr*, 'the Tower', with a number of Englishmen inside it, and an attack on Chester itself by Rheinallt's men, during which part of the city was set on fire.[34]

The fact that the poem survives in at least thirty copies, mainly from the sixteenth and seventeenth centuries, suggests that it held a particular resonance for the antiquarian gentry scholars of early modern Wales.[35] The poem, and the incident behind it, illustrate the overflow of social practice from one side of the border to the other; English institutional power coming out to meet Welsh resistance across the shared geographical landscape of Denbighshire, Flintshire and Cheshire. This is the 'place' which is read differently by the two cultural groups. To the men of Chester, these counties are configured as the estates of the English nobility, owned by the king. To the Welsh, the same landscape is read transgressively as the ancestral lands of an ancient nation whose sovereignty pre-dated the coming of the English.

Using a triumphalist military rhetoric, the poem maps out a Welsh nation built on tradition, heroic achievement and a long history of opposition to the English, of which this incident with the men of Chester is but the latest in an endless sequence:

> Gwayw Rheinallt, Oswallt, Iesu – croesed hwn,
> > Tân gwyllt wrth ymgyrchu;
> > Gwayw gwaedlyd i'r holl fyd fu,
> A gwayw Emrys i Gymru.
>
> Cymry ar y llu o'r llan – a'u gorchwyl
> > A gyrchodd Ddyw Calan;
> > Cael ar faes, coelier y fan,
> Cadw ac ymlid, Cad Gamlan (ll. 17–24).

(Spear of Rheinallt, of Oswald, may Jesus welcome it,
wild fire on the attack;
it was a bloody spear against the whole world,
and the spear of Ambrosius for Wales.

Welshmen upon the host from the parish, the task
of those who attacked on New Year's Day;
on a field – the place was trusted –
guarding and pursuing, they held the Battle of Camlan.)[36]

The invocation of famous names from the Arthurian past – Emrys (Aurelius Ambrosius), Oswald (the seventh-century Christian king of Northumbria) and the battle of Camlan at which Arthur was killed while fighting the English – provide a specifically Welsh reading of Rheinallt's victory over the men of Chester, while the long list of Englishmen cut down in the fray (Alac, Siac, Siôn, Wilcin) uses linguistic difference to under-score the cultural and political gulf between the two sides. In his bitter curses on Chester and the whole county, the poet not only draws attention to its Englishness ('dilyw ar swydd Gaer, dialedd Saeson', 'a flood upon Chester county, Saxon vengeance') but locates it as part of a much older history of the wars between British and Saxons. This is a mapping of north Wales and Cheshire which reveals the traces of the 'outside' ineluctably present on the inside, a way of seeing the territory as a single space, a single battlefield which has seen almost constant action for centuries. The revenge inflicted by Rheinallt on the men of Chester is, in the voice of the poet, not simply revenge for their destruction of his lands but for centuries of oppression by the English. Cheshire is called into being as a metonym for the whole of England and its institutional power; the Welsh challenge to this power rewrites the English-made borders as permeable and ineffec-tive against the Welsh-made map:

Trwy Ddyfed y try ddeufin,
Tryw'r Mers, mae trywyr am un,
Trwy Wynedd, tarw o Einion,
Try lwgwr hwnt, trwy Loegr hen (ll. 5–8).

(Through Dyfed he overruns two borders,
through the March, three men to one,
through Gwynedd, a bull out of Einion,
he unleashes havoc even further, through old England.)

The evidence of the Welsh poems discussed in this essay provides some-thing of a challenge to the received (English) view of Chester as a border city. Not only did the English themselves overflow into Wales, ignoring the

official border when it suited them, but the Welsh viewed Chester as part
of a larger political whole, one piece in a jigsaw of English urban colonization which spread throughout Wales and the March. Reading it from a
Welsh subject position, Chester was not a city on the Welsh border: it was
part of a regional neighbourhood which included Flintshire, Denbighshire
and much of Cheshire – English counties mapped over a Welsh landscape.
Whatever Chester thought about the Welsh, whether they were welcomed
or reviled, the Welsh themselves experienced city life on their own terms,
transgressing the limits imposed on them by the political border and the
city walls. They took what Chester and the other English cities had to offer,
particularly religious monuments and access to consumer goods, and their
engagement with the city left its traces on the streets, in the churches and
in the written record. This is how the poets write the Welsh into Chester, as
the 'presence-in-absence' within an English city.

APPENDIX

List of medieval Welsh strict-metre poems with Chester connections

Poems are listed by topic, first line, metre and author where known. Poems
which have been edited for the 'Mapping Medieval Chester' website
(*www.medievalchester.ac.uk*) are marked with an asterisk, and a brief
description of the different Welsh metres can be found on that site. Details
of printed editions and manuscript copies can be found in the 'Maldwyn'
catalogue of the National Library of Wales at *maldwyn.llgc.org.uk*. This
list is not guaranteed to be exhaustive but is reasonably comprehensive.

Religious poems to the Cross at Chester

First line	Metre	Author
Agorwch y dre gaerog	cywydd	Bedo Brwynllys (15th c.)
Bloeddiais ers hanner blwyddyn	cywydd	Ieuan Brydydd Hir (15th c.)
Caraf benrhaith côr arianwaith	awdl	Gruffudd ap Maredudd ap Dafydd (14th c.)
*Garllaes fûm o 'r gwayw oerllwm	cywydd	Maredudd ap Rhys (15th c.)
Pum gweli 'n golchi amgylchion moroedd	awdl	Bedo Brwynllys (15th c.)
Y grog erchwyniog chwenaw	awdl	Dafydd ap Hywel ab Ieuan Fychan (15th c.)

First line	Metre	Author
Y grog i bob dyn o gred	*cywydd*	Guto'r Glyn (15th c.)
Y grog odidog y doded dy lun	*awdl*	Llawdden (15th c.)
Y gŵr o Gaer nid gair gau	*cywydd*	Ieuan Brydydd Hir (15th c.)

Occasional poems

First line	Metre	Author
Annes aeron Siôn fy nghwrs enwi hael (praise poem to Annes)[37]	*awdl*	Lewys Glyn Cothi (15th c.)
*Du sy ar feirdd da sir Fôn (to a poet killed near Chester)	*cywydd*	(?) Tudur Aled (15th c.)
Galar maith gwelir am un (lament for Dafydd Miltwn, buried in St Peter's)[38]	*cywydd*	Lewis ab Edward (16th c.)
Un tad yn abad, wynebwr grasus (praise poem to John Birkenshaw, Abbott of Chester)[39]	*awdl*	Tudur Aled (15th c.)
Y grog wyn o Gaer a gaed (praise poem to Edudful ferch Cadwgan)[40]	*cywydd*	Lewys Glyn Cothi (15th c.)
Y gwynt oriog i'n tiroedd (sending the wind as a messenger to Chester)	*cywydd*	Huw Machno (16th–17th c.)
Y llew'n dwyn aur Llundain oedd (to Wiliam Siôn, keeper of Chester Park)	*cywydd*	Lewys Morgannwg (16th c.)

Satires

First line	Metre	Author
Hywel urddedig hoyw-walch (satire on a Grey Friar of Chester)[41]	*cywydd*	Iolo Goch (14th c.)
*I Reinallt mae cledd ar groenyn yn graf (satire on the men of Chester)	*awdl*	Lewys Glyn Cothi (15th c.)
*Naws eidral meddal sy'n meddwi (satire on the beer of Chester)	*englyn*	(?) Raff ap Robert (16th c.)
*Od ai di i Gaer arch i'r maer roi imi gyllell (satire on the mayor of Chester)	*englyn*	(not known – 16th c.?)

First line	Metre	Author
Teg o gynnyrch, hygyrch hardd (satire on a Grey Friar of Chester)	*cywydd*	Iolo Goch (14th c.)

Political poems

First line	Metre	Author
Deuwr hwnt fal blodau rhos	*cywydd*	Ieuan ap Tudur Penllyn (15[th]c.)
Nos da, llew onest llawen	*cywydd*	Hywel Cilan (15th c.)
*Tri llu aeth o Gymru gynt	*cywydd*	Guto'r Glyn (15th c.)
*Ŵyr Einion â'i ffon ffinied y Saeson	*awdl*	Tudur Penllyn (15th c.)

Notes

[1] Much of this court poetry has been edited but the editions are in Welsh and very few of the poems have been translated into English, apart from the work of the fourteenth-century poet Dafydd ap Gwilym, who worked mainly in south Wales and does not mention Chester.

[2] I have identified the 'Chester' poems using 'Maldwyn', the online index of medieval Welsh poetry which allows key-word searches. See *http://maldwyn.llgc.org. uk* (accessed 22 July 2009). The poems are listed by topic and first line in the Appendix above.

[3] On the significance of Chester as a Welsh pilgrim destination, see Barry Lewis, *Welsh Poetry and English Pilgrimage: Gruffudd ap Maredudd and the Rood of Chester* (Aberystwyth, 2005).

[4] These ideas were first outlined in detail by Henri Lefebvre. See especially *The Production of Space*, Donald Nicholson-Smith (trans.) (Oxford, 1991).

[5] Michel de Certeau, *The Practice of Everyday Life* (Berkeley, 1984), pp. 91–2.

[6] W. Natter and J. P. Jones, 'Identity, Space, and other Uncertainties', in *Space and Social Theory. Interpreting Modernity and Postmodernity*, ed. Georges Benko and Ulf Strohmayer (Oxford, 1997), pp. 141–161, p. 146.

[7] Philip Morgan, 'Cheshire and Wales', in H. Pryce and J. Watts (eds), *Power and Identity in the Middle Ages: Essays in Memory of Rees Davies* (Oxford, 2007), pp. 196–210, pp. 206 and 207.

[8] For discussion of the Welsh contribution to life in medieval Chester, for example, see Laughton in this volume, pp. 169–83.

[9] R. R. Davies, *Conquest, Coexistence and Change: Wales 1063–1415* (Oxford, 1987), p. 364.

[10] John Williams, *The Records of Denbigh and its Lordship*, vol. 1 (Wrexham, 1860), pp. 100–1.

[11] Davies, *Conquest, Coexistence and Change*, p. 371. See also Davies's reference

to a Welsh attempt in the late fourteenth century to dispute the entitlement of the lord of Dyffryn Clwyd to his lands (p. 441).

[12] For a full account of the rebellion, see R. R. Davies, *The Revolt of Owain Glyn Dŵr* (Oxford, 1995).

[13] Of these towns, only Ruthin had a history as a Welsh town before coming under English rule in 1282. By 1324, only one-third of the town's burgesses were Welsh. See Ian Soulsby, *The Towns of Medieval Wales* (Chichester: Phillimore, 1983), pp. 232–5.

[14] I have written elsewhere of the relationship between the Welsh and the plantation towns of the English. See H. Fulton, 'Trading Places: Representations of Urban Culture in Medieval Welsh Poetry', *Studia Celtica*, 31 (1997), 219–30.

[15] Davies, *Conquest, Coexistence and Change*, pp. 433–4.

[16] Davies, *Revolt of Owain Glyn Dŵr*, p. 283.

[17] Ibid., p. 291.

[18] Aberystwyth, National Library of Wales MS 3039B, 706. I have edited the poem as part of the 'Mapping Medieval Chester' project. See *www.medievalchester. ac.uk* (accessed 30 September 2009).

[19] See for example Iolo Goch's poem thanking his patron for the gift of a knife, in *Iolo Goch: Poems*, D. Johnston (ed.) (Llandysul, 1993), no. 11, '*Llywelyn eryr gwŷr gwych*'.

[20] Morgan, 'Cheshire and Wales', pp. 206–7. See also Jane Laughton, *Life in a Late Medieval City: Chester 1275–1520* (Oxford: Windgather Press, 2008), pp. 103–4.

[21] J. T. Driver, *Cheshire in the Later Middle Ages, 1399–1540* (Chester, 1971), p. 39. For further discussion of the participation of individuals of Welsh origin in official civic life, see Laughton in this volume, pp. 169–83.

[22] For the full poem and annotations see 'Mapping Medieval Chester' *www.medi-evalchester.ac.uk* (accessed 30 September 2009). For a Welsh edition, see Enid Roberts, *Gwaith Maredudd ap Rhys a'i Gyfoedion* (Aberystwyth, 2003).

[23] For the Welsh text of the poem, see T. Gwynn Jones, *Gwaith Tudur Aled* (Cardiff, 1926), no. 9, '*Un tad yn abad, wynebwr–grasus*' (listed in the Appendix above).

[24] For the Welsh poem with English translation and apparatus see *www.dafydd-apgwilym.net* (accessed 30 September 2009), poem no. 4, '*Lluniau Crist a'r Apostolion.*'

[25] As an example, see H. Lewis, T. Roberts and I. Williams (eds), *Cywyddau Iolo Goch ac Eraill* (Cardiff, 1937), no. 35, '*Rhedodd o'r ddaear hoywdeg*' (anon.).

[26] Leslie Harries (ed.), *Gwaith Huw Cae Llwyd ac Eraill* (Cardiff, 1953), no. 51, *Brodyr aeth i baradwys*.

[27] Driver, *Cheshire in the Later Middle Ages*, p. 35.

[28] Douglas Jones, *The Church in Chester, 1300–1540, Remains Historical and Literary Connected with the Palatine Counties of Lancaster and Chester*, Chetham Society Third Series VII (Manchester, 1957), p. 168. As Jones notes, another William Pellyn was a rector of St Peter's church in Chester in 1501, a rare example of a Welshman (or at least a man of Welsh descent) holding a religious office in the city.

[29] I have edited and translated this poem as part of the 'Mapping Medieval Chester' project. For another modern edition in Welsh, see D. Johnston (ed.), *Gwaith Lewys Glyn Cothi* (Cardiff, 1995), no. 215.

[30]   D. J. Bowen, *Barddoniaeth yr Uchelwyr* (Cardiff, 1959), no. 23, ll. 61–2. For an English translation of the whole poem, see J. P. Clancy (trans.), *Medieval Welsh Lyrics* (London, 1965), pp. 166–8.

[31]   T. Roberts (ed.), *Gwaith Tudur Penllyn ac Ieuan ap Tudur Penllyn* (Cardiff, 1958), p. 112.

[32]   *Rotuli Parliamentorum*, 512.

[33]   Ormerod, I, p. 233.

[34]   T. Roberts, 'Noddwyr Beirdd: Teuluoedd Corsygedol, Y Crynierth, a'r Tŵr', *Y Beirniad*, 8 (1919), 114–23, pp. 120–1.

[35]   Another poem in praise of Rheinallt which describes the same attack was composed by the fifteenth-century poet Hywel Cilan. See I. Jones (ed.), *Gwaith Hywel Cilan* (Cardiff, 1963), no. 8, '*Nos da, llew onest llawen*' (listed in the Appendix above). Jones suggests the attack took place on 1 May rather than 1 January (pp. xii–xiii). The attack is also mentioned in an elegy to Rheinallt and his cousin, Dafydd Llwyd of Abertanad, by Ieuan ap Tudur Penllyn (Roberts, *Gwaith Tudur Penllyn ac Ieuan ap Tudur Penllyn*, no. 50, 'Deuwr hwnt fal blodau rhos'), listed in the Appendix above.

[36]   See my edition and translation at 'Mapping Medieval Chester' *www.medieval-chester.ac.uk* (accessed 30 September 2009).

[37]   Annes was the wife of Gruffudd ab Ieuan, and both were connected, by blood or service, to the powerful Yorkist commander in north Wales, William Herbert. Lewys Glyn Cothi describes Annes and her husband, who were patrons of Welsh poets, as leaders of Chester society. See D. Johnston (ed.), *Gwaith Lewys Glyn Cothi*, no. 119.

[38]   Dafydd Miltwn (Milton) was sheriff of Chester in 1512 and mayor in 1523 and 1538. See R. T. Jenkins et al (eds), *Dictionary of Welsh Biography down to 1940*, Honourable Society of Cymmrodorion (London, 1959), p. 635.

[39]   John Birkenshaw was abbot of St Werburgh's in Chester from 1493 to 1524 and was responsible for major rebuilding in the abbey. He was also a chaplain to Henry VII. He died in 1537. See 'Houses of Benedictine Monks: The Abbey of Chester', in *VCH Ches.* 3, pp. 132–146.

[40]   The identity of this woman is uncertain. See the note in D. Johnston (ed.), *Gwaith Lewys Glyn Cothi*, p. 603.

[41]   The 'grey friars' were the Franciscans. On their house in Chester, see Laughton, *Life in a Late Medieval City*, p. 71 and pp. 98–102.

10

Mapping the Migrants: Welsh, Manx and Irish Settlers in fifteenth-century Chester

JANE LAUGHTON

Introduction

Medieval towns were unhealthy places. People lived in close proximity, many of them crowded together in poor quality accommodation and although there were piped water supplies in some towns, provision for the disposal of human, animal and industrial waste was limited to cesspits and open drains in the street. Epidemic diseases inevitably flourished and urban communities proved very vulnerable. Levels of infant and child mortality were always high and it was rare for families in fifteenth-century England to rear as many as two children.[1]

All medieval towns therefore depended upon a constant flow of immigrants to maintain their populations. For the period before 1350 we can attempt to determine the origins of these newcomers by studying the locative surnames of the townspeople. As surnames had not yet become fixed, the locative surnames probably indicated the places from which individuals or their fathers or grandfathers had come. This evidence suggests that the majority of newcomers to small towns came from within a ten-mile radius and few had travelled more than twenty miles, commonly taking the familiar route to an urban centre already known from visits to market or church festivals. Larger towns attracted immigrants from much further afield but even in major centres like York, Exeter and Nottingham, half of the places from which the names were taken lay within a twenty-mile radius.[2]

The figures for Chester are comparable, with surname evidence indicating that some 45 per cent of immigrants came from places lying within a twenty-mile radius and another 20 per cent from a distance of between twenty and forty miles.[3] Parts of north-east Wales lay well within this catchment area and among the newcomers were many from Flintshire and Denbighshire. Other immigrants had travelled considerable distances, drawn to a city which was the regional capital of the north-western plain and a major west coast port. One or two arrived from as far away as Cumberland and Bedfordshire, while others came across the sea from Ireland and the Isle of Man.

This paper focuses on settlers with Welsh, Manx and Irish origins, people who had themselves crossed cultural and administrative boundaries to reach the borderland city or who were descendants of those who had made the journey in the years before 1350. It deals with the period between the late fourteenth and early sixteenth century, when surname evidence is no longer considered reliable, but many of Chester's ethnic immigrants can still be identified by their names. Surnames of poorer immigrants like Emma Trim and Howell of Holyhead were meaningful, as were the somewhat derogatory names bestowed on newcomers by the resident community: Margaret Walshewoman, Agnes Irish and Gilbert Manskman. Moreover, many Welsh and Manx townsmen were readily identifiable by their names: the forenames David, Dyow, Elis, Gruff, Grono, Madoc and Res, and the patronymic 'ap' for the Welsh; the forenames Patrick, Donald and Gybbon, and the patronymic 'Mac' for Manxmen. Immigrants from Ireland cannot be identified in this way. The native Irish were evidently not attracted to Chester and the majority of those who did arrive came from the east coast, especially from the area under English control in the vicinity of Dublin, known from the late 1440s as the Pale.[4]

Once the ethnic immigrants have been recognized, attempts must be made to discover where they lived. Of paramount importance in this search are the records of Chester's mayors, sheriffs and treasurers, organized as they were in the late-medieval period under the heads of the four main streets. These main streets and gates had Roman origins but the local monk Lucian, writing in *c.*1195, saw deep religious symbolism in the cruciform layout, noting that the city,

> habet eciam plateas duas equilineas et excellentes in modum benedicte crucis, per transuersum sibi obuias et se transeuntes, que deinceps fiant quattuor ex duabus, capita sua consummantes in quattuor portis, mistice ostendens atque magnifice, magni Regis inhabitantem graciam se habere.

> (has two perfectly straight streets intersecting like the blessed cross, which form four roads, culminating at the four gates, mystically revealing that the grace of the Great King dwells in the very city.)[5]

The civic authorities valued the cruciform plan for a very practical and entirely secular reason, seeing it as a convenient mechanism for governing their city. From the thirteenth century, Chester was divided into four subdivisions based on the four main streets for administrative purposes and much civic business was recorded under street heads. Surviving lists of councillors, jurymen and constables, of fine-payers, wrong-doers and tenants of city land therefore reveal the quarter of Chester in which people lived, including the less affluent townsmen and women. Property deeds and the few surviving rentals also provide 'addresses' and there are occasional references in the court rolls.

This chapter seeks to determine whether these ethnic immigrants integrated with the long-established English families to form a hybrid community or whether they remained distinctive groupings with their own identities and loyalties.

Immigrants from Wales

The Welsh were the most numerous of the ethnic immigrants in the late medieval period. North-eastern Wales was locked into Chester's economic hinterland by the eleventh century and links became closer after the county of Flint, newly created in 1284 by the Statute of Rhuddlan, was attached to Cheshire for administrative purposes and controlled by a justice based at Chester.[6]

The Welsh approached Chester from the south and entered the city via the Bridgegate, occasionally called the Welsh gate.[7] Drovers bringing cattle to the livestock market in Bridge Street and Lower Bridge Street came this way, as did peasants coming with Welsh cheese and carters with loads of sea-coal from Flintshire, the iron-bound cart wheels regularly damaging the bridge over the Dee.[8] This was a familiar trading route and the vast majority of Welsh immigrants understandably chose to settle in the Bridge Street quarter, some of them living in large properties along the main street and others occupying one-up one-down dwellings in the back lanes. By the end of the fifteenth century, there may have been a particular concentration of Welsh settlers in Handbridge, the suburb south of the river. In 1487, both the brewers and six of the fourteen ale-sellers recorded in Handbridge were Welsh; in the 1480s and 1490s all five chaloners at work in Chester were Welsh and all were based there.[9]

Some Welsh immigrants found only labouring jobs and were always poor; others learned a craft and prospered as shoemakers, glovers and especially as tailors, eventually becoming freemen and serving as constables and jurymen. Some remained loyal to their homeland, among them Geoffrey the tailor who had lived in Chester since at least 1396 but who was charged in December 1401 with sending padded jackets to north Wales to equip the followers of Owain Glyndŵr. Other links posed no threat. The wife of David the corviser set out for Holywell with their three-year-old daughter in late October 1408, evidently intending to celebrate the feast of St Winifred on 3 November. A few miles from Chester the child was knocked to the ground by a man on horseback and suffered a fatal injury.[10]

For this level of society, no evidence survives which documents intermarriage with the resident English community but we may suspect that the practice was not uncommon. The Anglicization of some names hints at a process of acculturation. Madok the wright thatcher, attested in Chester in 1398, had changed his name to Matthew the thatcher by 1402; the butcher John ap Wyllym, active in the city in the 1450s, was also known as John William; the chaloner David ap Howell, working in Handbridge at the end of the century, was sometimes named David Powell.[11] The city clerks doubtless welcomed these changes because they struggled to spell Welsh names and evidently wrote them phonetically: 'Glwadys', 'Thlyke', 'Thlannelwey' and 'Dulgethle' for example.[12] The Welsh word 'godarte' found its way into local speech. The local monk Ranulph Higden, writing around the mid-fourteenth century, explained that these were vessels of white and red clay made in north Wales. Some were purchased in Chester by John Gruff in 1499 and a few years later a saddler threw a 'godert' filled with ale into the face of the tailor John Conwy. Drinking cups known as 'goddards' were still used in north Wales and especially in Anglesey, at the end of the nineteenth century.[13] Small amounts of pink and white pottery were found in the excavations at 5–7 Foregate Street in 1991, possibly the product of the late medieval pottery industry known at Ewloe (now in the modern day Flintshire), where such clay was found.[14]

The most successful Welsh migrants became very wealthy, joined the ruling elite and chose to live in grand houses along the main frontages of Bridge Street and Lower Bridge Street. John of Ewloe, five times mayor of Chester in the years 1405–10 and son of David of Ewloe, mayor from 1380 until 1383, may serve as an outstanding example. The family originated in Cilcain in Flintshire, where David was known as David ap Gwyllym Vellynyth, but on arrival in Chester in the 1360s, he either adopted or was given the locative surname Ewloe, from the place in Flintshire some seven miles west of Chester. It was perhaps chosen as the family name because the coal mines there were the original focus of their commercial interests and a major source of their wealth.[15] David of Ewloe rapidly joined the small group of powerful men who dominated the city and in 1368 he was granted the wardship of a wealthy local heiress, marrying her to his son John when she was under age and without the consent of the lord. John's second wife was another heiress with a considerable fortune.[16] These advantageous marriages increased John's status and he was able to nego-tiate good matches for his children, including that of his son to the daughter of John Done of Utkinton.[17] The Dones were a leading gentry family who had held the office of chief forester of Delamere and Mondrem since the middle of the fourteenth century and this marriage linked the Ewloes with the county elite. John and his younger son Edmund were both described as gentlemen in the indictment rolls of the county court in the early fifteenth century.[18]

John of Ewloe lived in an imposing house with extensive gardens on the west side of Bridge Street at the junction with Cuppin Lane. He associated closely with Welsh townsmen and many of his servants, tenants and debtors were Welsh, including Jevan the shepherd of Handbridge. His commercial interests in the coal mines at Ewloe ensured regular contacts with people living in Flintshire and his Welsh employees and retainers flocked to Chester to support him in his quarrels with elite citizens, including others of Welsh descent.[19] Yet he was elected mayor in October 1405, two years after the Welsh of Flintshire had joined Glyndŵr and when the rebellion still posed a major threat and was re-elected in the following four years. In January 1408, he became embroiled in a bitter dispute with the constable of Chester castle and both men were temporarily suspended from office in August 1409, Ewloe because he was 'tampering with the rebels' and his loyalty was suspect.[20]

In January 1420, when John's son Edmund was indicted for the attempted murder of the brothers John and Robert Hope, the court learned that John of Ewloe was 'wholly' Welsh, born in Wales of Welsh parents allegedly villein tenants of Lord Grey of Ruthin and that his original name was Janyn ap David ap Gwillym Vellynyth.[21] John and Robert Hope were also 'wholly' Welsh, sons of Hopkyn Caveglogh and Eva vergh David Saer ap Jo[ ] ap Ken[ ] ap Godve. The parents were buried in Chester's Carmelite church and the family had perhaps moved to the city during their lifetime. Their son, Jankyn ap Hopkyn Caveglogh was always known as John Hope, either because he had been born in the Welsh town or perhaps because he derived much of his wealth from his lease of the lord-ship of Hope and Hopedale.[22] He had a distinguished civic career, serving as sheriff in the years 1412–15, as mayor seven times between 1419 and 1428, and as murager in 1431–2. Robert Hope (Robyn ap Hopkyn Caveglogh) was sheriff in 1415–16, murager in 1419–20 and mayor in 1430–1. The two brothers lived in Bridge Street, probably in St Michael's parish; in 1439 John Hope left wax for candles to that church and 26s. 8d to make a window for his soul and for Robert's. He also remembered his Welsh roots, leaving money to repair the church at Hope and to roof the church at St Asaph.[23] His home was evidently spacious, containing hall, chamber and kitchen and furnished with costly silver and silver-gilt vessels.[24]

Edmund of Ewloe's attack on the Hope brothers was instigated by the wife of former mayor John of Overton, another citizen of Welsh origin. William of Hawarden, mayor in 1416–17 and 1418–19, was also from Flintshire and was imprisoned in the castle in 1416 for aiding and abetting his sons, one of them clerk of the Pentice, in an attack on two citizens.[25] Bitter feuds continued to divide the city's powerful Welsh elite long after Glyndŵr's rebellion was over. In subsequent decades, citizens of Welsh descent played a lesser role in city government, but in 1497 the mercer Tudor ap Thomas was elected sheriff; with Henry Tudor on the throne he was doubtless proud of his name. A possible immigrant from Beaumaris in Anglesey, Thomas enjoyed a long and successful career in the city and was still named among the aldermen twenty years after he had held the shrievalty. His life was affected by family tragedy. One child was killed by a stone falling from St Peter's church in 1491 and his wife, the daughter of a leading mercer, fell to her death down the stairs of their Bridge Street home in 1517.[26]

Immigrants from the Isle of Man

Manx immigrants, like the Welsh, chose to settle in the quarter of Chester familiar to them through trade and therefore naturally gravitated towards the Watergate, site of the late medieval harbour. In Lucian's day, the harbour lay to the south of the city but the progressive silting of the Dee led to its relocation on the western side of Chester and to the establishment of additional anchorages further down the estuary. Large ships berthed at these outports and their cargoes were transferred to shallow-draught boats or carts for carriage up to the city.[27]

The Isle of Man occupied a strategic location in the Irish Sea region and contact with Chester is attested from the tenth century.[28] Trading links were well-established by the later medieval period and traffic between city and island may well have increased when the bishopric of Sodor and Man became part of an English province of the Church in 1387 and especially after the appointment of the abbot of St Werburgh's to the bishopric in 1478. His monks regularly travelled to the island in the 1490s.[29] The grant of the lordship of Man with its crown to Sir John Stanley of Lathom (Lancashire) in 1406 also fostered trading links. Relatively few Manx vessels were recorded in the customs entries at that time, but by the 1450s they were arriving on a regular basis and activity intensified in the following decades.[30] Manx vessels traded around the Irish Sea and not all their cargoes originated in the Isle of Man. Merchandise included coarse woollen cloth and a little wheat from the island and large quantities of herring, salmon and eels.[31]

Manx immigrants arrived in increasing numbers over the course of the fifteenth century and the fish trade provided employment for many of them. For some, it was a profitable sideline rather than a main occupation, among them the tailors and carpenters who imported herring and eels.[32] Others prospered as fishmongers and shipowners. In the 1450s and 1460s, Richard Macally imported wheat and fish, employing boatmen to serve him on voyages from Chester to Mathafarn (Anglesey), Man and Ireland.[33] In later years, he perhaps worked for the Stanley family. His goods were listed aboard the *Mary of Stanley* in c.1470 and a decade later he was named as the former occupant of a messuage in Watergate Street owned by William Stanley of Hooton.[34] This house stood on the south side of the street, next to a property with a vaulted undercroft owned at the end of the century by a leading baker. Donald Maccane was employed as a servant in this household.[35]

Poorer immigrants lived in cramped cottage accommodation in the lanes skirting the religious houses, some of them supplementing their income by running brothels. Prostitution inevitably flourished in the harbour area and a list of the city's brothel keepers in 1475–6 recorded two apiece in Northgate Street and Eastgate Street, nine in Bridge Street and eighteen in Watergate Street. Among thirteen women accused of brothel keeping in 1463 were several from Watergate Street, including Alice Gibon, Margaret Scotte, Alice Scotte and Marion of Man, the last two evidently independent householders who contributed to local taxes.[36] It seems that a considerable number of Manx women lived alone, some perhaps because their husbands worked as boatmen and were away from home for long periods.

Manx settlers formed a close-knit, if not always harmonious community, providing board and lodging for new arrivals, advancing loans and acting as pledges when required.[37] The Watergate Street district was always the focus of their community; by 1539 the north aisle of Holy Trinity was dedicated to St Patrick, the patron of Man and in the seventeenth century the lane skirting the Franciscan friary was known as Manx Lane.[38] Did a swarthy complexion distinguish the islanders from other townspeople? The shipmaster Patrick Man *alias* Black Patrick, the brothel keeper Black Meg, and John Davy *alias* Blakjohn of the Isle of Man were recorded in Chester in the later fifteenth century.[39]

One or two Manxmen anglicized their names: Macroke to Croke and Macally to Kelly for example.[40] Donald Macwyn *alias* Saer was church-warden of Holy Trinity in 1496, steward of the Carpenters' guild in 1499 and constable for Watergate Street a few years later. He pursued debts for herring and Gascon wine and evidently dabbled in the import trade.[41] Fellow Manxmen also prospered, including the tailor Thomas Croke, new entrant to the franchise in 1475–6. He was regularly named in the customs entries in the 1480s and 1490s and evidently supplemented his income by importing salted herring and eels, usually in vessels based in the Isle of Man. He was still serving as councillor and as constable for Watergate Street in the early sixteenth century, thirty years after he became a freeman and was alderman of the Tailors' company in 1507.[42] Manx origin was no bar to progress and the wealthiest men could be elected sheriff and mayor.

The newcomer from the Isle of Man who achieved the most outstanding success was John the armourer, a wealthy merchant with trading interests around the Irish Sea and mayor of Chester for seven terms between 1385 and 1395. In his will drawn up in 1396, he made bequests to people living on the island, including his brother and sister and left a quarter share in his boat, the *St Mary*, to his apprentice David (who was probably Welsh). He asked to be buried in St Mary's chapel in Holy Trinity church and evidently lived in the parish, perhaps in a grand house along the main frontage of Watergate Street. He lived in considerable style, employing as many as four female servants and a private chaplain. Silver beakers and silver-gilt mazers were on display in his home; he wore fur-trimmed garments and silver-studded belts and sported a silver dagger at his girdle and a diamond ring on his finger.[43]

John the armourer was accepted and respected by Chester's ruling elite and was a founder member of the city's fashionable fraternity of St Anne, where he and his wife mingled with the local gentry. The couple were also members of the prestigious Trinity Guild at Coventry, an indication of the extent of John's mercantile interests and which perhaps explains his bequest to the maintenance of the causeway on the road to that city, some five miles north-west of Nantwich. After John's death his young widow (his second wife) took over the business and was a guild member in her own right, enjoying the title Mistress (*Domina*).[44]

Immigrants from Ireland

Chester's links with Ireland were longstanding. A Hiberno-Norse community involved in the Irish trade had been established to the south of the legionary fortress in the tenth century and medieval chroniclers considered Chester's location 'facing Ireland' a defining feature. The monk William of Malmesbury, writing in *c.*1125, noted that goods were exchanged between Chester and Ireland, 'ut quod minus natura soli habet labor negotiantium apportet' ('so that what the nature of the soil lacks, is supplied by the toil of the merchants').[45] The island remained the mainstay of the city's trade in the fourteenth and fifteenth centuries and most ships arriving in the port came from there. Yet it seems that few Irish chose to settle in the city in the late medieval period, although the absence of distinguishing names may of course render many of them invisible.

Irish settlers of lower social status can sometimes be identified because Chester's townspeople referred to them by names such as Marian labourer *alias* Marian of Ireland and John of Ireland labourer, both of them charged with trespass in the 1420s and 1430s. Occasionally we learn where they lived. Christian la Iryssh kempster (wool comber) owed eighteen pence for rent, bread and ale to a Foregate Street resident in 1395 and Alan le Irysshe was recorded in Northgate Street the following year.[46] Women linked with prostitution congregated in the Watergate Street district. Agnes Irish and Emma Trim were fined for keeping brothels there in 1463, as was Elizabeth Ireland in 1476. Thirty years later Katherine Irishwoman of Greyfriar Lane was accused of brothel-keeping.[47] Manx women did not have the trade to themselves.

Immigrants with brighter prospects may also have settled in and around Watergate Street. William Preston of Drogheda, one of only three Irishmen known to have entered the city's franchise in the fifteenth century, was evidently involved in maritime trade. When he became a freeman in 1419, his pledge was John Hatton, a wealthy merchant from Watergate Street who owned lands and tenements in Ireland and whose ships sailed regularly to the island with cargoes of woollen cloth and salt.The two men doubtless knew each other through their trading activities.[48] Preston may have chosen to live close to his sponsor in an area linked with his commercial interests but he perhaps soon moved back to his homeland. The merchant William Preston of Drogheda did much business with Chester's drapers and dyers in the late 1430s.[49] Robert Drane of Ireland, who became a freeman in 1420, was not mentioned again in the city's records and his stay in Chester may also have proved short-lived.[50]

Robert Nottervill, the third known entrant from Ireland, had twice served as mayor of Drogheda when he became a freeman in October 1460 and his move to Chester may have been connected with national politics.[51] The Duke of York fled to Ireland in October 1459 and spent time establishing a firm political base there. He returned to England in September 1460, landing at Red Bank in Wirral and spending a few days in Chester where he entrusted the castle to the keeping of John Stanley and rewarded the city's mayor for his support.[52] Robert Nottervill may have been a Yorkist supporter. His move to Chester proved a success; he served as sheriff in 1468–9, as mayor in 1478–9 and still took the oath as an alderman in 1486–7. He perhaps died the following year.[53] In a list of contributors to a local tax in 1462–3 Robert Nottervill was recorded in Bridge Street, named below the mercer who had acted as his pledge on his entry to the freedom, but a few years later he was living in Northgate Street.[54] He remained closely involved in trade with Ireland, handling merchandise imported by Dubliners and dealing in grey yarn and 'narrow Irish cloth'. Northgate Street was a convenient base for this trade. Carts bringing cloth unloaded at the Wirral outports entered the city via the Northgate and many drapers and linen weavers lived in Northgate Street.[55]

Conclusion

The evidence suggests that immigrants from Wales and the Isle of Man tended to settle in localities which they already knew and where they could expect to find fellow countrymen. It has proved impossible to 'map' the immigrants from Ireland with any certainty but there are hints in the sources that they may have been influenced by similar considerations. Although the Welsh and Manx newcomers congregated in particular districts, the Welsh in the south part of Chester and the Manx in the west, they did not live in ethnic enclaves. The lists of residents who contributed to the local tax in 1462–3 reveal that Manx taxpayers in Watergate Street had English neighbours and that Welsh taxpayers in Handbridge lived among English townspeople. In the rental of the Benedictine priory drawn up in 1526, eight of the twenty-four tenants recorded in Nuns Lane were from the Isle of Man. Four were named together in one group and three in another but their small cottages stood among cottages occupied by English tenants.[56]

Their working lives also brought the English, Welsh, Manx and Irish townspeople together. They laboured side by side on building projects, quarrying stone to pave the city streets and carting stone from the quarry near Dee bridge for repairs to the castle. They came into contact through employment as servants.[57] They met as fellow parishioners at weekly services, at major festivals of the church's year and at convivial church-ales. Many of the more well-to-do immigrants became freemen and participated fully in civic life, regularly sitting beside English-born citizens on juries and in council meetings. They became members of the city's craft guilds and took part in civic ceremonial. The most successful men served as sheriff and mayor and joined the civic elite. The experience of immigrants who failed to make their way was very different. Men like the labourer John le Irysshe, accused of theft in 1415 and Gilbert Beggar, fined in 1509 because he was deemed able-bodied and fit to work, were treated with suspicion and remained outsiders.[58] Prejudice was doubtless widespread, then as now, but this did not prevent Chester from becoming a multicultural society.

The merchant Otiwell Corbet may serve as an example of this hybridity. Originally from the Isle of Man, he was probably a relative of the shipmaster David Corbet whose vessel regularly entered Chester's port in the 1450s and 1460s. Thirty years later the merchants Robert, Thomas and Otiwell Corbet, themselves occasionally described as shipmasters, were carrying goods to the city on ships with home ports around the Irish Sea.[59] They handled some wine and iron but their main trade was in eels and salted herring.[60] Occasional references in the 1490s to salmon and to dealings with men from Carrickfergus in Ulster suggest that the Corbets were already involved with the famous salmon fishery on the river Bann, as they certainly were by 1505. Some fifteen years later, Otiwell leased the fishery for £60 a year.[61]

The Corbets evidently considered Chester the most suitable base for their business and all three were living in the city by the 1490s, Robert and Thomas with their wives. Robert, perhaps the eldest, became a freeman in 1491–2 and was dead by 1507–8; Thomas and Otiwell entered the franchise in 1500–1 and Otiwell was still importing salmon in 1526.[62] His mercantile dealings brought him into contact with traders from Ireland, Anglesey and the Isle of Man; in 1502 he acted as pledge for John Ramsey 'scotte'.[63] He served as councillor for Watergate Street in 1507–8 and evidently lived in this quarter of Chester.[64] He and his family were drawn into the circle of the city's most powerful men and perhaps aimed to emulate their lifestyle, purchasing furs, expensive horses and birds of prey.[65] They were inevitably drawn into the bitter feuds which divided the civic elite. When Otiwell was attacked in Watergate Street by one leading merchant in 1501 he defended himself with a 'skeyne', a type of knife or dagger used by Irish foot soldiers as one of their chief weapons and inflicted a fatal blow.[66] The use of an Irish 'skeyne' in Chester by a citizen of Manx origin demonstrates very clearly the cross-cultural linkages at play within the urban community.

Notes

[1]   C. Dyer, *Standards of Living in the Later Middle Ages: Social Change in England c.1200–1520* (Cambridge, 1989), p. 192.

[2]   P. McClure, 'Patterns of migration in the later middle ages: the evidence of English place-name surnames', *Economic History Review*, Second Series 32 (1979), 167–82; D. Keene, *Survey of Medieval Winchester*, 2 vols (Oxford, 1985), vol. 1, pp. 371–9 and C. Dyer, *Making a Living in the Middle Ages: The People of Britain 850–1520* (London, 2002), pp. 193–4.

[3]   J. Laughton, *Life in a Late Medieval City: Chester 1275–1520* (Oxford, 2008), pp. 89–90.

[4]   A. Cosgrove, 'The emergence of the Pale, 1399–1447', in A. Cosgrove (ed.), *A New History of Ireland*, II: *Medieval Ireland, 1169–1534* (Oxford, 1987), pp. 533–56, p. 533.

[5]   *DLC*, fol. 13r.

[6]   I. Brown, *Discovering a Welsh Landscape: Archaeology in the Clwydian Range* (Macclesfield, 2004), pp. 104–5.

[7]   CCALS, ZMUR / 1, m. 3.

[8]   A. T. Thacker, 'Markets', in *VCH Ches*. 5. ii, pp. 94–100, p. 98 and CCALS, ZMB 4, mm. 32v, 51, 72v.

[9]   CCALS, ZMB 6, fol. 169v; ZSR 338, m. 1; ZSR 372, m. 1d; ZSR 377, m. 1; ZSR 378, m. 1d; ZSR 406, m. 1d; ZSR 454, m. 1 and ZSR 455, m. 1.

[10] CCALS, ZSR 114, m. 1 and TNA: PRO, CHES 25/10, mm. 8d, 32d.

[11] CCALS, ZMB 1, fol. 26v; ZMB 2, fol. 3; ZSB 1, fol. 154; ZSB 3, fol. 96 and ZSB 4, fol. 31v.

[12] TNA: PRO, CHES 25/8, m. 15d; CCALS, ZSR 220, m. 1 and ZSR 226, m. 1.

[13] CCALS, ZSB 4, fol. 121v; ZSR 478, m. 1d; OED, sv. *goddard*. Was it a corruption of the French *godet*, a drinking cup?

[14] S. Ward, *Chester City Ditches: A Slice of History*, Chester Archaeological Service: Guidebook No. 1 (Chester, 1992), pp. 16–17.

[15] TNA: PRO, CHES 25/11, m. 18; SC 6/772/15, m. 1; SC 6/774/6, m. 1; *Report of the Deputy Keeper of the Public Records (DKR)*, 36, Appendix II (London, 1875), pp. 177 and 344 and *DKR*, 37 (London, 1876), p. 357.

16   TNA: PRO, SC 6/786/8, mm. 7, 7d; SC 6/793/8, m. 1d and BL Harley MS 2037, fols 209–210v.

17   TNA: PRO, SC 6/786/8, m. 7d and 36 *DKR*, pp. 153–4.

18   D. J. Clayton, *The Administration of the County Palatine of Chester 1442–1485*, Chetham Society 35 (Manchester, 1990), p. 192 and TNA: PRO, CHES 25/11, mm. 6, 17d, 18.

19   CCALS, ZMB 1, fol. 10v; ZSR 107, m. 1; ZSR 121, m. 1; ZSR 122, m. 1 and TNA: PRO, CHES 25/11, mm. 7, 7d, 8.

20   36 *DKR*, pp. 83, 104 and 493 and R. H. Morris, *Chester in the Plantagenet and Tudor Reigns* (Chester, 1893), p. 47.

21   TNA: PRO, CHES 25/11, m. 18.

22   TNA: PRO, CHES 25/11, mm. 17–17d and SC 6/794/4, m. 14.

23   *The Cheshire Sheaf*, Series 3, 17 (1920), 105.

24   TNA: PRO, CHES 25/11, mm. 17–18 and BL Harley MS 2020, fol. 403 (reference to ground cellar of Robert Hope on (probably) the east side of Bridge Street). In 1415, John Hope had a large garden containing a malt kiln near Castle Lane (CCALS, ZMB 3, fol. 3v).

25   TNA: PRO, CHES 25/11, m. 9 and M. J. Bennett, *Community, Class and Careerism; Cheshire and Lancashire Society in the Age of Sir Gawain and the Green Knight* (Cambridge, 1983), p. 120.

26   CCALS, ZMB 8, fol. 125v; ZMB 9, fol. 3v; ZSB 3, fol. 9v; QC/1/1; BL, WALE 29/F114 and Ormerod, I, pp. 233–4.

27   S. Ward, 'The course of the River Dee at Chester', in P. Carrington (ed.), '*Where Deva spreads her Wizard Stream': Trade and the Port of Chester* (Chester, 1996), pp. 4–11, pp. 9–10; J. Laughton, *Life in a Late Medieval City*, pp. 171–3 and L. Toulmin Smith (ed.), *The Itinerary of John Leland in or about the years 1535–1543*, 5 vols (London, 1964), vol. iii, p. 91.

28   A. T. Thacker, 'Early Medieval Chester, 400–1230', in *VCH Ches.* 5. i, p. 20.

29   E. B. Fryde, D. E. Greenway, S. Porter and I. Roy (eds) *Handbook of British Chronology*, Royal Historical Society (London, 1986), p. 273; R. H. Morris, *Chester in the Plantagenet and Tudor Reigns*, p. 146; CCALS, ZSB 1, fol. 131v; ZSB 2, fol. 50; ZSB 3, fol. 112; ZSB 4, fols 14, 19, 80 and ZSR 265, mm. 1, 1d; ZSR 268, m. 1d.

30   J.R. Dickinson, *The Lordship of Man under the Stanleys: Government and Economy in the Isle of Man, 1580–1704*, Chetham Society 41 (Manchester, 1996), pp. 1 and 4–6; CCALS, ZMB 3, fol. 33v; ZSB 3, fols 14, 29 and ZSB 4, fol. 40.

31   CCALS, ZSR 318, m. 1d; ZSR 356, m. 1d; ZSR 363, m. 1; ZSR 378, m. 1d; ZSR 437, m. 1; ZSR 448, m. 1; ZMB 6, fol. 81; ZSB 3, fol. 75; ZSB 4 and fols 19, 141v.

32   Thomas Croke tailor: BL Harley MS 2158, fol. 58v; CCALS, ZSB 3, fol. 112, ZSB 4, fols 14, 15, 18v, 19, 37, 37v, 40, 41, 56v, 57, 59, 81 and 103 and ZMB 9, fols 3, 11v. Donald Saer carpenter: CCALS, ZMB 9, fol. 5v, 9; ZSR 419, m. 1d; ZSR 432, m. 1d; ZSR 448, m. 1 and ZSR 468, m. 1.

33   CCALS, ZSR 311, m. 1; ZSR 319, m. 1d; ZSR 326, m. 1 and ZSB 2, fol. 13.

34   CCALS, ZSB 3, fol. 14; ZSR 332, m. 1d and BL Harley MS 2046, fol. 27v.

35   CCALS, ZSR 411, m. 1d; BL Harley MS 2037, fol. 309v.

[36] CCALS, ZSB 2, fol. 8; ZSB 3, fol. 39v and BL Harley MS 2158, fol. 47.

[37] CCALS, ZSR 325, m. 1d; ZSR 326, m. 1; ZSR 349, m. 1d; ZSR 351, m. 2; ZSR 358, m. 1; ZSR 386, m. 1d; ZSR 418, m. 1; ZSR 439, m. 1; ZSR 451, m. 1d; ZSR 452, m. 1d; ZSR 463, m. 1; ZSB 2, fols 8, 21, 25v; ZSB 3, fol. 66v and ZSB 4, fols 31, 48, 53.

[38] A. T. Thacker, 'Medieval parish churches', in *VCH Ches*. 5. ii, p. 134; *PN Ches*. V (I:i), p. 15.

[39] CCALS, ZSB 1, fol. 167; ZSB 2, fols 59, 68, 70v, 71v and ZSR 356, m. 1d.

[40] CCALS, ZMB 6, fol. 168 and ZSR 385, m. 1d.

[41] CCALS, ZMB 9, fols 5v and 9; ZSR 419, m. 1d; ZSR 432, m. 1d; ZSR 448, m. 1 and ZSR 468, m. 1.

[42] BL Harley MS 2158, fol. 58v; CCALS, ZSB 3, fol. 112; ZSB 4, fols 14, 15, 18v, 19, 37, 37v, 40, 41, 56v, 57, 59, 81, 104, 112, 138, 138v, 140v, 141v, 147, 150, 150v, 151v and 152; ZMB 8, fols 61 and 126; ZMB 9, fols 3 and 11v and ZSR 480, m. 1.

[43] TNA: PRO, WALE 29/291.

[44] *Calendar of Patent Rolls 1391–6*, pp. 248–9; M. D. Harris (ed.), *Register of the Guild of the Holy Trinity, St Mary, St John the Baptist and St Katherine of Coventry*, Dugdale Society 13 (London, 1935), p. 28.

[45] William of Malmesbury, *De Gestis Pontificum Anglorum*, N. E. S. A. Hamilton (ed.), Rolls Series 52 (London, 1870), p. 308 and D. M. Palliser (ed.), *Chester: Contemporary Descriptions by Residents and Visitors* (Chester, 1980), p. 6.

[46] CCALS, ZSR 108, m. 1d; ZSR 112, m. 1; ZSR 160, m. 1d and ZSR 190, m. 1.

[47] CCALS, ZSB 2, fol. 8; ZSB 3, fol. 39v and ZSB 6, fol. 10.

[48] CCALS, ZMB 3, fol. 56v; ZSR 153, m. 1d; ZSR 157, m. 1; ZSR 170, m. 1d; ZSR 171, m. 1d; ZSR 172, m. 1d; ZMB 3, fols 93, 94v, 96 and 96v and *Cheshire Sheaf*, Series 3, 36 (1941), 9.

[49] CCALS, ZSR 220, m. 1; ZSR 236, m. 1d and ZSR 239, m. 4d.

[50] CCALS, ZMB 3, fol. 105v.

[51] CCALS, ZMB 5, fol. 45v.

[52] J. Laughton, *Life in a Late Medieval City*, p. 56.

[53] CCALS, ZMB 7, fol. 3.

[54] BL Harley MS 2158, fols 45v and 46v and CCALS, ZMB 5, fols 85v and 109v.

[55] J. Laughton, *Life in a Late Medieval City*, pp. 51–5, 104–5 and 143–4. A linen smoother was found in an excavation in Hunter Street (off Northgate Street) (Information from Julie Edwards, Chester Archaeology.)

[56] BL Harley MS 2158, fols 45v, 46v and 47 and W. F. Irvine, 'Notes on the history of St Mary's nunnery, Chester', *Journal of the Chester Archaeological Society*, 13 (1907), 105–9.

[57] TNA: PRO, E 101/488/7, m. 1 and E 101/545/25, m. 1d; CCALS, ZMUB/1, fols 10–11; ZSR 303, m. 1d; ZSR 306, m. 1d; ZSR 406, m. 1d and ZSR 411, m. 1d.

[58] CCALS, ZMB 3, fol. 12v and ZSB 5, fol. 61.

[59] CCALS, ZSB 4, fols 37, 62, 79, 102 and 107v (shipmasters); Liverpool (ZSB 4, fols 127 and 151v); Houth (ZSB 4, fols 107v and 148v) and Beaumaris (ZSB 4, fol. 152).

[60] CCALS, ZSB 4, fols 14 and 140v; ZSR 445, m. 1d; ZSR 451, m. 1; ZSR 459, m. 1; ZSR 460, m. 1d; ZSR 461, m. 1 and ZSR 464, m. 1d.

[61] CCALS, ZSR 403, m. 1; ZSR 412, m. 1d; ZSR 442, m. 1d and ZSR 465, m. 1d.

[62] CCALS, ZSB 4, fol. 94; ZSB 5, fol. 177v; ZSR 371, m. 1; ZSR 460, m. 1 and ZTAR 1/5, m.1.

[63] CCALS, ZSR 451, m. 1d; ZSR 456, m. 1; ZSR 471, m. 1d; ZSR 515, m. 6 and ZMB 9, fol. 31v.

[64] CCALS, ZMB 9, fols 4 and 4v and BL Harley MS 2037, fols 309v–310.

[65] CCALS, ZSR 459, m. 1d and ZSR 460, m. 1d. The falcons may have been imported from Ireland.

[66] CCALS, ZMB 9, fols 32v–3.

11

Leeks for Livery: Consuming Welsh Difference in the Chester *Shepherds' Play*

ROBERT W. BARRETT, JNR

I want to begin with a brief overview of the Chester *Shepherds' Play*, the text under discussion in this essay. This pageant, seventh of twenty-four Chester Whitsun plays, was produced throughout its Tudor lifetime by the Painters', Glaziers', Embroiderers', and Stationers' Company. The earliest known performance of the play took place sometime during the mayoral year 1515–16: in BL MS Harley 2125, Chester herald painter and antiquarian Randle Holme II reports that 'the shepards play & the Assumption of our lady was playd in St Iohns churchyard' at that time.[1] The Painters' 1534 charter mentions 'þe plae of þe shepperds Wach with þe Angells hyme.'[2] There are extant accounts for the 1568, 1572 and 1575 performances of the play.[3] After the final production of the Chester cycle in 1575, the last Tudor reference to the play comes in 1577–8: numerous local chronicles report that Henry Stanley, fourth Earl of Derby and his son Ferdinando, then Lord Strange, took in a performance of the pageant at the High Cross in the city centre.[4] The play would not be staged again until 1906, the year that Nugent Monck's Early Drama Society presented the pageant to audiences in London and Chester as the first episode of a three-part *Nativity* sequence.[5]

We cannot say for certain that the *Shepherds' Play* recorded in the extant manuscripts of the cycle is the same pageant witnessed by the Stanleys in 1578; the text of the Chester cycle underwent constant revision during its sixteenth-century heyday. But there is evidence that the pageant in performance resembled the version written down in the 1590s and 1600s – at least the pageant as it was enacted in the waning years of the Whitsun plays' production. In his list of irreligious 'absurdities' to be found in the cycle's 1572 performance, former Genevan exile and Protestant divine Christopher Goodman complains about aspects of the play that can be found in the five versions recorded for posterity by local antiquarians. Goodman decries 'The foolish descanting of the Shepherds upon Gloria in excelsis' (ll. 376–435), 'The angels suspected of the Shepherds to be sheep-stealers. With a lewd merry song' (ll. 394–5 and the stage direction after line 447 that calls for the shepherds to sing 'troly, loly, loly, loo'), 'Their kissing of the cratch & clothes' (ll. 490–1), and 'They forsake their vocation, not mentioned in Scripture' (but nonetheless present in ll. 651–79 of the play-text).[6] I will return to this last 'absurdity' later on; for now, it is enough to note that Goodman's list allows us to tentatively accept that the play we have today was actually performed at some point in the 1570s, if not earlier and later as well.

The plot of Pageant 7 embellishes the action of Luke 2: 8–20 as follows: the shepherds Hankeyn, Harvey and Tudd make their entrances in order, each boasting about his skill as a shepherd. Once all three men are met, they sit down for a meal of outrageous proportions. The shepherds finish their repast and decide to share it with their hireling, Trowle, who is still out in the fields watching the sheep. The rude and explicitly obscene Trowle refuses to accept their hospitality, but does accept Tudd's offer of a wrestling match. He defeats all three shepherds, gathers up the remains of the feast, and retreats to his post. The weary herdsmen are suddenly surprised by the appearance of the Star of Bethlehem; an equally stupefied Trowle rejoins them. An angel appears, singing 'Gloria in excelsis Deo'; the shepherds and Trowle engage in a spirited (and comically ignorant) explication of the heavenly song and then head off to Bethlehem to visit the Christ Child, singing the secular tune 'Troly, loly, loly, loo' all the way. Upon arriving at the stable, they do obeisance to the Child, gain an understanding of the Nativity's meaning from Mary and Joseph and then present Christ with a series of humble gifts: a bell, a spoon, a cap and (from Trowle) 'a payre of my wyves ould hose' (l. 591).[7] Four hitherto silent shepherds' boys make similar offerings, giving the child a bottle, a hood, a pipe and a nut hook. The shepherds and Trowle then all agree to abandon secular life in favour of religious vocation: Harvey will become a preacher, Tudd a missionary, Trowle an anchorite and Hankeyn a hermit. They share a kiss and part company singing.

There is one crucial detail missing from this synopsis of the play's action: the shepherds' ethnicity. As their names suggest, Hankeyn, Harvey, Tudd and Trowle are not historically accurate shepherds from biblical

Palestine. However, neither are they the deliberately anachronistic and anachoristic Englishmen of the other extant shepherds' plays (those of Coventry, Towneley and York). Chester's shepherds are explicitly Welsh shepherds: Hankeyn, the *primus pastor*, opens the play by boasting that there is no 'better shepperd' than he 'From comlye Conwaye unto Clyde' – that is, from the River Conwy to the River Clwyd, both rivers in north Wales (ll. 7, 5). 'Tudd', the name of the *tertius pastor*, is short for Welsh 'Tudor,' and the scholar David Mills has suggested that Hankeyn's designation of Tudd as 'Tybbys sonne' (in ll. 65 and 69) 'jocularly inverts Welsh patronymic styling.'[8] The clinching justification for assigning the shepherds Welsh identity is the presence of stereotypically Welsh leeks on the 'menu' of their feast. First mentioned by Harvey in line 114, 'leekes' reappear in lines 155–6: asked by Hankeyn to summon Trowle, Harvey vows not to stop blowing his horn 'tyll that lad have some of our leekes'. Tudd eggs him on, noting that this dish is well suited to Trowle: 'Leekes to his liverye is likinge.'

Acknowledgement of the shepherds' Welsh origins is fairly routine in scholarly discussions of Play 7. However, analysis usually stops there. Indeed, David Mills has been the only critic to develop a more extended reading of the shepherds' Welshness. He argues that the shepherds' ethnic otherness is a feature deliberately exploited by the Painters' play:

> These Welsh shepherds are incomers from a different culture, both ethnic and rural . . . But, like the shepherds of the Bible, they are outsiders who have been granted a revelation that is denied to the insiders of the town . . . Though comic in their boisterous alterity during the first part of the play, they warrant respect as well as amusement because of that special knowledge. Having brought that knowledge into the city, they leave the community, not as literal pastors but as novitiates in spiritual pastoralism, to be hermit, preacher, missionary, and anchorite.[9]

The dynamic here is one of assimilation and conversion, a *translatio pastorum* that takes place on multiple levels. One is religious: as Rosemary Woolf points out, the sequence of pageants in Chester (Play 7 follows Play 6, the Wrights' *Annunciation and Nativity*, even though the action of the two plays is simultaneous) means that the shepherds begin their performance under the governance of the Old Law. The result of 'this regression in time' is that the shepherds simultaneously serve as both their own type and anti-type.[10] They undergo supersession and emerge as advocates for Christ's New Law – as shepherds of men. Mills acknowledges this reading in his closing nod to 'spiritual pastoralism.'

The other *translatio* in the play is the one Mills adds to the discussion: the shepherds' ethnic transformation from Welsh to English. Here Welsh outsiders – what Mills will later call 'people from an alien culture'[11] – first gain entrance to an English Christian community centred on the infant in the manger and then journey forth from Bethlehem/Chester to augment that community, converting ignorant outsiders (Tudd goes 'over the sea' in l. 657) and lapsed insiders (Hankeyn, Harvey and Trowle all continue to inhabit an insular landscape). For Mills, the process of assimilation is smooth; he repeatedly stresses the play's 'amused but sympathetic' treatment of the shepherds.[12] Possessing a 'simple dignity', they in no way resemble 'the foolish country folk whom we see in the two Towneley Shepherd plays.'[13] Mills is guided here (as he explicitly acknowledges) by the overall integration of the Welsh into Chester's late medieval and early modern civic society. While Chester's status as the northern bulwark of the Welsh Marches meant that it was often pitted against the Welsh, serving as the point of departure for English imperial incursions into *Wallia pura*, the city was also a site of more peaceful interchange. Welsh families owned property in the city, spoke Welsh in its streets, sued one another in its courts and served in its oligarchic government.[14] Indeed, the anti-Welsh ordinances that the Chester authorities issued in the aftermath of Owain Glyndŵr's early fifteenth-century uprising were the harshest in England largely due to the extensive Welsh presence in the city. In a time of crisis, it was precisely proximity that urgently demanded separation.

What I want to do in this essay is bring a more thoroughly historicist approach to Mills's essentially thematic reading of the play (that is, his point about difference being converted into identity). While Mills asserts that Play 7 'has to be set not only in this local context, but in the national context of the Tudor dynasty, the reconciliation of England and Wales in contemporary literature, of which Shakespeare's Captain Fluellen in *Henry V* is perhaps the best known', he fails to follow through on the implications of his statement.[15] Influenced by the New British History and post-colonial studies, Shakespeare scholars working on *Henry V* and other Shakespearean plays depicting the Welsh – *Cymbeline*, *1 Henry IV*, and *The Merry Wives of Windsor* – see something more complicated than 'the affectionately humorous presentation of the Welsh' in the play.[16] Writing about *Cymbeline*, Garrett Sullivan notes that 'whereas one strain of English thinking about Wales downplayed the differences between the two cultures, even subsumed them in a notion of Britishness, another figured the Welsh as difficult to assimilate as [cartographer John] Norden found their land to measure'.[17] Christopher Highly discusses 'English suspicions of complicity between the lower orders of Wales and the Irish rebels' of the late 1500s, seeing in *Henry IV*'s Welshwomen a 'threat from the Celtic fringe' that Shakespeare couches 'in terms of the overthrow of a masculine English identity through castration'.[18] Lisa Hopkins considers the way in which 'Wales's status as physically marginal makes it prone to being treated as psychologically marginal too, a place where rationality is prone to sudden, violent, almost Gothic encounters with its Others'.[19] Perhaps most relevant for my own purposes is Patricia Parker's reading of Act 5, Scene 1 of *Henry V*, the scene 'in which a notorious English pilferer [Pistol] is made to "eat" the "leek" of the Fluellen whose name recalls the last true "Prince of Wales."'[20] Here Parker identifies 'both a Welsh "correction" and the cycle of revenge (in both directions) which in these histories works against any final teleological closure or "perfection," breaching the concluding language of "peace" and union in these final scenes of *Henry V*.[21] She finds Shakespeare's play unable to solve 'the problem of continence and containment in both senses – of ungoverned sound and of incorporating troublesome borderers into the "body" of England'.[22]

I do not want to rule out the possibility of regional differences in Welsh stereotypes (although it is worth noting that Welsh immigration made Welshmen and women nearly as familiar in metropolitan London as they were in provincial Chester). But I do believe that the Shakespeare scholars convincingly demonstrate the limitations of reading Chester's shepherds as gentle parodies and harmless stereotypes. Parker's 'leeks' (which she reads alongside *Henry V*'s 'breaches' as punning evocations of 'fissures . . . and faults both territorial and bodily') call into question readings of the Chester 'leekes' as innocent symbols of ethnic difference (or, as we will see, signs of human frailty).[23] The Anglo-Welsh interface in post-Glyndŵr Chester is not characterized by open, constant hostility – but neither does it represent a perfectly smooth transition from one identity to another. From the moment of its early sixteenth-century inception, the Chester *Shepherds' Play* is a post-colonial drama, a pageant caught up in the vexed negotiations of ethnicity along the English frontier. Mills is not wrong to see an integrative impulse in the play – the shepherds do 'become' English over the course of the play. As I hope to show, the feast scene is perhaps the primary vehicle for this process of incorporation. But this acquisition of Englishness (or, more specifically and accurately, Cestrianness) is temporary at best: the play ends with the Welsh shepherds once again precariously positioned on the borders of the community. They may acquire pastoral authority, but only Harvey has any chance of exercising that authority within the walls of Chester (and thus within the city's body politic). Hankeyn, Tudd, and Trowle all find themselves moving away from the city as swiftly as they once approached it.

Before the play can expel the shepherds as the tenaciously foreign agents they are, it must first ingest them – the function of the notorious feasting scene. Writing about a similarly 'grotesque' feast in the Towneley *Prima Pastorum*, A. C. Cawley could account for the social diversity and sheer quantity of the dishes named by the shepherds only by dismissing the meal as 'a ludicrous gallimaufry that can never have existed except in his [the playwright's] imagination'.[24] In Cawley's reading, the Towneley shepherds' repast is pure wish-fulfilment. There is no such critical recourse in analyses of the Chester play: the Painters' account books clearly list the extensive amounts spent on food for the performances of 1568 and 1572.[25] The shepherds' 'liverye' was physically displayed 'on stage'. Harvey is the first to show 'such store as my wife had' (l. 109), producing 'bredd this daye was bacon, / onions, garlycke, and leekes, / butter that bought was in Blacon, / and greene cheese that will greese well your cheekes' (ll. 113–16). Tudd's wife is even more generous in supplying her husband:

And here ale of Halton I have,
and whot meate I had to my hyer;
a puddinge may noe man deprave,
and a jannock of Lancastershyre.

Loe, here a sheepes head sowsed in ale,
and a grayne to laye on the greene,
and sowre milke. My wyffe had ordained
a noble supper, as well is seene (ll. 117–24)

He goes on to promise his 'fellowes' additional 'hott meate . . . gambonns and other good meate in fere, / a puddinge with a pricke in the ende' (ll. 129–32). In the version of Hankeyn's speech provided by R. M. Lumiansky and Mills in their critical edition of the plays, his contribution is limited to 'a pigges foote from puddings purye' (l. 128) but one of the extant manuscripts (BL MS Harley 2124) augments that offering with a 'panch-cloute', a 'womb-clout', a 'lyveras', and a 'chitterling boyled'. Finally, when Trowle enters the play, he makes mention of additional dishes: 'Fye on your loynes and your liverye, / your liverastes, livers, and longes, / your sose, your sowse, your saverraye' (ll. 202–4).

The critics have tended to read this smorgasbord in exegetical terms. On the *in bono* side is V. A. Kolve's evocation of 'Christmas feasting and plenty' in the aftermath of Advent 'fasting and privation.'[26] Here the emphasis is on the action of the play not in its immediate Whitsuntide moment but in its diegetic context of Christmas Eve: 'Christ's body and blood, the spiritual food of Christians, are born that night, and the Sacrament of the Altar was often spoken of as a kind of banquet which had its beginning on Christmas Day.'[27] Lauren Lepow's celebratory reading of the feast in the Towneley *Prima Pastorum* could just as easily be applied to the meal in the Chester play: 'Like the foods provided for their feast, the shepherds themselves, and the audience for whom they are surrogates, are an eclectic group; yet each is equally cleansed by God's Word, Christ, and by their communion with him.'[28] However, the more dominant readings of the feast are *in malo*. Rosemary Woolf finds the shepherds 'more interested in feeding themselves than in feeding their flocks, a selfishness 'indicative of an unredeemed world'.[29] Peter Travis further develops this analysis, calling the feast 'a disguised and deformed "Old Testament" adumbration of the Nativity *epiphania*, the feast for the eyes with which the pageant concludes'.[30] The shepherds' 'gross banquet' is nothing more than a 'profane and "fictional" inversion' of the Eucharist, a material expression of a spiritual 'inner appetite which is weak and undernourished'.[31] Robert Adams sums up this line of approach, reading Harvey's 'onions, garlycke, and leekes' *pace* R. E. Kaske as Egyptian temptations right out of Numbers 11:5 and Tudd's 'sowre milke' as 'a violation (according to rabbinical tradition) of the injunction against boiling a kid in its mother's milk (Exodus 23:19).'[32] 'The gluttons' feast', he concludes, 'is essential in characterizing the corrupt spiritual leadership of the Old Law'; the shepherds, 'allegorical representatives of the Levitical priesthood.'[33]

In what follows, I do not want to reject such readings outright (although it is worth noting that Lisa Kiser's recent ecocritical reading of the Chester and Towneley shepherds' plays convincingly demonstrates that the shepherds are actually quite good at caring for their sheep).[34] The feast certainly has its theological implications. But it has also has distinct ethnic repercussions that have hitherto been almost entirely ignored. Harvey's 'leekes' potentially allude to Numbers 11:5, but they definitely signify Welshness; so too does his 'greene cheese that will greese well your cheekes' – Gillian Brennan's catalogue of foreigners in Elizabethan literature includes 'the "cheese-mad" Welshman.'[35] However, the dishes that interest me the most in this scene are the distinctly *English* delicacies that the shepherds consume: the butter bought in Blacon (a town 1.25 miles northwest of Chester), the ale from Halton (10 miles northeast of Chester), and the jannock or 'oaten cake' from Lancashire, Cheshire's northern neighbour. Critical commentary usually glosses these three items as the sort of localizing details contributing to the cycles' anachorism and anachronism and then moves on to other matters. I want to slow down for a moment and consider the biosocial implications of the Welsh shepherds' consumption of English food.

The sociologist Claude Fischler writes that 'To incorporate a food is, in both real and imaginary terms, to incorporate all or some of its properties: we become what we eat.'[36] Put simply, 'Incorporation is a basis of identity.'[37] He goes on to note that this incorporation also has a distinct social dimension:

> Human beings mark their membership of a culture or a group by asserting the specificity of what they eat, or more precisely – but it amounts to the same thing – by defining the otherness, the difference of others . . . it can be said that the absorption of a food incorporates the eater into a culinary system and therefore into the group which practices it, unless it irremediably excludes him.[38]

By ingesting English cheese, ale and cake, the Welsh shepherds find themselves incorporated into the English 'culinary system' and thus into the English body politic as well. Here the anthropological approach meets up with the *in bono* school of exegetical criticism: if the shepherds' feast is a type of the Eucharist, then eating its contents begins the process of bringing the shepherds into Christian communion. The generous spirit in which the shepherds offer Trowle some of the food is likewise a forerunner of their play-ending evangelical efforts. Sharing food with others becomes a means of sharing the Word with the other.

That said, incorporation does not necessarily culminate in utopian communion. Fischler goes on to note the 'fundamental gravity and deeply rooted anxiety' that accompanies eating.[39] Borrowing a term from the psychoanalyst Melanie Klein, he points out that 'incorporation of the bad object' is always a possibility to be feared: 'An object inadvisedly incorporated may contaminate him, insidiously transform him from within, possess him or rather depossess him of himself.'[40] In ethnic terms, incorporation into the Cestrian body politic is a potential relinquishing of Welsh identity. Jeffrey Jerome Cohen gets at this more negative dynamic in his account of the feast held by Henry II for the northern Irish in 1171:

> He arranged an extravagant feast prepared *Anglicanae mense* – a terminology that nicely draws attention to the fact that the Irish did not, like the English, eat at tables. The formal dinner was an act of aggression, meant to overawe the Irish royals by the copiousness of the food as well as its elegant presentation. The Irish were forcibly anglicized in the process, not just because to sit at Henry's English table was to acknowledge the superiority of his court but also because the chieftains had to eat the foreign dishes served . . . the princes make their submission both verbally and gustatorily, exiting the repast with a little bit of Henry's England incorporated into their Irish flesh.[41]

Play 7 might also be read in this fashion: the shepherds are 'anglicized' as a result of their feast, submitting to a Christian communion implicitly designated English by the playwright's anachoristic and anachronistic techniques (formal tropes are not politically neutral.) The Eucharist – the edible Christ Child the playwright identifies in line 451 as 'fruyt' – would function in this regard as 'an act of aggression'.

If that is the case, I must nonetheless admit that the shepherds fail to recognize it as such. The equanimity with which they accept incorporation into Cestrian Christendom is noteworthy. It may result from what Mills calls 'the reality of Chester society, with its unique ethnic mixture'.[42] Robert Appelbaum's work on early modern foodways would tend to support such a reading. Appelbaum observes that 'foodways operate in flux', a flux derived from 'the commonly hybrid quality of cultural life'.[43] The systems of incorporation abstractly described by Fischler are actually 'formed by social groups who live not in absolute spatial and temporal isolation, but rather in contact with other social groups and other regional practices'.[44] As the 'great homogenizer' (Appelbaum's term), food in Welsh-inflected Chester is necessarily hybrid: we don't know the exact means by which Harvey and Tudd's wives acquire the English food they pack in their husbands' lunches, but the implication of regular economic and cultural traffic across the Anglo-Welsh border is clear.[45]

Of course, we might also locate the shepherds' lack of anxiety surrounding the English food they consume in the fact that they were quite probably portrayed by Englishmen: Chester-dwelling members of the Painters' Company and semi- or fully-professional actors hired for the occasion. Mills points out that the 'kind of foreign exoticism' lent to the English foods via the shepherds' Welshness actually 'strengthens our sense of their "otherness"'.[46] I agree: in looking at the ethnicity of the shepherds play, the Welsh subject position of the fictional shepherds matters less than the primarily English subject positions of the actors and spectators. The 'bad objects' being consumed in Play 7 are not Blacon butter, Halton ale and Lancashire jannock. Instead, the 'bad objects' are four Welsh herdsmen named Hankeyn, Harvey, Tudd and Trowle. Christian theology requires communion with the other, but that meal need not go down easily. Indeed, lest the body politic suffer from food poisoning, it may be necessary to purge the system of the dangerous meal.[47]

We see this expulsion take shape at the end of the pageant. Joseph initiates matters by giving the shepherds and their boys their evangelical charge: 'Therefore goes forth and preach this thinge, / all together and not in twynne: / that you have seene your heavenly kinge / common all mankynde to mynne' (ll. 536–9). However, when the shepherds do depart from the stable, they fail to follow Joseph's directive to remain 'all together and not in twynne.' Trowle is the first to be excluded from the newly-Christianized (and anglicized) shepherd fellowship, cut out of the group by Harvey's unspoken reduction of their number to three: 'Brethren, lett us all three / singinge walke homwardlye' (ll. 651–2). Trowle's previous integration with his masters (which begins in l. 367 when the boy joins the shepherds' debate about the meaning of the angel's song and is subsequently confirmed in lines 444–51 when he leads the shepherds – and possibly the audience – in their song of 'Troly, loly, loly, loo') gives way here to the same separation that preceded his entrance into the play. Trowle appears to have been anxious about this outcome during the preceding gift-giving scene, presenting his wife's 'ould hose' to the Christ Child so that 'my state on felloweshippe that I doe not lose' (l. 589). That is to say, even the humble gifts of the shepherds (Hankeyn's bell, Harvey's spoon and Tudd's cap) belong to a process of homosocial competition. 'Fellowshippe' is a status that must be aggressively maintained if it is not to be lost.

Unfortunately for Trowle, 'fellowshippe' is precisely what he loses with his omission from Harvey's invitation. Four once again become three. Moreover, as Christina Fitzgerald points out, Trowle's choice of pastoral vocation leaves him 'strikingly alone', back in the state of isolation he occupied at the start of the play: 'Sheppardes craft I forsake; / and to an anker herby / I will in my prayers wach and wake' (ll. 666–8).[48] None of the other three shepherds ends up this isolated. Harvey vows to 'preach all that I can and knowe', gesturing toward the liturgical duties of the parish priest: 'Singinge awaye hethen will I' (ll. 654, 656). Tudd will go 'over the sea' and 'preach this thinge in every place' – that is, in every heathen place (ll. 657, 659). And even Hankeyn, who announces his intention to become a 'hermitte' and 'in wilderness to walke for aye,' still anticipates the possibility of social communion: 'And I shall noe man meete / but for my livinge I shall him praye, / barefoote one my feete' (ll. 669, 673–5) (The 'livinge' for which Hankeyn will beg is another meal generating Christian community.)

Fitzgerald links these social inclusions and exclusions to the homosocial politics of the Painters and other Chester guilds:

> In their focus on fraternity and community, the Chester plays concerning the shepherds and the Three Kings . . . construct a guild fantasy of the 'social body' while simultaneously revealing the exclusionary tactics of such community building, along with its concomitant anxieties. These shepherds and Magi, like

the guilds who produced and performed them, define themselves in part by an exorcism of the unwanted; and they do not always have an idealized relation to the larger social body.[49]

Fitzgerald's concern here is primarily with 'the sexual or social other who must be contained, controlled, or kept at bay'.[50] But we can, of course, also define this 'larger social body' in ethnic terms, extending the 'exorcism of the unwanted' to the Welsh shepherds. Even as he argues for Play 7's commensality, Mills has to admit that the shepherds' 'presence in Chester serves to define the civic community negatively as "non-Welsh"'.[51] Philip Morgan makes a similar point in his study of medieval Chester's relations with its Welsh neighbours (and citizens): '"Being Cheshire" might entail recourse to a rhetoric of Welsh otherness.'[52] The shepherds' departure from the very community they joined in the stable at Bethlehem here becomes the city's means of preserving its 'non-Welsh' identity. Trowle ends up locked in an anchorhold (which, if we follow the lead of the play's anachoristic localization, could 'place' him outside the city walls in the vicinity of Chester's own Redcliff anchorhold), Tudd crosses the Channel (leaving behind his insular identities) and Hankeyn's life of religious vagrancy places himself everywhere – and thus precisely nowhere. Harvey's commitment to preaching might potentially allow him to remain within the fortified boundaries of Chester's community, but the same speech where he announces his change of vocation also begins with the aforementioned invitation to 'walke homwardlye'. The implication here is that he's Wales-bound, looking for more converts to Anglo-Christian *communitas*.

What strikes me most about the end of the *Shepherds' Play* is its resemblance to the conclusion of the Croxton *Play of the Sacrament*. As numerous critics have noted, the Croxton *Play*'s seemingly straightforward narrative of conversion and integration is undone by the very ending that claims to establish it. Christened by the Bishop, Jonathas and his fellow Jews leave the playing area in lines 968–9: 'Now we take owr leave at lesse and mare – / Forward on owr vyage we wyll us dresse.'[53] Their plan is to 'walke by contre and cost, / Owr wyckyd lyvyng for to restore' (ll. 964–5). Lisa Lampert has this to say about their itinerary:

> The Jews are converted, but they will remain perpetual foreigners on a penitential 'vyage,' leaving a community to which they did not belong in the first place. Ambiguous Jewish presence threatens the final stability and unity upon which the resolution of the play's action depends. The play ends with a feeling of unity, but it is a unity specific to a particular vision of the Christian, one that finally cannot acknowledge Christianity's Jewish origin or contain Christians with Jewish origins.[54]

Robert Clark and Claire Sponsler agree, noting that 'This conversion followed by exodus conveniently leaves untested the ability of the Christian community to integrate the Jews on a permanent resident basis.'[55] So does Ruth Nisse: 'When the "baptized" Jews leave the city at the end of the Croxton Play, this new expulsion from East Anglia undermines any untroubled reading of the play as an affirmation of "penance and healing acceptance".'[56] I am of course not claiming any kind of source relationship between the two plays. But I do find their structural parallels to be striking: each text organizes itself around the problematic integration of troublesome 'internal others' (Geraldine Heng's term for England's Jews, but an equally apt designation for Chester's Welsh populace).[57] Like Jonathas the Jew, the Welsh shepherds explicitly engage in penance for their sins. Trowle advises that 'wee us agree / for our mysdeedes amendes to make' (ll. 661–2), a restoration that resembles the restitution promised by Jonathas. Hankeyn also vows that 'this world I fully refuse, / my mysse to amend with monys' (ll. 678–79). Indeed, because the Chester play lacks an Aristorius figure (that is, a guilty insider), there is no member of the idealized Cestrian body politic to be implicated in sin here – only outsiders from over the Dee.

In my estimation, this exclusionary reading of Play 7 was definitely available to sixteenth-century Cestrian spectators, many of whom were well aware of what Philip Morgan calls the '"Welsh version" of Cheshire history'.[58] Morgan is using 'Welsh version' here as shorthand for an ongoing awareness of Chester's medieval military struggle with the Welsh, an imperial history that never goes away, that proves essential to Chester's own self-definition as an urban community (I would even suggest that Chester's sixteenth-century history as the springboard for Elizabeth's Irish campaigns might serve as a typically westward *translatio* of that struggle.) Morgan asserts (and I concur) that there is always a 'cognitive dissonance' between this historical narrative of conflict and the lived experiences of English Cestrians and their Welsh neighbours.[59] That 'dissonance''' is precisely the sort of ambiguity discussed above. We cannot assume with Mills that the shepherds' Welshness was always met with 'amused' tolerance on the part of the play's spectators.

For example, BL MS Harley 2125 – the same manuscript that records the first performance of the pageant in 1515–16 – also reports a riot that broke out 'on Holy Rode Eve [14 September] 1515, betwixte some citizens of Chester and diverse Waylshe gents at St Werburgh's lane end, but little hurte doune because the Welshmen fled'.[60] Cestrian victory over the Welsh is also a constant feature of Henry Bradshaw's *Life of St Werburge*, a text most likely produced in the city's Benedictine monastery between the years 1506 and 1513. Throughout Book 2 of this work (the portion devoted to the saint's Cestrian miracles), Bradshaw constantly reminds his local audience that the Welsh live 'in the montaynes segregate, / Euer to the Saxons hauynge inwarde hate' (ll. 686–7), that the River Dee is 'a sure diuision' between the two populations (l. 701), and that the Welsh are 'Ennemies to englisshemen' (l. 692), 'wicked' villains who 'made insurrection, inwardly gladdyng' (ll. 1423–5), and 'wyld . . . without humanite' (l. 1436).[61] If we momentarily entertain the hypothesis that the Chester shepherds were Welshmen as early as their play's first recorded appearance, then we can see the pageant's account of Anglo-Welsh relations emerging from a local culture as characterized by ethnic animosity as it is by ethnic amity.

Looking at the opposite end of Play 7's archival record (that is, the 1578 performance at the High Cross for the Stanleys), we can identify similar sentiments at work in Chester. For example, there is a 1580s petition to the Privy Council from the citizens of Chester asking for government assistance in repairing the city harbour. Not only do the petitioners claim that these repairs are necessary to enable the launching of English expeditions against the Irish, but they also betray their lurking suspicion of the city's closest Celtic neighbours: 'since such tymes as have bene may be agayne. . . walles maye rebel.'[62] In addition, there is Morgan's observation that 'the dark presence of the Welsh is a leitmotif of the Chester ritual calendar.'[63] Morgan has in mind the 1584 Christmas Watch speech written for Mayor Robert Brerewood by Clerk of the Pentice William Knight. The annual Christmas Watch patrol of the city by the Mayor and his retinue was one of the ways in which the citizens of Chester staked out their territory: 'The walls and their gates redefined the city and their boundary was ceremonially reinforced by the Christmas and Midsummer Watches.'[64] Having learned his speech 'by hart,' the illiterate Mayor Brerewood began the ceremony by invoking the memory of Welsh enmity: 'as this manor of seruice first arosse, as I learne in tyme of warrs with the welch: this citty beinge most endangered by the Enimy at christmas tyme, so it is Contynued of duty for such terms'.[65] The citizens are therefore called once again to arms as a martial community, 'as wachmen hauinge the Care & charge of this citty refferred to you', and they are pitted against a variety of internal others: 'lewd Roges or vacobonds or other disordred persons'.[66] The inclusion of this rhetoric within Tudor Chester's official celebration of Christmas – the feast celebrating the inauguration of the Christian community in the stable at Bethlehem – has potentially strong implications for contemporary reception of a play depicting that inauguration.

The seventy-year continuity of Morgan's 'Welsh version' – the currency of anti-Welsh sentiment from Bradshaw to Brerewood – reminds us that we cannot continue to treat the Chester plays as either ahistorical arte-facts of theology or straightforward reflections of society. Instead, we would do better to follow the path laid out by Theresa Coletti in her recent survey of religious culture in Tudor Chester: 'More promising than simply parsing Catholic and Protestant in the Chester plays, however, is the emerging critical consensus that the cycle's religious ideology is as mobile as its sixteenth-century pageant wagons.'[67] Indebted to 'a revisionary religious history' that replaces 'stable categories of religious identity' with 'a complex cultural field of such identity production', Coletti ulti-mately argues for a Chester cycle that is 'theologically and ideologically hybrid'.[68] Early modern Chester's ethnic identities and regional affilia-tions were similarly hybrid – a point that I have made elsewhere although not hitherto in reference to the Whitsun plays.[69] The Chester *Shepherds'* *Play* cannot be read as outright demonization of a foreign other by civic insiders; prejudice against the Welsh was not total during the heyday of the Chester cycle. But neither can the shepherds be effortlessly integrated into holistic fantasies of civic and national community. Their Welshness resists naturalization: Halton ale goes down smooth, but Hankeyn, Harvey, Tudd and Trowle all cause indigestion.

Notes

1. Elizabeth Baldwin, Lawrence M. Clopper and David Mills (eds), *Cheshire including Chester*, Records of Early English Drama, 2 vols, vol. 1, p. 67. In *The Chester Mystery Cycle: Essays and Documents* (Chapel Hill, 1983), R. M. Lumiansky and David Mills suggest that the play emerged as part of Chester's Corpus Christi pageant sometime between 1500 and 1515–16 (p. 174). However, they have no evidence for their assertion – only the assumption that Thomas Smith, mayor of Chester in 1515–16, 'would not have called upon a guild to present an untried play' (p. 172).

2. *Cheshire including Chester*, p. 73.

3. Ibid., pp. 122–5 (for 1568), pp. 139–41 (for 1572) and pp. 165–7 (for 1575).

4. Ibid., pp. 181–2.

5. David Mills, *Recycling the Cycle: The City of Chester and its Whitsun Plays* (Toronto, 1998), pp. 208–11.

6. *Cheshire including Chester*, p. 147.

7. This and all other quotations of the text of Play 7 are taken from the edition of the pageant provided in vol. 1 of the Lumiansky and Mills edition of *The Chester Mystery Cycle*.

8. 'The Chester Mystery Plays and the Limits of Realism', p. 231.

9   Ibid., p. 233.
10 Rosemary Woolf, *The English Mystery Plays* (Berkeley, 1972), p. 185.
11 Mills, *Recycling the Cycle*, p. 177.
12 David Mills, 'The Chester Mystery Plays and the Limits of Realism' in Tom Scott and Pat Starkey (eds), *The Middle Ages in the North-West: Papers Presented at an International Conference Sponsored Jointly by the Centres of Medieval Studies of the Universities of Liverpool and Toronto* (Oxford, 1995), pp. 221–36, p. 230.
13 David Mills, *Recycling the Cycle*, p. 177.
14 For further discussion of the involvement of individuals of Welsh origin in Chester civic society and government, see Fulton and Laughton in this volume (pp. 149–68 and pp. 169–83).
15 Mills, *Recycling the Cycle*, p. 176.
16 Ibid.
17 Garrett A. Sullivan, Jr., 'Civilising Wales: *Cymbeline*, Roads and the Landscape of Early Modern Britain', *Early Modern Literary Studies*, 4 (1998), *http://extra.shu.ac.uk/emls/04–2/sullshak.htm* (accessed 30 September 2009, n. pag., paragraph 21).
18 Christopher Highly, 'Wales, Ireland, and *1 Henry IV*', *Renaissance Drama*, New Series 21 (1990), 91–114, p. 102. The Welsh shepherds of Play 7 also joke about castration: just before the wrestling match begins, Trowle warns his masters to be 'warre lest your golyons glent' (l. 247). Nominally the only genitals threatened here are Welsh ones; we must nonetheless remember that the shepherds are almost certainly being played by Englishmen, a performance fact that complicates the ethnic affiliation of the actors' masculinity.
19 Lisa Hopkins, 'Welshness in Shakespeare's English Histories', in Ton Hoenslaars (ed.), *Shakespeare's History Plays: Performance, Translation and Adaptation in Britain and Abroad* (Cambridge, 2004), pp. 60–74, p. 66.
20 Patricia Parker, 'Uncertain Unions: Welsh Leeks in David J. Baker and Willy Maley (eds), '*Henry V*', in *British Identities and English Renaissance Literature* (Cambridge, 2002), p. 97.
21 Ibid.
22 Ibid., p. 98.
23 Ibid., p. 83.
24 A. C. Cawley, 'The "Grotesque" Feast in the *Prima Pastorum*', *Speculum*, 30 (1955), 213–17, p. 215.
25 Again, see Baldwin et al. (eds), *Cheshire including Chester*, pp. 122–5 (for 1568) and 139–41 (for 1572).
26 V. A. Kolve, *The Play Called Corpus Christi* (Stanford, 1966), p. 163.
27 Ibid., p. 165.
28 Lauren Lepow, '"What God Has Cleansed": The Shepherds' Feast in the *Prima Pastorum*', *Modern Philology*, 80 (1983), 280–3, p. 282.
29 Woold, *The English Mystery Plays*, pp. 187 and 188.
30 Peter W. Travis, *Dramatic Design in the Chester Cycle* (Chicago, 1982), p. 123.
31 Ibid., pp. 122 and 120.
32 Robert Adams, 'The Egregious Feasts of the Chester and Towneley Shepherds', *The Chaucer Review*, 21 (1986), 96–107, pp. 102 and 103.
33 Ibid., pp. 102 and 105.

[34] See Lisa Kiser, '"Mak's Heirs": Sheep and Humans in the Pastoral Ecology of the Towneley *First* and *Second Shepherds' Plays'*, *Journal of English and Germanic Philology*, 108 (2009), 336–59, pp. 347–9.

[35] Gillian Brennan, 'The Cheese and the Welsh: Foreigners in Elizabethan Literature', *Renaissance Studies*, 8 (1994), 40–64, p. 64.

[36] Claude Fischler, 'Food, Self, and Identity', *Social Science Information*, 27 (1988), 275–92, p. 279.

[37] Ibid.

[38] Ibid., 280–1.

[39] Ibid., 281.

[40] Ibid.

[41] Cohen, *Hybridity, Identity, and Monstrosity in Medieval Britain*, p. 21.

[42] Mills, *Recycling the Cycle*, p. 176. For more on the late medieval integration of the Welsh into the Cestrian community, see Laughton, *Life in a Late Medieval City*, pp. 103–4.

[43] Robert Appelbaum, *Aguecheek's Beef, Belch's Hiccup, and Other Gastronomic Interjections: Literature, Culture, and Food amongst the Early Moderns* (Chicago, 2006), p. 11.

[44] Ibid.

[45] Ibid., p. 13.

[46] Mills, 'The Chester Mystery Plays and the Limits of Realism', p. 231.

[47] Writing about early modern perceptions of 'the Irish diet', Joan Fitzpatrick observes 'a fear that the absorption of strange foodstuffs will make strange the English body and initiate a wider social corruption which will inevitably undermine English cultural superiority' (Fitzpatrick, 'Food and Foreignness in *Sir Thomas More*', *Early Theatre*, 7 (2004), p. 42.) Her observation could be applied to Welsh foods as well. Nevertheless, while it remains possible that some of the food purchased for use in performance by the Painters had Welsh origins, the play's greatest anxiety is reserved for its faux-Welsh shepherds.

[48] Christina M. Fitzgerald, *The Drama of Masculinity and Medieval English Guild Culture* (New York, 2007), p. 106.

[49] Ibid., p. 101.

[50] Ibid., p. 103.

[51] Mills, *Recycling the Cycle*, p. 177.

[52] Philip Morgan, 'Cheshire and Wales', p. 201.

[53] All quotations from the Croxton *Play of the Sacrament* are taken from the edition of the play in John Coldewey's *Early English Drama: An Anthology*, Garland Reference Library of the Humanities 1313 (New York, 1993).

[54] Lisa Lampert, *Gender and Jewish Difference from Paul to Shakespeare* (Philadelphia, 2004), p. 115.

[55] Robert L. A. Clark and Claire Sponsler, 'Othered Bodies: Cross-Dressing in the *Mistere de la Sainte Hostie* and the Croxton *Play of the Sacrament*', *Journal of Medieval and Early Modern Studies*, 29 (1999), 61–87, p. 73.

[56] Ruth Nisse, *Defining Acts: Drama and the Politics of Interpretation in Late Medieval England* (Notre Dame, 2005), p. 122.

[57] Geraldine Heng, *Empire of Magic: Medieval Romance and the Politics of Cultural Fantasy* (New York, 2003), p. 84.

[58] Morgan, 'Cheshire and Wales', p. 196.

[59] Ibid., p. 201.

[60] Quoted in Morris, *Chester in the Plantagenet and Tudor Reigns*, p. 66.

[61] All of these quotations are taken from Carl Horstmann's EETS edition of Bradshaw's *Life*.

[62] Quoted in D. M. Woodward, *The Trade of Elizabethan Chester*, Occasional Papers in Economic and Social History 4 (Hull, 1970), p. 89.

[63] Morgan, 'Cheshire and Wales', p. 199.

[64] Mills, *Recycling the Cycle*, p. 23.

[65] Baldwin et al., *Cheshire including Chester*, pp. 203 and 204.

[66] Ibid., p. 204.

[67] Theresa Coletti, 'The Chester Cycle in Sixteenth-Century Religious Culture', *Journal of Medieval and Early Modern Studies*, 37 (2007), 531–47, p. 535.

[68] Ibid., 536 and 537.

[69] See the introduction to my *Against All England*, pp. 1–23. I am not alone in making such assertions about Cestrian identity: for important accounts of Cestrian hybridity, see Cohen, *Hybridity, Identity, and Montrosity*, pp. 103–4; Pamela Clare Ingham, *Sovereign Fantasies: Arthurian Romance and the Making of Britain* (Philadelphia, 2001), pp. 107–36 and Rhonda Knight, 'All Dressed Up with Someplace to Go: Regional Identity in *Sir Gawain and the Green Knight*', *Studies in the Age of Chaucer*, 25 (2003), 259–84. But these accounts largely focus on travel writing and chivalric romance; until now, the ethnic implications of Chester's biblical drama have not been objects of sustained critical attention.

12

Remembering Anglo-Saxon Mercia in late medieval and early modern Chester

CATHERINE A. M. CLARKE

The focal point of the Benedictine abbey of St Werburgh's, Chester, in the later medieval period was the elaborate shrine of St Werburgh itself, located in the presbytery, behind the high altar. Probably built in the 1340s, the stone structure has been described as 'representing a miniature two-storeyed chapel, the lower storey forming the base and the upper housing the reliquary containing the saint's remains'.[1] The lower section, with votive niches for pilgrims making supplication to Werburgh, seems never to have been completed: J. M. Maddison suggests that this may have been due to the interruption of the Black Death in the mid-fourteenth century.[2] The upper section, however, was richly decorated with carved tracery and small gilded statues of thirty-four Anglo-Saxon saints and royal figures, holding scrolls which showed their names in Latin. The majority of these statues represented key figures from the history of the Anglo-Saxon kingdom of Mercia, whilst others were connected through kinship with the Mercian noblewoman and saint Werburgh herself.[3] The stone shrine then, formed the focus for devotion to Werburgh in the later Middle Ages, commemorating her sanctity and her ongoing patronage of Chester, as well as the prestige and authority of the Benedictine community of St Werburgh's as custodian of her cult. But, visually, the shrine also offered a striking monument to the Mercian heritage and identity of Chester, celebrating not only the genealogy of its patron saint, but also the venerable ancestry of the city itself in this ancient Anglo-Saxon kingdom. The prominence of Anglo-Saxon Mercia in the fourteenth-century shrine of St Werburgh is not unique: a range of texts associated with late medieval and early modern Chester also place particular emphasis on the Mercian heritage of the city, often using the shrine itself as the starting point for the exploration and imaginative reconstruction of early medieval history. These texts offer fascinating examples of the emergent interest in Anglo-Saxon history, culture and language, as well as the development of broader antiquarian interests and methods, in the sixteenth century onwards. Yet, in Chester itself, the memory of Anglo-Saxon Mercia has specific meaning and cultural and political value. The memorialisation of Mercia in both textual and material sources offers an alternative cultural geography which moves Chester from the periphery of England to the centre of an autonomous, powerful, ancient kingdom, re-asserting the city's importance and status. The idea of Mercia forms part of the development of a local Chester identity which is contiguous – but not synonymous – with 'England' and 'Englishness', playing a key role in the formulation and articulation of a distinct regional identity for Cheshire in the period.[4]

The shrine which is extant in St Werburgh's Cathedral in Chester today bears the marks of its complex, troubled history and various phases of destruction, decay and restoration. During the Reformation, the relics of Werburgh were removed and the shrine was dismembered, with the remnants later forming the burial place for Bishop Downham and then, from 1635, part of the new episcopal throne. After a partial restoration in 1748 of the sections of the shrine incorporated into the throne, all the remaining pieces were collected in 1888 by Arthur Blomfield and re-assembled in their current site in the Lady Chapel, behind the high altar.[5] Evidence of former violence and decay remains: several figures in the upper section have lost their heads and others are in fact mis-matched heads and bodies put together by the later restorers. Yet, whilst the extant shrine is an imperfect, compromised version of the fourteenth-century original posited by art historians, its visible traces of earlier moments in its physical history call attention to processes of destruction, loss and recuperation of the past. The nineteenth-century reconstruction which stands in St Werburgh's today represents just one response to the challenges of historical loss and recovery which have been associated with Werburgh's shrine in its various forms across the centuries. Whilst Blomfield's nineteenth-century enterprise responded to (and sought to correct) the absence of Werburgh's shrine within the fabric of the medieval cathedral, the very earliest history of Werburgh's shrine at Chester is inextricably connected with issues of loss, absence and imaginative recuperation. The hagiographers of Werburgh tell us that, at the first translation of her relics in Hanbury, the saint's body is found to be wholly intact and incorrupt 'quasi in dulci stratu obdormire' ('as if sleeping in a soft bed') – a conventional sign of sanctity.[6] However, in the period of the Danish invasions, when the saint's body is moved to Chester for protection, it is found to have 'resolued unto powder'.[7] Henry Bradshaw, following earlier hagiographers, interprets this as a divine miracle, performed

> Lest the cruell gentils / and wiked myscreantes
> With pollute handes full of corrupcion
> Shulde touche her body / by indignation . . .[8]

These ingenious explications of the decay of Werburgh's relics suggest an alternative insight into the function of the elaborate fourteenth-century shrine. Like the explanatory accounts of Florence, Goscelin or Bradshaw, the shrine seeks to negotiate an absence, to fill the gap left by Werburgh's vanished relics. The ornate, imposing stone shrine serves to euphemise the loss of Werburgh's material body, and to replace the saint's dissolved physical remains with tangible new relics of Chester's spiritual and cultural heritage – the carved figures of Mercian kings and saints. This ongoing process of imaginative recovery and re-invention, so evident in the fabric and history of Werburgh's shrine, resonates across late medieval and early modern texts which engage with the Mercian heritage of Chester.

Written around 1513,[9] Henry Bradshaw's *Life of Saint Werburge* shows a strong interest in the Mercian heritage of Werburgh as well as that of Chester itself. Recent work on the *Life of St Werburge* has identified Bradshaw's propagandist aims to advance the interests of the Benedictine abbey of St Werburgh's, of which he himself was a member, and to resist the increasing power of the secular civic authorities (as well as the more distant influence of the English Crown) in Chester. Throughout the medieval period, overlaps and tensions existed between the spheres (and physical spaces) of influence of St Werburgh's and the city's secular rulers.[10] Robert Barrett emphasizes the ways in which Bradshaw's text 'directly intervenes in the long-running struggle between the mayor and the abbot for control of Chester', a struggle that intensified with the award of the Great Charter by Henry VII in 1506, which formalised a new civic constitution and gave control to a secular civic assembly led by the mayor.[11] With the jurisdiction and authority of St Werburgh's diminishing, the *Life of St Werburge* insists on an urban topography with the saint's shrine at its very heart, re-asserting the abbey's position as the spiritual, cultural and political centre of the city. The *Life of St Werburge* stresses the crucial role played by Werburgh as the patron and protector of the city and by the Benedictine abbey as the guardian of her relics and custodian of

Chester's heritage. In the final chapters of Book II, Bradshaw moves from a catalogue of Werburgh's many miracles performed as patron of Chester to a direct address to 'all the inhabytauntes within the countie palatine of Chestre', reminding them of the venerable history of the abbey and its role in the spiritual and cultural development of the city. The repeated end-line in these stanzas exhorts the citizens that they should 'to the monasterie be neuer vnkynde'.[12] Whilst royal intervention enabled and authorised the growing power of the secular civic authorities in Chester, undermining the former prestige of the abbey, it also formed a more direct potential threat to the monastery of St Werburgh's. In his 1848 facsimile edition of the *Life of St Werburge*, Edward Hawkins recognizes the cultural and political implications of the text's early sixteenth-century date, noting that 'the Reformation was approaching, the shadows of coming events were already apparent, and were exerting their almost unobserved influence upon the feelings and opinions of the people'.[13] For Henry Bradshaw then, contemporary Chester is beset by threats to its historic identity and heritage and subject to the pernicious interference of the English Crown. The *Life of St Werburge* remembers Anglo-Saxon Mercia as a Golden Age for the power, prestige and autonomy of Chester and its region, offering a response to the troubled politics of local identity in Bradshaw's present.

Following earlier hagiographers, Bradshaw gives sustained attention to the complex genealogy of Werburgh, which brings together four Anglo-Saxon kingdoms (Mercia, Northumbria, Kent, and East Anglia) as well as the Frankish royal line.[14] Bradshaw's imagery of the 'royall rose' and swete ryuer' to envision Werburgh's mixed noble ancestry recalls the use of the same metaphors by Goscelin of Saint-Bertin to represent her geneaology.[15] But Bradshaw places particular emphasis on Werburgh's Mercian identity, exploiting the idea of Mercia to reinforce the affinity between the saint and Chester (a potential difficulty, as she was buried at her own request at Hanbury and only translated to Chester two centuries later) and to create opportunities for exploring the early history of the city. For Bradshaw, Werburgh is 'rose of merciens' (II: 317): a model of virginity, virtue and piety as well as an important figure in Anglo-Saxon history. Book I of his *Life of St Werburge* focuses on the saint's earthly life, while Book II goes on to chronicle her role as patron saint of Chester and extends its focus to other key figures in the development of the city. Again, throughout Book II, Anglo-Saxon Mercia features strongly, with figures such as Offa, Earl Leofric and, in particular, Æthelflæd 'Lady of the Mercians' given particular prominence in Bradshaw's account of the early history of Chester.[16]

In Book I, Bradshaw offers a description of Mercia (or *Merselande*) which begins with an account of the bounds of the historical Anglo-Saxon kingdom.

> The bounds and lorshyppes / of the sayd Mercyens,
> As shewen duyers bokes hystoryall,
> Were large and mighty / and of great prehemynens,
> Where the sayd kynge [Wulfhere] reigned by power imperyall.
> This realme to dyscrybe / begyn we shall
> At the Cytee of Chester / and the water of Dee,
> Bytwene Englande and Wales / of the west partye . . .[17]

Bradshaw continues to outline the bounds of Mercia to the east, south and north, reaching as far as the east coast of England, London and the river Humber. This presentation of the territory of Mercia at its maximum extent strengthens the impression of the power, influence and 'pre-eminence' of the Anglo-Saxon kingdom, but is also, of course, a necessity if Chester is to be included within its bounds.[18] Bradshaw sets out his intention to begin his description of Mercia with Chester itself, centring the kingdom on the city and reinforcing its importance. Bradshaw's description of the 'myghty kyngdome' of Mercia goes on to catalogue its '[m]any noble Cytees' and 'townes and burghes royall', listing fourteen settlements including Lincoln, Bristol, Oxford and Cambridge.[19] Bradshaw also celebrates the many 'royall ryuers' of Mercia and its fertile, productive lands, asserting that 'no part of all this lande // May be compared / to this foresaid Merselande'.[20] This lengthy account of the Anglo-Saxon kingdom of Mercia provides more than simply background to the genealogy of Werburgh. For Bradshaw, Mercia offers an alternative cultural and political geography to that of his own contemporary England, presenting Chester as a principal city within an autonomous, powerful and prestigious kingdom. On the sixteenth-century map of England, Chester is geographically peripheral and marginal, located far from the increasingly influential centres of power and government at the very edge of the English kingdom where it borders with Wales, and on the margins of the island itself. The idea of Mercia enables Bradshaw to re-situate Chester at the heart of a powerful and autonomous kingdom, moving the city from a position of geographical and cultural marginality into an important centre.

Yet, clearly this notion of Chester at the heart of the Anglo-Saxon kingdom of Mercia presents difficulties which Bradshaw is forced to negotiate or elide. Geographically, Chester was only ever at the very edge of Mercian territory, and even then only at the period of the kingdom's greatest extent. Bradshaw's response to this challenge draws on the rhetorical and linguistic resources of the poet to offer an alternative, verbal mapping which overwrites the realities of history and geography. His explicit intention to begin his verbal map of Mercia '[a]t the Cytee of Chester' skilfully places Chester, in rhetorical and textual terms, as the kingdom's principal town. Later, Bradshaw offers an etymology for the name *Merselande*, again exploiting the potentials of language to support his own ideological map of Mercia. He notes that the northern boundary of the kingdom was formed by the river Mersey.

> Of the foresaid ryuer / and water of Mersee
> The kynge of Mercyens / taketh his name,
> As moost sure dyuydent / to be had in memorye,
> Mesurynge and metynge / the bondes with great fame
> Of Mersee and Northumberlande / kynges of the same,
> Bitwene chesshyr & lancashyr theyr kingdoms, certayne,
> As auncyent Cronycles descryben it full playne.[21]

Mercia in fact derives from the Old English *mearc* ('border, boundary'), reflecting the origins of Mercia at the 'edges' between other early king-doms within Britain, but Bradshaw's false etymology again directs emphasis to the north-west region and the area close to Chester. This etymologically-justified emphasis on the north-western periphery of Mercia again achieves a re-ordering of cultural and political geography which asserts the importance of Chester. Bradshaw's etymology ensures that, even within Mercia, Chester moves from being a city on the margins to a city at the very centre in terms of history, heritage and identity.

Siginificantly, whilst Bradshaw's account of Mercia in Book I of the *Life of St Werburge* begins in the historical past, with descriptions firmly in the preterite, it slips almost imperceptibly into a present tense which insists on the validity and authority of Mercian identity in the author's own period. From the statement that '[m]any royall ruyers / were conteyned in the same', Bradshaw moves to the assertion that:

> . . . this royall realme / *holdeth*, as we fynde,
> Habaundance of fuytes / pleasaunt and profytable [my emphasis]. . .[22]

Bradshaw then continues to discuss 'the people of Mercyens' in the present tense, referring to the tradition of their prowess as archers and their success 'In all actes Marcyall / eyer hauynge the vyctoyre.'[23] He remarks that:

> If they be well ordred / vnder a sure capytayne
> And set to suche busynesse / theyr honour to auaunce,
> The tryumph they optayne – / knowen it is certayne
> In Englande and Scotlande / & in the realme of Fraunce;

Fewe of them have countred / by manhoode and valeaunce
Great nombre of enemyes / with knyghthode & policy,
We meane them moost specyall / in the Weest-party.[24]

Bradshaw's celebration of the ancient kingdom of Mercia slips into a politically-charged assertion of cultural difference and autonomy in his own historical present. The stanza reminds its readers of the power and martial strength of the Mercians, explicitly comparing Mercia with – and thus distinguishing it from – Scotland, France and England. The success of the Mercians over their enemies in the 'Weest-party' (Wales) forms the basis for Bradshaw's celebration of their power and military prowess here. But the implicit deficit of similar 'manhoode and valeaunce' in England, Scotland and France suggests the potential of the Mercians – the men of Bradshaw's own Cheshire – to assert their superior strength if needed.

The textual history of the *Life of St Werburge* means that we must consider a dual audience for Bradshaw's assertions about present-day Mercian identity and potential, with different implications for the text's different readerships. Originally addressed to 'the inhabytauntes within the countie palatine of Chestre', including 'lordes, barons / ye rulers of the countre' as well as '[m]archauntes' and 'honest matrons',[25] Bradshaw's comments on Mercia offer a specific political message for the people of Chester. Whilst celebrating their Mercian heritage, he warns of the need for the people to be 'wel ordred' and for good leadership under 'a sure capytayne' – possibly a caution relating to the secular civic government and the need for the city to choose its allegiances carefully. He fore-grounds the concept of 'honour', celebrating the prestigious heritage and renowned achievements of the Mercians, but also hinting at the proper 'busynesse' to be undertaken, should this honour ever be threatened or denigrated. For the Chester audience, these lines could be read as a call to remain loyal to Mercian identity, heritage and honour and to resist external interference (from London and the Crown) in the affairs of the city. In the context of early sixteenth-century Chester and Benedictine anxieties about the meddling of the Crown and threats to the abbey's jurisdiction and authority, this stanza crackles with political challenge and threat.

Yet in its surviving form, Henry Bradshaw's *Life of St Werburge* exists only in the London publication of 1521, printed by Richard Pynson, the King's Printer, for an audience beyond Chester. Several recent studies have explored the implications of its transition from local to national text and the ways Bradshaw's work might be re-positioned for a national audi-ence within wider discourses of anti-Lutheranism, didactic literature for women, or formulations of national identity. In her analysis of Pynson's edition of the text, Catherine Sanok emphasizes the ways in which Chester – the bastion city defended from its enemies by its spiritual patron – functions as a 'metonym for England itself', identifying 'elisions of a national paradigm and a regional one'.[26] Whilst her argument makes a persuasive case for the ways in which Chester history in the *Life of St Werburge* might have a national resonance, Sanok overlooks the ways in which Bradshaw's idea of Mercia militates against the notion of a monolithic, unified national identity in which the region is merely a mirror for the nation. For a London audience, Bradshaw's comments about the ongoing validity and power of Chester identity – and the capacity of its citizens to 'auaunce' their interests – offer a reminder of the distinctive identity and power of the regions in general and of Chester, with its history of autonomy as a palatinate, in particular. For Bradshaw, Mercia is more than simply a remote, defunct historical kingdom. The idea of Mercia shapes his sense of Cestrian identity, underscoring its difference from the wider culture of 'England' and 'Englishness' and its potential to re-assert itself in response to threat or denigration. Of course, even within late medieval Chester, Bradshaw is still a partisan voice, speaking on behalf of the Benedictine abbey in opposition to the growing power of the city's secular authorities. Yet he appropriates the authority of Mercia to underpin his vision of Chester with the abbey and Werburgh's shrine, at its centre.

Werburgh's shrine features prominently in Book II of Bradshaw's *Life of St Werburge*, where it appears in the form of a portable reliquary, taken out of the abbey and into the streets of the city at times of danger. In his account of the great 1180 fire of Chester for example, the procession of Werburgh's shrine through the streets of the city extinguishes the blaze and Bradshaw gives the following words (II: 1680–1) to the thankful citizens:

> we shall neuer able be
> The place to recompence for this ded of charite.

Barrett relates this episode to Bradshaw's propagandist strategies on behalf of the abbey, describing this as the notion of 'impossible debt, of a charity so great that it can never be matched', and explores the ways in which this 'idea of impossible recompense [functions] as a pre-emptive strike against a citizenry all too ready to enter into conflict with the abbey – and all too capable of winning that struggle'.[27] Repeatedly in Book II, Werburgh's shrine itself is the focal point for the spiritual patronage and protection of the city. Writing in the early sixteenth century, we can assume that Bradshaw knew the fourteenth-century stone shrine in St

Werburgh's abbey, although there is no direct description of it in the *Life of St Werburge*. However, its carvings of the kings and saints of Mercia may have influenced his interest in and emphasis on Mercian history in the *Life*, and his account of Werburgh's genealogy (I: 260–420) may well have been structured around the figures represented on the shrine, such as 'Penda', 'Wulfer', 'Cryda' and so on.

At the Dissolution – just a few years after the completion of Bradshaw's *Life of St Werburge* – the shrine of St Werburgh was dismembered as a papist cultural relic. Yet, in the decades after the Reformation, the shrine begins to take on new valencies and cultural uses as a symbol of Protestant cultural authority and the long tradition of a specifically English Christianity and religious practice. *The Vale-Royall of England, or, The County Palatine of Chester*, published by Daniel King in London in 1656, also shows a prominent interest in the Mercian history of Cheshire. However, here the interest is motivated by an emergent antiquarian approach to the recovery and recording of the past, as well as a Protestant interest in the early history of England and English religious and cultural institutions. The essays collected within the volume show a particular attention to the Mercian history of Chester and the early development of the city and St Werburgh's. A general overview of the kingdom of Mercia offers a correction of the false etymology espoused by Bradshaw, stating that:

> This kingdom of *March*, reached from *London* to the River of *Marsey*, which parteth *Cheshire* from *Lancashire*; of which River, some write it should take name: But that I cannot believe; but think rather it was so called, because it marched or bordered upon all the other.[28]

Throughout, the emphasis of the volume is on sound scholarship and rigorous empiricism, revealed in the words of the author which preface a 'Tract' on the Kings of Mercia.

> My main design is, by Chronological Characters, to fix the rise and period of the Mercian Monarchy, together with the true times of each kings attainment of the Royall Scepter, so far forth, as the company of most, if not all the ancient and modern Writers extant on this Subject will give light: who are generally so full of absurd contradictions, and Anachronisms, that I almost despaired to attain my proposed end.[29]

Whilst the Mercian heritage of Werburgh and the early English origins of religious institutions in Chester are evidently a focus for pride and celebration in *The Vale-Royall*, Werburgh's shrine itself becomes here a troubling absence or gap in the evidence for continuity of Anglo-Saxon heritage and custom. In this period, the now-dismembered shrine was incorporated into the Episcopal throne in the Choir of Chester cathedral. Yet 'N.N.', writing in 'A Discourse of the Foundation and Endowment of St Werburgs in Chester', is reluctant to accept its continued existence. He writes:

> In the most probable guesse, by view of all the Monuments at that Church [St Werburgh's] at this present, I can affirm nothing for certainty, either of the matter of her Shrine, or place where it stood, and yet am loath to be incredulous, as not to believe them which think that one good part of it is there seen, whether in the place where it first stood, which I think not; or removed to the place where now at the upper end of the Quire on the right hand it serves to be a supporter to a fair Pue erected for the Lord Bishop of the Diocese to sit to hear the Preacher of the Weekly Lecture, the Pulpit being opposite to sit on the other side.[30]

For 'N.N.', these uncertainties about the preservation and continued existence of Werburgh's shrine suggest an ambivalent attitude towards the Mercian past which it represents. Whilst *The Vale-Royall* throughout devotes sustained attention to the Anglo-Saxon history of Cheshire and the venerable Mercian origins of buildings, customs and institutions, the loss of Werburgh's shrine suggests a discontinuity or severance from that remote early medieval past. Whilst some writers might indulge in 'absurd contradictions, and Anachronisms', the treatises in *The Vale-Royall* insist on their basis in unequivocal material evidence and empirical proof. The apparent absence of Werburgh's shrine raises an anxiety about the strength of connection and continuity with Mercian history and perhaps a lack of confidence in the ongoing identity of Chester and its citizens as distinctively Mercian.

In 1749, about a year after the partial restoration of the fragments of Werburgh's shrine incorporated into the Episcopal throne, an anonymous 'Citizen of Chester' produced a pamphlet, published by Elizabeth Adams, for the benefit of the Chester Bluecoat School. The pamphlet sets out:

> A Summary of the Life of St. *Werburgh*
> With an Historical Account
> OF THE
> *Images* upon Her SHRINE,
> (Now the Episcopal Throne)
> IN the CHOIR of *CHESTER*.
> Collected from ancient Chronicles, and old Writers.[31]

The detailed description of Werburgh's shrine begins on page nine of the pamphlet, where it is preceded by a small engraving (Figure 9). Whilst apparently a minor detail within the pamphlet as a whole, this engraving in fact situates and informs reception of the subsequent text, offering

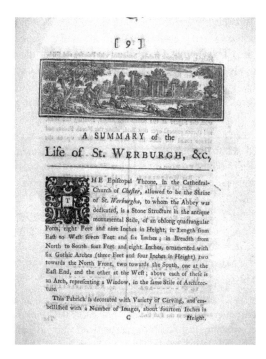

Figure 9. Elizabeth Adams, *A Summary of the Life of St Werburgh* (Chester, 1749), p. 9 (detail), used by permission of Cheshire Archives and Local Studies.

valuable clues about the politics and aesthetics of the volume. Here, in recognisably romantic style, we have two gentleman seated in a pastoral setting, surveying a picturesque ruin. One of the gentlemen appears to be painting a picture of the scene. The ruins themselves are an ahistorical fantasy of architectural styles – classical columns, Romanesque arches and neat rectangular Georgian-style windows – all in the process of being absorbed back into nature by the plants and trees which grow out of the crumbling stone. The two gentlemen observers are clearly in postures of leisure and repose: accompanied by their dog they sit on the grassy bank, under the shade of a tree (the classic pastoral *locus amoenus*). Whilst one paints his picture, the other lies semi-recumbent and gestures towards the ruins which are the object of their gaze. Yet the gentlemen are separated from the alluring ruins by a lake or river: the object of their attention remains held in the distance, recoverable only through the painter's art. This image of course, is not a mimetic representation of a particular ruin

– least of all Werburgh's shrine – but it does function as a clear exposition of the imaginative *idea* of the ruin and its position in relation to the viewer. The opening image is suggestive of the ways in which the author of the Bluecoat pamphlet will approach and engage with the fragments of history represented by Werburgh's shrine and also calls attention to a tension between two concurrent discourses running throughout the pamphlet. On the one hand, the author adopts the language of diligent, rigorous empirical analysis and historical endeavour. Yet, simultaneously, the early medieval past is located within an aesthetic of nostalgia and retreat, romanticised and removed from contemporary experience. Of course, it could be argued that this fundamental duality or ambivalence is at the core of the developing mode of antiquarian writing within the period.[32] Certainly in the Bluecoat pamphlet, this duality has complex and intriguing implications for the author's sense of relationship with Chester's Mercian past.

The pamphlet makes reference to the recent repairs to the remains of Werburgh's shrine, suggesting that this may have revived interest in the Anglo-Saxon history of Chester.

> The Chapter of *Chester* having lately begun to beautify their Cathedral, the decayed Decorations on the Episcopal Throne engaged their Attention: This fine Piece of Antiquity had been ornamented with Carving and Statuary, both which had greatly suffered, not by Time, but by Violence: They have therefore endeavoured to repair the one, & to restore the other, so that the little IMAGES which have for so many centuries guarded, as it were, this ancient Monument, and were so injuriously defaced, are, by a commendable Care, now made whole again.[33]

The pamphlet gives particular attention to the figures around the top of the shrine, representing Mercian kings and saints. The author notes that:

> Each of these held in one Hand a Scroll or Label, upon which were inscribed in *Latin*, but in the Old *English* Character, the Names of Kings and Saints of the Royal Line of MERCIA. Many of the Labels are broke off, others are so much defaced, that only a Syllable or two can be read.[34]

The author then offers a reconstruction of the legible names on the shrine (Figure 10) and also includes a genealogy of the kings of Mercia. Once again, the reconstruction of Anglo-Saxon Mercia is the ultimate focus of this antiquarian enterprise, leading on from the shrine itself to more general recollections and comments, including discussion of Offa and his triumphant defence of 'Mercian lands' against the Welsh. The author muses on Offa's punishment of Welsh intruders into Mercia with the rather quaint couplets:

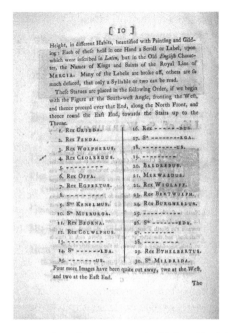

[10]

Height, in different Habits, beautified with Painting and Gild-
ing : Each of thefe held in one Hand a Scroll or Label, upon
which were infcribed in *Latin*, but in the Old *Englifh* Character, the Names of Kings and Saints of the Royal Line of
MERCIA. Many of the Labels are broke off, others are fo
much defaced, that only a Syllable or two can be read.

Thefe Statues are placed in the following Order, if we begin
with the Figure at the South-weft Angle, fronting the Weft,
and thence proceed over that End, along the North Front, and
thence round the Eaft End, towards the Stairs up to the
Throne.

1. REX GRIEDA.	16. REX - - - - - -DUS.
2. REX PENDA.	17. Sᵗ - - - - - - - -RGA.
3. REX WOLPHERUS.	18. - - - - - - - - -US.
4. REX CEOLREDUS.	19. - - - - - - - -
5. - - - - - - - - -	20. BALDREDUS.
6. REX OFFA.	21. MERWALDUS.
7. REX EGBERTUS.	22. REX WIGLAFF.
8. - - - - - - - -	23. REX BERTWULPH.
9. Sᵗ KENELMUS.	24. REX BURGHREDUS.
10. Sᵗ MILBURGA.	25. - - - - - - - -
11. REX BEORNA.	26. Sᵗ - - - - - -EDA.
12. REX COLWLPHUS.	27. - - - - - - - -
13. - - - - - - - - -	28. - - - - - - - -
14. Sᵗ - - - - - -LDA.	29. REX ETHELBERTUS.
15. - - - - - - -US.	30. Sᵗ MILDRIDA.

Four more Images have been quite cut away, two at the Weft,
and two at the Eaft End.

The

Figure 10. Reconstruction of the names on St Werburgh's shrine, Elizabeth
Adams, *A Summary of the Life of St Werburgh* (Chester, 1749), p. 10, used by
permission of Cheshire Archives and Local Studies.

You could, great Offa, with deep Dykes enclose
Within their Bounds, your rugged Cambrian foes;
Nor dar'd they range into the Mercian lands,
Dreading the Doom of amputated Hands.[35]

Here again, the idiom of the pamphlet slips easily from scholarly reconstruction into folklore or fairytale. The world of Offa and his Mercian
warriors is remote and mythic, signalled by the archaising language of the
verse and the neat end-rhymes themselves, which translate history into the
imaginative and rhetorical world of romance.

The duality of the Bluecoat pamphlet's approach to its material – both
scholarly and self-consciously amateur – extends throughout. For example,
whilst it offers a very thorough and careful analysis of the extant carved
figures (complete with acknowledgement of names which cannot be recov-
ered in full) and a painstaking record of the dimensions of the shrine, the
author insists that the work was produced 'in a very few Days, for his own
Amusement'. Here, as in the opening engraving, we have an insistence on

the model of the gentleman amateur, brought to his subject by imaginative attraction and interest rather than necessity (supposedly) free from the
political agendas or obligations of patronage associated with the profes-
sional writer. The relationship between the Anglo-Saxon past outlined in
the pamphlet and the author's own present in eighteenth-century Chester
is similarly ambivalent. Anglo-Saxon Mercia is presented as the underpin-
ning of contemporary Cestrian identity, traditions and Christian heritage.
Yet the Anglo-Saxon past is also presented as a space of retreat and
nostalgia, removed from immediate contemporary concerns and pressures,
in which the author can find 'amusement' and pleasure through imaginative engagement with a different, remote cultural world. Even as the
Bluecoat pamphlet recuperates Mercian history, it others and distances it,
representing it as an object of desire and imaginative reconstruction rather
than as an integral and inalienable part of Cestrian identity. As visualized
metaphorically in the opening engraving of the two gentlemen and the
ruin, Chester's Mercian past remains distant and intangible, as if beyond
a stretch of water: an object of nostalgia and imaginative escape which is
recoverable only through artistic enterprise.

The interest in Mercian history demonstrated by these Chester texts
reflects of course, a wider emergent history in Anglo-Saxon history, culture
and language in the late medieval and early modern period. Influential
early figures include Elizabeth I's first Archbishop of Canterbury, Matthew
Parker (1504–75), who gathered together early manuscripts and began
their study, or Laurence Nowell, working on Old English and Anglo-
Saxon laws in the 1560s. This early scholarship on Anglo-Saxon culture
and language was developing throughout the period covered by the
texts discussed here, informing a wider interest in Anglo-Saxon heritage
which extended beyond Cheshire and the idea of Mercia.[36] Interestingly,
evidence for the early reception of Henry Bradshaw's *Life of St Werburge*
suggests that this text was read by audiences with a particular attention to
Anglo-Saxon history. The 1521 Richard Pynson edition held in the British
Library (shelfmark C.21.c.40) includes inscriptions and marginal annotations in several early modern (late sixteenth-century) hands, which offer
a valuable insight into the reception of Bradshaw's work and the ways in
which the text was read by its audiences.[37] Throughout, dates are supplied
for key events if they are not given in the main text (for example, in reference to the death of William the Conqueror: '*Anno* 1087'). Dates given in
Roman numerals in the main text are also helpfully converted into Arabic
numbers. There are prolific glosses relating in particular to figures of
Anglo-Saxon history – for example, Æthelflæd, 'Lady of the Mercians',

or King Edgar – and evidence of a specific interest in Anglo-Saxon royal genealogy. At the beginning of the book, opposite the second woodcut, there is a carefully-written list of key figures in Anglo-Saxon history (from 'Hengistus' and 'R(ex) Vortygerne' onwards) and next to it, an even longer list of Anglo-Saxon saintly women, including 'L(ady) Werburga' and 'Lady Hilda'. Bradshaw's text seems to have been used by these early annotators primarily as a source (and repository) for the key names and dates of Anglo-Saxon history.

This kind of interest in the *Life of St Werburge* suggests ways in which the text could be used to explore and assert ideas of heritage, identity and 'Englishness' more widely. However, the specific interest in Mercia in late medieval and early modern Chester examined in this essay fits within very specific issues involved in the formation of a local identity which is distinct from that of 'England.' Cheshire, the region, resists its marginalization from centres of power and government in the south of England – its relegation to the periphery – with an alternative cultural geography which places it at the centre of an autonomous, prestigious and ancient kingdom. Writing about Mercia in late medieval and early modern Chester echoes the rhetoric of the Palatinate and the long tradition of independent or distinct regional identity for Cheshire. The idea of Mercia offers a persistent vocabulary for articulating local identity and for privileging the heritage and interests of the region over those of the (modern) nation. At the nexus of these texts and discourses is Werburgh's shrine itself with, at its own centre, that generative absence of the saint's vanished physical relics. Indeed, R. V. H. Burne even raises questions about whether the translation of Werburgh from Hanbury to Chester ever actually took place, noting that it appears for the first time only in Higden's *Polychronicon*, and that the view of many modern historians that Chester was 'lying waste at the time of the alleged translation' presents further difficulties for accepting the account.[38] This essay can only be a starting point for exploring Werburgh's shrine as a cultural signifier in late medieval and early modern Chester, leaving its own absences, gaps and unknowns for future study. We might ask why the elaborate stone tomb was constructed in the mid-fourteenth century – what did Mercia mean to audiences in Chester at that time, and why might interest in the Anglo-Saxon past have been prominent in that period? Why does Mercia become such a potent (yet unlikely) cultural symbol for a city which was only ever on its extreme periphery? The ready re-interpretation of the shrine from symbol of Papist idolatry to a relic of an innate, always-Protestant English religious identity in the years after the Reformation also deserves further investigation. In the later texts and discourses surrounding

Werburgh's shrine, the idea of Anglo-Saxon Mercia usurps the place of the saint, becoming the primary object of veneration and contemplation. Late medieval and early modern texts write within the inviting absences at the heart of both the shrine and Chester's obscure early history, filling them with their own configurations of Cestrian heritage, identity and future potential. These texts respond to the difficult – yet ultimately productive – absence of authentic, contemporary documents from the city's Anglo-Saxon past, as well as the later losses written on the material fabric of the shrine, by inventing a new corpus of writing on which to found Chester's identity. This fundamental process of loss, recovery and re-invention goes back to the fourteenth-century construction of Werburgh's shrine itself, when the carved, gilded figures of Mercian kings and saints were placed as the new material bodies – the new spiritual and cultural relics of Chester – within the saint's empty tomb.

Notes

1. A. T. Thacker, 'Cathedral and Close' in *VCH Ches*. 5. ii, pp. 185–204, p. 191.
2. J. M. Maddison, *St Werburgh's Shrine*, Extract from the Friends of Chester Cathedral Annual Report (Chester, 1984), p. 17.
3. Werburgh was the daughter of King Wulfhere of Mercia and also had genealogical connections with other (Anglo-Saxon and Frankish) royal houses. For a short account of the life and cult of St Werburgh, see R. V. H. Burne, *The Monks of Chester: the History of St Werburgh's Abbey* (London, 1962), pp. 1–2. For an earlier Life of the saint, Rosalind C. Love (ed. and trans.), *Goscelin of Saint-Bertin: The Hagiography of the Female Saints of Ely* (Oxford, 2004) and Henry Bradshaw, *The Life of Saint Werburge of Chester by Henry Bradshaw*, Carl Horstman (ed.), EETS OS 88 (London, 1887), as well as the selective edition of Bradshaw (with full Introduction) by Catherine A. M. Clarke at *www.medieval-chester.ac.uk* (accessed 30 September 2009). For a description of the shrine see A. T. Thacker, 'Cathedral and Close', pp. 190–1 and Sally-Beth MacLean, *Chester Art* (Kalamazoo, 1982), pp. 81–5.
4. For an overview of Anglo-Saxon Mercia, see *Mercian Studies*, Ann Dornier (ed.) (Leicester, 1977) or *Mercia: An Anglo-Saxon Kingdom in Europe*, Michelle P. Brown and Carol Ann Farr (eds) (London, 2001).
5. See A. T. Thacker, 'Cathedral and Close', p. 191 and Sally-Beth MacLean, *Chester Art*, pp. 81–5.
6. Rosalind C. Love, *Goscelin of Saint-Bertin*, pp. 48–9.
7. *Life of St Werburge*, rubric to Book I, Ch. XXXIII.
8. *Life of St Werburge*, I: 3472–4.
9. Although the poem does not survive in manuscript, this date is inferred from the closing 'balade to the auctour' in Richard Pynson's printed edition of 1511. Only Catherine Sanok has challenged this dating, suggesting an alternative of 1485–93,

based on her understanding of historical context and her interpretation of the acrostic signature in the 'other balade to saynt werburge' appended to Pynson's edition. See Catherine Sanok, *Her Life Historical: Exemplarity and Female Saints'Lives in Late Medieval England* (Philadelphia, 2007), p. 204.

[10] Recently, Jane Laughton has dealt with these tensions between civic and monastic power in a discussion entitled 'Challenges to Urban Government', in which she observes that '[t]he jurisdiction of the Benedictine abbey posed a ... serious threat to social harmony' in later medieval Chester. Jane Laughton, *Life in a Late Medieval City: Chester 1275–1520* (Oxford, 2008), p. 130.

[11] Robert W. Barrett, Jnr, *Against all England: Regional Identity and Cheshire Writing, 1195–1656* (Notre Dame, 2009), p. 47 and more generally pp. 47–51. See also Laughton, *Life in a Medieval City*, pp. 38–9.

[12] *Life of St Werburge*, II: XXII.

[13] Edward Hawkins (ed.), *The holy lyfe and history of Saynt Werburge, by Henry Bradshaw* (facsimile) (London, 1848), p. xiv. Recent commentators on the *Life of St Werburge*, myself included, would not however agree with Hawkins's subsequent suggestion that 'Bradshaw had evidently less faith in the miraculous legends of his monastery, than had been enjoyed by his predecessors; in truth there appears to be occasionally a lurking humour in his description, which displays as much disbelief in his own narrative, as the temper of the times, and the still lingering credulity of his contemporaries would permit'. This attempt to make a proto-Protestant out of Bradshaw simply does not fit with the emphasis on devotion to Werburgh, saintly miracles, and the authority of the abbey as custodian of her relics in the *Life of St Werburge*.

[14] *Life of St Werburge*, I: 260–420.

[15] See Rosalind C. Love, *Goscelin of Saint-Bertin*, pp. 28–33. The extensive use and explication of these organic metaphors in Goscelin and Bradshaw may be an attempt to transform any unease about Werburgh's hybrid, mixed ancestry into a positive model of assimilation and unity.

[16] See for example II: 519–26 (Offa); II: 1206–40 (Leofric) and II: 583–666 (Æthelflæd)

[17] *Life of St Werburge*, I: 183–9.

[18] For a discussion of the boundaries of the kingdom and territories of Mercia see Cyril Hart, 'The Kingdom of Mercia', in *Mercian Studies*, Ann Dornier (ed.), pp. 43–62.

[19] *Life of St Werburge*, I: 204, 205 and 207–10.

[20] Ibid., I: 223–4.

[21] Ibid., I: 197–203.

[22] Ibid., I: 218–219.

[23] Ibid., I: 229. Bradshaw also alludes here to the tradition of Cestrians as formidable archers, noting that they are 'moost valyaunt in artylere' (I: 228).

[24] *Life of St Werburge*, I: 232–8.

[25] Ibid., I: rubric to Ch. XXII, 1794, 1810 and 1826.

[26] Sanok, *Her Life Historical*, pp. 84, 91.

[27] Robert W. Barrett, Jnr, *Against all England*, pp. 44–5.

[28] Daniel King, *The Vale-Royall of England, or, The County Palatine of Chester.*

Performed by William Smith, and William Webb, Gentlemen (London, 1656), p. 1 (NB page numbering begins from 1 again several times through this volume.)

[29] King, *The Vale-Royall*, p. 9.

[30] Ibid., p. 32.

[31] Elizabeth Adams, *A Summary of the Life of St. Werburgh* (Chester, 1749), title page. The nineteenth-century historian George Ormerod casts some light on the authorship of this text, referring to it as 'Cowper's Summary of the Life of St. Werburgh' which is 'an enlargement of an account of the Shrine, by Mr Stones, rector of Coddington, which exists in his hand-writing, among the Cowper collections'. See Ormerod, I, p. 298, n. 'a'.

[32] For recent discussion of early antiquarianism in Britain, see Sarah McCarthy, Bernard Nurse and David Gaimster, *Making History: Antiquaries in Britain, 1707–2007* (London, 2007) and S. Pearce (ed.), *Visions of Antiquity: the Society of Antiquaries, 1707–2007* (London, 2007).

[33] Adams, *A Summary of the Life of St Werburgh*, p. 5.

[34] Ibid., pp. 9–10.

[35] Ibid., p. 19. This verse is referred to as from 'a Poem published by a young Nobleman of *Oxford*, about eight Years ago' and is given in Latin as well as English.

[36] See further discussion on this topic in Carl T. Berkhout and Milton McC. Gatch (eds), *Anglo-Saxon Scholarship: the first three centuries* (Boston, 1982) or Allen J. Frantzen and John D. Niles (eds), *Anglo-Saxonism and the Construction of Social Identity* (Gainesville, 1997).

[37] This is the copy of the text which is digitized on *Early English Books Online www. eebo.chadwyck.com* (accessed 30 September 2009), though the resolution is not clear enough to show all the annotations and markings.

[38] R. V. H. Burne, *The Monks of Chester: The History of St Werburgh's Abbey* (London, 1962), pp. 1–2.

Bibliography

Manuscripts

BL, Harley MS 1046.
BL, Harley MS 2162.
Oxford, Bodleian Library, Bodley MS 672.

Primary Sources

Adams, Elizabeth, *A Summary of the Life of St. Werburgh* (Chester, 1749).

Appleby, J. T. (ed.), *The Chronicle of Richard of Devizes of the Time of King Richard the First* (London, 1963).

Babbington, C. and J. R. Lumby (eds), *Polychronicon Ranulphi Higden monachi Cestrensis*, Rolls Series 41, 9 vols (London, 1879–86).

Baldwin, Elizabeth, Lawrence M. Clopper and David Mills (eds), *Cheshire Including Chester*, Records of Early English Drama, 2 vols (Toronto, 2007).

Barclay, Alexander, *The Life of St George*, William Nelson (ed.), EETS OS 230 (London, 1955).

Barraclough, G. (ed.), *The Charters of the Anglo-Norman Earls of Chester, c.1071–1237*, Record Society for the Publication of Original Documents relating to Lancashire and Cheshire 126 (Gloucester, 1988).

Benson, L. D., *The Riverside Chaucer* (Oxford, 1987).

Bowen, D. J., *Barddoniaeth yr Uchelwyr* (Cardiff, 1959).

Bowerman, Anthony, 'Walk Around Chester Walls', with a pictorial map by Chris Bullock (Tattenhall, 1998).

Bradshaw, Henry, *The Life of Saint Werburge of Chester*, Carl Horstmann (ed.), EETS OS 88 (London, 1887).

Broster, John, *A Walk Around the Walls and City of Chester* (Chester, 1821).

Butler, H. E. (trans.), 'A description of London by William Fitz Stephen', in F. M. Stenton (ed.), *Norman London: An Essay*, Historical Association Leaflet 93 / 94 (London, 1934), 25–35.

Calendar of the Charter Rolls Preserved in the Public Record Office (London, 1903–27).

Calendar of the Close Rolls Preserved in the Public Record Office (London, 1900–63).

Calendar of the Patent Rolls Preserved in the Public Record Office (London, 1891–1916).

Cheney, C. R. and B. E. A. Jones (eds), *Canterbury 1162–1190*, English Episcopal Acta 2 (Oxford, 1986).

Cheney, C. R. and E. John (eds), *Canterbury 1193–1205*, English Episcopal Acta 3 (Oxford, 1986).

Cheshire Sheaf, The, Series 3.

Christie, R. Copley (ed.), *Annales Cestrienses; or chronicle of the Abbey of S. Werburg, at Chester*, Record Society for the publication of original documents relating to Lancashire and Cheshire 14 (Chester, 1886).

Clancy, J. P. (trans.), *Medieval Welsh Lyrics* (London, 1965).

Clover, H. and M. M. Gibson (eds), *The Letters of Lanfranc Archbishop of Canterbury* (Oxford, 1979).

Coldewey, John, *Early English Drama: An Anthology*, Garland Reference Library of the Humanities 1313 (New York, 1993).

Constable, G. and B. Smith (eds), *Libellus de Diversisi Ordinibus et Professionibus qui sunt in Aecclesia* (Oxford, 1972).

Daniel, Iestyn (ed.), *Gwaith Llwadden* (Aberystwyth, 2006).

Darlington, R. R. and P. McGurk (eds), *The Chronicle of John of Worcester*, J. Bray and P. McGurk (trans), 3 vols (Oxford, 1995–98).

Domesday Book, seu Liber Censualis Willelmi Primi, 2 vols (London, 1783).

Dugdale, William, *Monasticon Anglicanum*, 6 vols (repr. Farnborough, 1970).

Epistolae Cantuarienses, in *Chronicles and Memorials of the Reign of Richard I*, William Stubbs (ed.), 2 vols, Rolls Series 38 (London, 1864–65), 2 (1865).

Erler, Mary Carpenter (ed.), *Robert Copland: Poems* (Toronto, 1993).

Fox, Richard, *The Letters of Richard Fox, 1486 –1527*, P. S. Allen and H. M. Allen (eds) (Oxford, 1929).

Franklin, M. J. (ed.), *Coventry and Lichfield 1072–1159*, English Episcopal Acta 14 (Oxford, 1997).

—— (ed.), *Coventry and Lichfield 1160–1182*, English Episcopal Acta 16 (Oxford, 1998).

—— (ed.), *Coventry and Lichfield 1183–1208*, English Episcopal Acta 17 (Oxford, 1998).

Friedberg, E. (ed.), *Liber Extra (= Decretales Gregorii IX): Corpus Iuris Canonici*, ii (Leipzig, 1881).

Furnivall, F. J (ed.), *The Stacions of Rome*, EETS OS 25 (London, 1867).

Giraldus Cambrensis, 'Itinerarium Kambriae', in Opera, James F. Dimock (ed.) (London, 1868).

Gesta Stephani,. K. R. Potter (ed. and trans.) (Oxford, 1976).

Gildas, *The Ruin of Britain*, Michael Winterbottom (ed. and trans.) (London, 1978).

Görlach, Manfred (ed.), *Kalendre of the Newe Legende of Englande* (Heidelberg, 1994).

Harries, L. (ed.), *Gwaith Huw Cae Llwyd ac Eraill* (Cardiff, 1953).

Harris, M. D (ed.), *Register of the Guild of the Holy Trinity, St Mary, St John the Baptist and St Katherine of Coventry*, Dugdale Society 13 (London, 1935).

Hawkins, Edward (ed.), *The holy lyfe and history of Saynt Werburge, by Henry Bradshaw* (facsimile) (London, 1848).

Hegel, G. W. F., *Philosophy of Right*, S. W. Hyde (trans.) (Kitchener, 2001).

Jaffé, P., *Regesta Pontificum Romanorum ad annum 1198*, S. Loewenfeld, F. Kaltenbrunner, and P. W. Ewald (eds) 2 vols (Leipzig, 1885–88).

James, Henry, *English Hours* (Oxford, 1981).

—— *The Ambassadors*, S.P. Rosenbaum (ed.) (New York, 1994).

Jocelini Cronica, in *Memorials of St Edmund's Abbey*, T. Arnold (ed.), Rolls Series 96 (London, 1890).

John of Salisbury, *Letters*, W. J. Mellor and H. E. Butler (eds) (London, 1955).

Johnston, Dafydd (ed.), *Iolo Goch: Poems* (Llandysul, 1993).

—— (ed.), *Gwaith Lewys Glyn Cothi* (Cardiff, 1995).

Jones, I. (ed.), *Gwaith Hywel Cilan* (Cardiff, 1963).

Jones, T. G., *Gwaith Tudur Aled* (Cardiff, 1926).

King, Daniel, *The Vale-Royall of England, or, The County-Palatine of Chester. Performed by William Smith, and William Webb, Gentlemen* (London, 1656).

Kolve, V. A., *The Play Called Corpus Christi* (Stanford, 1966).

Legg, John Wickham (ed.), *The Sarum Missal* (Oxford, 1916).

Lewis, H., T. Roberts and I. Williams (eds), *Cywyddau Iolo Goch ac Eraill* (Cardiff, 1937).

Love, Rosalind C. (ed. and trans.), *Goscelin of Saint-Bertin: The Hagiography of the Female Saints of Ely* (Oxford, 2004).

Lumiansky, R. M. and David Mills (eds), *The Chester Mystery Cycle*, 2 vols, EETS Supp. S. 3 and 9 (London, 1974–86).

—— *The Chester Mystery Cycle: Essays and Documents* (Chapel Hill, 1983).

McClure, J. and R. Collins (eds), *Bede: The Ecclesiastical History of the English People* (Oxford, 1999).

Melville, A. D. (ed.), *Ovid: Metamorphoses* (Oxford, 1998).

Migne, J. P. (ed.), *Patrologiae cursus completus, series latina* (*Patrologia latina*), 221 vols (Paris, 1841–64).

Millett, Bella (ed.), *Ancrene Wisse: A Corrected Edition of the Text in Cambridge, Corpus Christi College, MS 402 with Variants from Other Manuscripts*, 2 vols, EETS OS 325 (Oxford, 2005).

Morris, John (ed.), *Domesday Book*, 34 vols (Chichester, 1974–86).

Palliser, D. M. (ed.), *Chester: Contemporary Descriptions by Residents and Visitors* (Chester, 1980).

Pantin, William H. (ed.), *Documents Illustrating the Activities of the General and Provincial Chapters of the English Black Monks*, vol. 3 (London, 1937).

Priscian, *Prisciani Caesariensis Opuscula*, Marina Passalacqua (ed.), Sussidi Eruditi 40 + 48, 2 vols (Rome, 1987–99).

Quintillian, *The Orator's Education*, D. A. Russell (ed.), 5 vols (Cambridge, Mass., 2001).

Register of Edward, the Black Prince, preserved in the Public Record Office, 4 vols (London 1930–3).

Roberts, E., *Gwaith Maredudd ap Rhys a'i Gyfoedion* (Aberystwyth, 2003).

Robertson, James Cragie (ed.), *Materials for the History of Thomas Becket, Archbishop of Canterbury*, Rolls Series 67, 7 vols (London, 1875–85).

Rotuli Parliamentorum, 7 vols (London, 1783–1832).

Savage, Anne and Nicholas Watson (eds and trans), *Anchoritic Spirituality* (Mawah, 1991).

Savage, H. E. (ed.), *The Great Register of Lichfield Cathedral, known as Magnum Registrum Album*, Collections for a History of Staffordshire edited by the William Salt Archaeological Society (Kendal, 1924).

Stewart-Brown, R. (ed.), *Cheshire in the Pipe Rolls, 1158–1301*, Record Society for the publication of original documents relating to Lancashire and Cheshire 92 (London, 1938).

Stubbs, W. (ed.), *The historical works of Gervase of Canterbury*, W. Stubbs (ed.), 2 vols, Rolls Series 73 (1879–80).

Tait, J. (ed.), *The Domesday Survey of Cheshire*, Remains Historical and Literary Connected with the Palatine Counties of Lancaster and Chester, Chetham Society New Series 75 (Manchester, 1916).

—— (ed.), *The Chartulary or Register of the Abbey of St Werburgh Chester*, Chetham Society New Series 79 (Part 1) and 82 (Part 2) (Manchester, 1920, 1923).

Taylor, M. V. (ed.), *Extracts from the MS* Liber luciani de laude Cestrie, Record Society for the publication of original documents relating to Lancashire and Cheshire 64 (Chester, 1912), 1–78.

Toulmin Smith, Lucy (ed.), *The Maire of Bristowe is Kalendar by Robert Ricart, Town Clerk of Bristol 18 Edward IV* (London, 1872).

—— (ed.), *The Itinerary of John Leland in or about the years 1535–43*, 5 vols (London, 1964).

William of Malmesbury, *De gestis pontificum Anglorum*, N. E. S. A. Hamilton (ed.), Rolls Series 52 (London, 1870).

William of Newburgh, *Historium Rerum Anglicarum* in *Chronicles of the reigns of Stephen, Henry II, and Richard I*, R. Howlett (ed.), 4 vols, Rolls Series 82 (1884–9), vol. 1.

Williams, I. and J. Ll. Williams (eds), *Gwaith Guto 'r Glyn* (Cardiff, 1939).

Woolf, Rosemary, *The English Mystery Plays* (Berkeley, 1972).

Secondary Sources

Adams, Robert, 'The Egregious Feasts of the Chester and Towneley Shepherds', *The Chaucer Review*, 21 (1986), 96–107.

Alexander, J. W., *Ranulf of Chester. A Relic of the Conquest* (Athens, Georgia, 1983).

Alldridge, N. J., 'Aspects of the topography of early medieval Chester', *Journal of the Chester Archaeological Society*, 64 (1981–3), 5–31.

Appelbaum, Robert, *Aguecheek's Beef, Belch's Hiccup, and Other Gastronomic Interjections: Literature, Culture, and Food among the Early Moderns* (Chicago, 2006).

Balibar, E., and P. Macherey, 'On literature as an ideological form', in *Untying the Text: A Post-Structuralist Reader*, R. Young (ed.) (London, 1981), pp.79–99.

Banks, Robert, *Paul's Idea of Community: The Early House Churches in their Historical Setting* (Exeter, 1980).

Barbieri, A. L., 'Nazirites', *New Catholic Encyclopedia*, vol. 10, pp. 287–8.

Barnes, Trevor and James Duncan (eds), *Writing Worlds: Discourse, Text and Metaphor in the Representation of Landscape* (London, 1992).

Barron, Caroline M., *London in the Middle Ages: Government and People 1200–1500* (Oxford, 2000).

Barrett, Robert W., Jr., *Against All England: Regional Identity and Cheshire Writing, 1195–1656* (Notre Dame, 2009).

Bartlett, Robert, *Gerald of Wales* (Oxford, 1982).

Bennett, H. S., *English Books & Readers 1475–1557* (Cambridge, 1952).

Bennett, M. J., *Community, Class and Careerism: Cheshire and Lancashire Society in the Age of* Sir Gawain and the Green Knight (Cambridge, 1983).

Berkhout, Carl T. and Milton McC. Gatch (eds), *Anglo-Saxon Scholarship: the first three centuries* (Boston, 1982).

Blunt, C. E. et al., *Coinage in Tenth-Century England* (Oxford, 1989).

Bowker, Margaret, *The Henrician Reformation: The Diocese of Lincoln under John Longland, 1521–1547* (Cambridge, 1981).

Boffey, Julia, 'Early printers and English lyrics: sources, selections, and presentation of texts', *Papers of the Bibliographic Society of America* 85 (1991), 11–26.

Brayman Hackel, Heidi, *Reading Material in Early Modern England: Print, Gender, and Literacy* (Cambridge, 2005).

Brennan, Gillian, 'The Cheese and the Welsh: Foreigners in Elizabethan Literature', *Renaissance Studies* 8 (1994), 40–64.

Brown, A. (ed.), *The Rows of Chester. The Chester Rows Research Project*, English Heritage Archaeological Report 16 (London, 1999).

Brown, I., *Discovering a Welsh Landscape: Archaeology in the Clwydian Range* (Macclesfield, 2004).

Brown, Michelle P. and Carol Ann Farr (eds), *Mercia: An Anglo-Saxon Kingdom in Europe* (London, 2001).

Bühler, Curt F., 'Note on the "Balade to Saynt Werburge"', *Modern Language Notes* 68 (1953), 538–9.

Burne, R. V. H., *The Monks of Chester: The History of St Werburgh's Abbey* (London, 1962).

Burrow, J. A., *The Poetry of Praise* (Cambridge, 2008).

Cannon, Christopher, *The Grounds of English Literature* (Oxford, 2004).

Carlson, David R., *English Humanist Books: Writers and Patrons, Manuscript and Print, 1475–1525* (Toronto, 1993).

Cartwright, Jane, *Feminine Sanctity and Spirituality in Medieval Wales* (Cardiff, 2007).

Cawley, A. C., 'The "Grotesque" Feast in the *Prima Pastorum*', *Speculum* 30 (1955), 213–17.

Cerfaux, Lucien, *The Church in the Theology of St Paul*, Geoffrey Webb and Adrian Walker (trans), second edition (New York, 1959).

Chenu, M. D., *Nature, Man and Society in the Twelfth Century: Essays on New Theological Perspectives in the Latin West*, Jerome Taylor and Lester K. Little (trans), Medieval Academy Reprints for Teaching 37 (Toronto, 1997).

Cheshire and Chester Archives and Local Studies, *Printed Maps in the Cheshire Record Office* (Chester, 2001).

Chewning, Susannah M. (ed.), *The Milieu and Context of the Wooing Group* (Cardiff, 2009).

Clark, Robert L. A. and Claire Sponsler, 'Othered Bodies: Cross-Dressing in the *Mistere de la Sainte Hostie* and the Croxton *Play of the Sacrament*', *Journal of Medieval and Early Modern Studies*, 29 (1999), 61–87.

Clarke, Catherine A. M., *Literary Landscapes and the Idea of England, 700–1400* (Cambridge, 2006).

Classen, Carl Joachim, *Die Stadt: im Spiegel der Descriptiones und Laudes Urbium in der antiken und mittelalterlichen Literatur bis zum Ende des zwölfen Jahrhunderts*, Beiträge zur Altertumswissenschaft Band 2 (Hildesheim, 1980).

Clayton, D. J., *The Administration of the County Palatine of Chester 1442–1485*, Chetham Society 35 (Manchester, 1990).

Cohen, Jeffrey Jerome, *Hybridity, Identity, and Monstrosity in Medieval Britain: On Difficult Middles* (New York, 2006).

Coletti, Theresa, 'The Chester Cycle in Sixteenth-Century Religious Culture', *Journal of Medieval and Early Modern Studies*, 37 (2007), 531–47.

Cosgrove, A., 'The emergence of the Pale, 1399–1447', in *A New History of Ireland,* II: *Medieval Ireland, 1169–1534*, A. Cosgrove (ed.) (Oxford, 1987), pp. 533–56.

Cosgrove, Denis E., 'Introduction: mapping meaning', in *Mappings*, D. E. Cosgrove (ed.) (London, 1999), pp. 1–23.

—— and Stephen Daniels (eds), *The Iconography of Landscape: Essays on the Symbolic Representation, Design and Use of Past Environments* (Cambridge, 1988).

Davies, Gerald, *Lordship and Society in the March of Wales* (Oxford, 1987).

Davies, R. R., *Conquest, Coexistence and Change: Wales 1063–1415* (Oxford, 1987).

—— *The Revolt of Owain Glyn Dŵr* (Oxford, 1995).

De Certeau, M., *The Practice of Everyday Life* (Berkeley, 1984).

Desborough, D. E., 'Politics and Prelacy in the Late Twelfth Century: The

Career of Hugh de Nonant, Bishop of Coventry, 1188–98', *Bulletin of the Institute of Historical Research*, 64 (1991), 1–14.

Diamond, E., 'An Israelite self-offering in the priestly code: a new perspective on the Nazirite', *The Jewish Quarterly Review*, New Series 88 (1997), 1–18.

Dickinson, J. R., *The Lordship of Man under the Stanleys: Government and Economy in the Isle of Man, 1580–1704*, Chetham Society 41 (Manchester, 1996).

Dodgson, J. McN., *The Place-Names of Cheshire*, 5 vols in 7, English Place-Name Society (1970–97).

Doran, J., 'Authority and care. The significance of Rome in twelfth-century Chester', in *Roma Felix – Formation and Reflections of Medieval Rome*, É. Ó Carragáin and C. Neuman de Vegvar (eds) (Aldershot, 2008), pp. 307–32.

Dornier, Ann (ed.), *Mercian Studies* (Leicester, 1977).

Driver, Felix, *Geography Militant: Cultures of Exploration and Empire* (Oxford, 2001).

Driver, J. T., *Cheshire in the Later Middle Ages, 1399–1540* (Chester, 1971).

Driver, Martha W., 'Nuns as patrons, artists, readers: Bridgettine woodcuts in printed books produced for the English market', in *Art into Life: Collected Papers from the Kresge Art Museum Medieval Symposia*, Carol Garrett Fisher and Kathleen L. Scott (eds) (East Lansing, MI, 1995), pp. 237–67.

—— 'Pictures in print: late fifteenth- and early sixteenth-century English religious books for lay readers', in *De Cella in Seculum: Religious and Secular Life and Devotion in Late Medieval England*, Michael G. Sargent (ed.) (Cambridge, 1989), pp. 229–44.

Duncan, James, *City as Text: The Politics of Landscape Interpretation in the Kandyan Kingdom* (Cambridge, 1990).

—— and David Ley (eds), *Place / Culture / Representation* (London, 1993).

Dyer, C., *Standards of Living in the Later Middle Ages: Social Change in England c.1200–1520* (Cambridge, 1989).

—— *Making a Living in the Middle Ages: The People of Britain 850–1520* (London, 2002).

Eales, R., 'Ranulf (III) [Ranulf de Blundeville], sixth earl of Chester', *DNB*, vol. 46, pp. 56–9.

Edney, Matthew H., 'The Origins and Development of J. B. Harley's Cartographic Theories', *Cartographica*, 40 (2005), 1–143.

Edson, Evelyn, 'World maps and Easter Tables: medieval maps in context', *Imago Mundi*, 48 (1996), 25–42.

—— *Mapping Time and Space: How Medieval Map-makers Viewed their World* (London, 1999).

Edwards, A. S. G., 'From manuscript to print: Wynkyn de Worde and the printing of contemporary poetry', *Gutenberg-Jahrbuch* (1991), 143–8.

—— and Carol M. Meale, 'The marketing of printed books in late medieval England', *The Library*, 6th series, 15 (1993), 95–124.

Eliade, M., *The Sacred and Profane: The Nature of Religion* (Orlando, 1987).

Emmison, Frederick and Roy Stephens (eds), *Tribute to an Antiquary* (London, 1976).

Erler, Mary C., 'Devotional Literature', in *The Cambridge History of the Book in Britain*, vol. 3 (Cambridge, 1998), pp. 495–525.

Fasnacht, Ruth, *A History of the City of Oxford* (Oxford, 1954).

Fenster, Tovi, 'The Right to the Gendered City: Different Formations of Belonging in Everyday Life', *Journal of Gender Studies*, 14 (2005), 217–31.

Fischler, Claude, 'Food, Self and Identity', *Social Science Information*, 27 (1988), 275–92.

Fitzgerald, Christina M., *The Drama of Masculinity and Medieval English Guild Culture* (New York, 2007).

Fitzpatrick, Joan, 'Food and Foreignness in *Sir Thomas More*', *Early Theatre*, 7 (2004), 33–47.

Fox, Alistair, *Politics and Literature in the Reigns of Henry VII and Henry VIII* (Oxford, 1989).

Franklin, M. J. 'Nonant, Hugh de', DNB, vol. 40, pp. 991–3.

—— 'The bishops of Coventry and Lichfield, *c.*1072–1208', in *Coventry's First Cathedral. The Cathedral and Priory of St Mary. Papers from the 1993 anniversary symposium*, G. Demidowicz (ed.) (Stamford, 1994), pp. 118–38.

Frantzen, Allen J. and John D. Niles (eds), *Anglo-Saxonism and the Construction of Social Identity* (Gainesville, 1997).

Fryde, E. B., D. E. Greenway, S. Porter, and I. Roy (eds), *Handbook of British Chronology*, Royal Historical Society (London, 1986).

Fulton, H., 'Trading places: representations of urban culture in medieval Welsh poetry', *Studia Celtica*, 31 (1997), 219–30.

Ganim, John M., 'The experience of modernity in late medieval literature: urbanism, experience and rhetoric in some early modern descriptions of London', in *The Performance of Middle English Culture: Essays on*

Chaucer and the Drama in Honor of Martin Stevens, James J. Paxson, Lawrence M. Clopper and Sylvia Tomasch (eds) (Cambridge, 1998), pp. 77–96.

Gem, R., 'Romanesque architecture in Chester c. 1075 to 1117', in *Medieval Archaeology, Art and Architecture at Chester*, A. T. Thacker (ed.), The British Archaeological Association Conference Transactions, 22 (Leeds, 2000), pp. 31–44.

Gilbert, Pamela *Mapping the Victorian Social Body* (New York, 2004).

Goodich, M., *Miracles and Wonders: The Development of the Concept of Miracle 1150–1350* (Aldershot, 2007).

Gransden, Antonia, 'Realistic observation in twelfth-century England', *Speculum* 47 (1972), 29–51.

Gregory, Ian N. and Paul S. Ell, *Historical GIS. Technologies, Methodologies and Scholarship* (Cambridge, 2007).

Gwyn, Peter, *The King's Cardinal: The rise and fall of Thomas Wolsey* (London, 1990).

Hadfield, Andrew, *Literature, Politics and National Identity: Reformation to Renaissance* (Cambridge, 1994).

Harley, J. B., 'Maps, Knowledge and Power', in I*conography of Landscape: Essays on the symbolic representation, design and use of past environments*, Denis Cosgrove and Stephan Daniels (eds) (Cambridge, 1988), pp. 277–312.

——— 'Deconstructing the map', *Cartographica*, 26 (1989), 1–20.

——— *The New Nature of Maps. Essays in the History of Cartography*, Paul Laxton (ed.) (Baltimore, 2001).

Harris, B. E. (ed.), *A History of the County of Chester*, Victoria History of the Counties of England, 5 vols, vol. 3: *Religious Houses* (London, 1980).

Harvey, Paul, 'Local and regional cartography in medieval Europe', in *History of Cartography: Cartography in Prehistoric, Ancient, and Medieval Europe and the Mediterranean*, J. B. Harley and David Woodward (eds), vol. 1 (Chicago, 1987), pp. 464–501.

Heng, Geraldine, *Empire of Magic: Medieval Romance and the Politics of Cultural Fantasy* (New York, 2003).

Highly, Christopher, 'Wales, Ireland, and *1 Henry IV*', *Renaissance Drama*, N.S. 21 (1990), 91–114.

Higson, P. J. W., 'Pointers towards the structure of agriculture in Handbridge and Claverton prior to parliamentary enclosure', *Transactions of the Historic Society of Lancashire and Cheshire*, 142 (1993), 56–71.

Hodnett, Edward, *English Woodcuts 1480–1535*, second edition (Oxford, 1973).

Holdsworth, C., 'Baldwin [Baldwin of Forde] (*c.*1125–1190), Archbishop of Canterbury', DNB, vol. 3, pp. 442–5.

Hopkins, Lisa, 'Welshness in Shakespeare's English Histories', in *Shakespeare's History Plays: Performance, Translation and Adaptation in Britain and Abroad*, Ton Hoenselaars (ed.) (Cambridge, 2004), pp. 60–74.

Horner, Shari, *The Discourse of Enclosure: Representing Women in Old English Literature* (New York, 2001).

Howe, Nicholas, *Writing the Map of Anglo-Saxon England. Essays in Cultural Geography* (London, 2008).

Hyde, J. K., 'Medieval descriptions of cities', *Bulletin of the John Rylands University Library of Manchester*, 48 (1966), 308–40.

Ingham, Patricia Clare, *Sovereign Fantasies: Arthurian Romance and the Making of Britain* (Philadelphia, 2001).

Irvine, Wm. Ferguson, 'Notes on the history of St Mary's Nunnery, Chester', *Journal of the Architectural, Archaeological and Historic Society for the County and the City of Chester and North Wales*, New Series 13 (1907), 67–109.

Jansen, V., 'Attested but opaque: the early Gothic east end of St Werburgh's', in *Medieval Archaeology, Art and Architecture at Chester*, A. T. Thacker (ed.) (Leeds, 2000), pp. 57–65.

Jedin, Hubert, *A History of the Council of Trent*, trans. Ernest Graf, vol. 1 (London, 1957).

Jenkins, R. T. et al. (eds), *Dictionary of Welsh Biography down to 1940*, Honourable Society of Cymmrodorion (London, 1959).

Johnson, Stanley Howard, 'A study of the career and literary publications of Richard Pynson' (unpublished Ph.D. thesis, University of Western Ontario, 1977).

Jones, D., *The Church in Chester 1300–1540*, Remains Historical and Literary Connected with the Palatine Counties of Lancaster and Chester, Chetham Society Third Series, VII (Manchester, 1957).

Keene, D., *Survey of Medieval Winchester*, 2 vols (Oxford, 1985).

—— 'Text, visualisation and politics: London, 1150–1250', *Transactions of the Royal Historical Society*, 6th series 18 (2008), 69–99.

Kettle, Ann J., 'The hospital of St Giles, Chester', *VCH Ches.* 3, pp. 178–80.

Kissan, B. W., 'An early list of London properties', *London and Middlesex Archaeological Society*, N.S. 8 (1940), 56–69.

Kiser, Lisa, '"Mak's Heirs": Sheep and Humans in the Pastoral Ecology of the Towneley *First* and *Second Shepherds' Plays*', *Journal of English and Germanic Philology*, 108 (2009), 336–59.

Knight, Rhonda M., 'All Dressed Up with Someplace to Go: Regional Identity in *Sir Gawain and the Green Knight*', *Studies in the Age of Chaucer*, 25 (2003), 259–84.

Knowles, David, *The Religious Orders in England, Volume III: The Tudor Age* (Cambridge, 1959).

—— *The Monastic Order in England. A history of its development from the times of St Dunstan to the Fourth Lateran Council 940–1216*, second edition (Cambridge, 1963).

Kuskin, William, *Symbolic Caxton: Literary Culture and Print Capitalism* (Notre Dame, 2008).

—— (ed.), *Caxton's Trace: Studies in the History of English Printing* (Notre Dame, 2006).

Lagorio, Valerie M., 'The evolving legend of St Joseph of Glastonbury', *Speculum*, 46 (1971), 209–31.

Lampert, Lisa, *Gender and Jewish Difference from Paul to Shakespeare* (Philadelphia, 2004).

Laughton, Jane, *Life in a Late Medieval City: Chester 1275–1520* (Oxford, 2008).

Lavezzo, Kathy, *Angels on the Edge of the World: Geography, Literature, and English Community, 1000–1534* (Ithaca, 2006).

Lees, Clare A., and Gillian R. Overing (eds), *A Place to Believe In: Locating Medieval Landscapes* (Philadelphia, 2006).

Lefebvre, Henri, *The Production of Space*, Donald Nicholson-Smith (trans.) (Oxford, 1991).

Lepow, Lauren, '"What God Has Cleansed": The Shepherds' Feast in the *Prima Pastorum*', *Modern Philology*, 80 (1983), 280–3.

Lewis, B., *Welsh Poetry and English Pilgrimage: Gruffudd ap Maredudd and the Rood of Chester* (Aberystwyth, 2005).

Lewis, C. P., 'English and Norman government and lordship in the Welsh borders 1039–87' (unpublished DPhil thesis, Oxford University, 1985).

——, 'Avranches, Hugh d', first earl of Chester (*d.*1101), magnate and founder of Chester Abbey', DNB, vol. 3, pp. 1–3.

—— and A. T. Thacker (eds), *A History of the County of Chester*, Victoria History of the Counties of England, 5 vols, vol. 5. i: *The City of Chester: General History and Topography* (Woodbridge, 2003) and vol. 5. ii *The City of Chester: Culture, Buildings, Institutions* (Woodbridge, 2005).

Lewis, Katherine J., 'History, historiography and re-writing the past', in *A Companion to Middle English Hagiography*, Sarah Salih (ed.) (Woodbridge, 2006), pp. 122–40.

Lilley, Keith D., 'Mapping the medieval city: plan analysis and urban history', *Urban History*, 27 (2000), 5–30.

—— 'Landscape mapping and symbolic form: drawing as a creative medium in cultural geography', in *Cultural Turns/Geographical Turns*, Ian Cook, David Crouch, Simon Naylor and James Ryan (eds) (London, 2000), pp. 231–45.

—— *City and Cosmos. The Medieval World in Urban Form* (London, 2009).

—— Christopher D. Lloyd, Steven Trick and Conor Graham, 'Analysing and mapping medieval urban forms using GPS and GIS', *Urban Morphology*, 9 (2005), 1–9.

Livingstone, David, *The Geographical Tradition: Episodes in the History of a Contested Enterprise* (Oxford, 1993).

Longley, Paul A., Michael F. Goodchild, David J. Maguire and David W. Rhind (eds), *Geographical Information Systems. Principles, Techniques, Management and Application* (second edition, abridged) (Hoboken NJ, 2005).

MacLean, Sally-Beth, *Chester Art* (Kalamazoo, 1982).

Maddison, J. M., *St Werburgh's Shrine*, Extract from the Friends of Chester Cathedral Annual Report (Chester, 1984).

Marotti, Arthur F., *Manuscript, Print, and the English Renaissance Lyric* (Ithaca, 1995).

Matthews, Keith, *Excavations at Chester. The Evolution of the Heart of the City, Investigations at 3–15 Eastgate Street 1990/1* (Chester, 1995).

Matthews, S., 'The content and construction of the *Vita Haroldi*', in *King Harold II and the Bayeux Tapestry*, G. R. Owen-Crocker (ed.) (Woodbridge, 2005), pp. 65–73.

McAvoy, Liz Herbert (ed.), *Rhetoric of the Anchorhold: Space, Place and Body within Discourses of Enclosure* (Cardiff, 2008).

McCarthy, Sarah, Bernard Nurse and David Gaimster, *Making History: Antiquaries in Britain, 1707–2007* (London, 2007).

McClure, P., 'Patterns of migration in the late middle ages: the evidence of English place-name surnames', *Economic History Review*, Second Series 32 (1979), 167–82.

Millett, Bella, 'The Genre of *Ancrene Wisse*', in *A Companion to Ancrene Wisse*, Yoko Wada (ed.) (Cambridge, 2003).

—— *Annotated Bibliographies of Old and Middle English Literature: Ancrene Wisse, the Katherine Group and the Wooing Group* (Cambridge, 2006).

Mills, David, 'The Chester Mystery Plays and the Limits of Realism', in *The Middle Ages in the North-West: Papers Presented at an International Conference Sponsored Jointly by the Centres of Medieval Studies of the Universities of Liverpool and Toronto*, Tom Scott and Pat Starkey (eds) (Oxford, 1995), pp. 221–36.

—— *Recycling the Cycle: The City of Chester and Its Whitsun Plays* (Toronto, 1998).

Minear, Paul S., *Images of the Church in the New Testament* (London, 1961).

Morgan, Philip, 'Cheshire and Wales' in *Power and Identity in the Middle Ages: Essays in Memory of Rees Davies*, Huw Pryce and John Watts (eds) (Oxford, 2007), pp. 195–210.

Morris, Rupert H., *Chester in the Plantagenet and Tudor Reigns* (Chester, 1893).

Natter, W. and J. P. Jones, 'Identity, space, and other uncertainties', in *Space and Social Theory. Interpreting Modernity and Postmodernity*, G. Benko and U. Strohmayer (eds) (Oxford, 1997), pp. 141–61.

Nisse, Ruth, *Defining Acts: Drama and the Politics of Interpretation in Late Medieval England* (Notre Dame, 2005).

Ormerod, G., *The History of the County Palatine and City of Chester*, revised and enlarged edition by Thomas Helsby, 3 vols (London, 1882).

Parker, Patricia, 'Uncertain Unions: Welsh Leeks in *Henry V*', in *British Identities and English Renaissance Literature*, David J. Baker and Willy Maley (eds) (Cambridge, 2002), pp. 81–100.

Pearce, S. (ed.), *Visions of Antiquity: the Society of Antiquaries, 1707–2007* (London, 2007).

Pernot, Laurent. *La Rhétorique De L'éloge Dans Le Monde Gréco-Romain*, Collection Des Études Augustiennes: Série Antiquité 137, 2 vols (Paris, 1993).

Phillips, Helen, 'Aesthetic and commercial aspects of framing devices: Bradshaw, Roos and Copland', *Poetica*, 43 (1995), 37–65.

Pickles, John, *A History of Spaces: Cartographic Reason, Mapping, and the Geo-coded World* (London, 2003).

Pollard, A. W. and G. R. Redgrave (eds), *A Short-title Catalogue of Books Printed in England, Scotland and Ireland, and of English Books Printed Abroad 1475–1640*, second edition (London, 1991).

Ralph, Elizabeth, 'Bristol, *circa* 1480', in *Local Maps and Plans from Medieval England*, Richard A. Skelton and Paul D. A. Harvey (eds) (Oxford, 1986), pp. 309–16.

Rhodes, J. T., 'Syon Abbey and its religious publications in the sixteenth century', *Journal of Ecclesiastical History*, 44 (1993), 11–25.

Ringler, William A., Jr., *Bibliography and Index of English Verse Printed 1476–1558* (London, 1988).

Roberts, T., 'Noddwyr beirdd: teuluoedd Corsygedol, y Crynierth, a'r Tŵr', *Y Beirniad*, 8 (1919) 114–23.

—— (ed.), *Gwaith Tudur Penllyn ac Ieuan ap Tudur Penllyn* (Cardiff, 1958).

Robinson, I. S., *The Papacy 1073–1198* (Cambridge, 1990).

Rogoff, Irit, *Terra Infirma: Geography's Visual Culture* (London and New York, 2000).

Rutter, Russell, 'William Caxton and literary patronage', *Studies in Philology* 84 (1987), 440–70.

Saenger, Michael, *The Commodification of Textual Engagements in the English Renaissance* (Burlington, 2006).

Sanok, Catherine, *Her Life Historical: Exemplarity and Female Saints' Lives in Medieval England* (Philadelphia, 2007).

Saunders, J.W., 'From manuscript to print: a note on the circulation of poetic MSS in the sixteenth century', *Proceedings of the Leeds Philosophical and Literary Society, Literary and Historical Section* 6 (1951), 507–28.

Scattergood, John, 'Misrepresenting the city: genre, intertextuality, and William Fitz Stephen's *Description of London (c.*1173)', in *London and Europe in the Later Middle Ages*, Julia Boffey and Pamela King (eds), Westfield Publications in Medieval Studies 9 (London, 1995), pp. 1–34.

—— *Manuscripts and Ghosts. Essays on the transmission of medieval and early Renaissance literature* (Dublin, 2006).

Sharpe, Reginald R (ed.), *Calendar of the Wills Proved and Enrolled at the Court of Hustings*, 2 vols (London, 1889–90).

Soulsby, I., *The Towns of Medieval Wales* (Chichester, 1983).

Strohm, Paul, 'Three London itineraries: aestheic purity and the composing process', in his *Theory and the Premodern Text* (Minneapolis, 2000), pp. 3–19.

Sweetinburgh, Sheila, *The Role of the Hospital in Medieval England: Gift-Giving and the Spiritual Economy* (Dublin, 2004).

Thacker, A. T., 'Chester and Gloucester: Early Ecclesiastical Organization in Two Mercian Burhs', *Northern History*, 18 (1982), 199–211.

—— 'The cult of King Harold at Chester', in *The Middle Ages in the North West*, T. Scott and P. Starkey (eds) (Oxford, 1995), pp. 155–76.

——, 'Werburh', DNB, vol. 58, pp. 164–5.

Thorn, F.R., 'Hundreds and wapentakes', in *The Cheshire Domesday [Introduction and Translation]* (London, 1991).

Thornton, Tim, 'Opposition drama and the resolution of disputes in early Tudor England: Cardinal Wolsey and the abbot of Chester', *Bulletin of the John Rylands Library*, 81 (1999), 25–47.

Travis, Peter W., *Dramatic Design in the Chester Cycle* (Chicago, 1982).

Ward, Simon M., *Excavations at Chester. The Lesser Medieval Religious Houses, Sites Investigated 1964–1983* (Chester, 1990).

—— *Chester City Ditches: A Slice of History*, Chester Archaeological Service Guidebook No. 1 (Chester, 1992).

—— 'The course of the river Dee at Chester', in *'Where Deva spreads her Wizard Stream': Trade and the Port of Chester*, P. Carrington (ed.) (Chester, 1996), pp. 4–11.

—— *Chester, A History* (Chichester, 2009).

Warf, Barney and Santa Arias (eds), *The Spatial Turn. Interdisciplinary Perspectives* (Oxford, 2009).

Warren, Ann K., *Anchorites and their Patrons in Medieval England* (Berkeley, 1986).

Watson, Sethina, 'The origins of the English hospital', *Transactions of the Royal Historical Society*, 6th series 16 (2006).

Watt, Diane, 'Faith in the Landscape: Overseas Pilgrimages in *The Book of Margery Kempe*, in *A Place to Believe In: Locating Medieval Landscapes*, Clare A. Lees and Gillian R. Overing (eds) (Philadelphia, 2006), pp. 178–87.

White, G., 'Ranulf (II) [Ranulf de Gernon], fourth earl of Chester (*d.*1153), magnate', DNB, vol. 46, pp. 53–6.

Williams, Franklin B., Jr, 'Commendatory verses: the rise of the art of puffing', *Studies in Bibliography*, 19 (1966), 1–14.

Williams, J., *The Records of Denbigh and its Lordship*, vol. 1 (Wrexham, 1860).

Woodward, D. M., *The Trade of Elizabethan Chester*, Occasional Papers in Economic and Social History 4 (Hull, 1970).

Index

Page numbers in italics refer to illustrations.